Peter Redgrove was born on 2 Ja
Taunton School, Somerset and a
where he was Open and State Sc
became a founder-member of 'the
a scientific journalist and editor. In
to travel to the USA as Visiting I
York. In 1962 he returned to England to become Gregory Fellow
in Poetry at Leeds University for three years. After this he
freelanced for a year before joining the Falmouth School of Art
from 1966–83 in order to teach creative studies. During 1974–5
he was O'Connor Professor of Literature at Colgate University,
New York. He is now a freelance writer and has gained a wide
reputation in several interlinked fields: as a poet, a novelist, a
playwright and in psychological practice. He lives in Cornwall with
his partner Penelope Shuttle, who was the co-author of *The Wise
Wound* and is also a poet and a short-story writer. Her most recent
book of poems is called *Adventures With My Horse.*

PETER REDGROVE

The Black Goddess

and the Sixth Sense

PALADIN
GRAFTON BOOKS
A Division of the Collins Publishing Group

LONDON GLASGOW
TORONTO SYDNEY AUCKLAND

Paladin
Grafton Books
A Division of the Collins Publishing Group
8 Grafton Street, London W1X 3LA

Published in Paladin Books 1989

First published in Great Britain by
Bloomsbury Publishing Ltd 1987

Copyright © Peter Redgrove 1987

ISBN 0-586-08762-1

Printed and bound in Great Britain by
Collins, Glasgow

Set in Ehrhardt

To Nuith

' . . . In brief, conceive light
invisible, and that is a spirit . . . '
Religio Medici

CONTENTS

ACKNOWLEDGMENTS

On the Inner, before the beginning, to N.L.R.; to S.M., *fons chymicae veritatis*; to J.L. and G.M.; to D.L., once my student, who saw the invisible and still teaches in pictures; to C.A. who demanded so many answers with his just questions and for whom the first steps were taken; to F.H. who bestowed her death-dream of the Friend on me as a life-gift; to S.C., who appeared when it was time; to K. who saluted him by name, and to R. and D. for help as yet unplumbed.

On the Outer, indispensable help, gratefully acknowledged, was given by Rosemary Yates and Keith Trickey, Kathleen Raine, Frank Kermode, John Latham, Sylvia and Noel Kantaris, Jacqueline Korn, Roger Cardinal, John Beer, Stewart Brown, David Gouedard, Ann Hoffmann and W. H. Stevenson. Particular tribute, on account of their long-standing patience, must be paid to Derek Toyne and Jean Wood and to the other staff at the Library of the Falmouth School of Art (Angela Sheldon-Fentem, Inge Deeks and Linda Crook). My grateful acknowledgments are also due to the Leverhulme Trust for the award of an Emeritus Fellowship during 1985–7.

The author and publishers would like to thank A. P. Watt Ltd on behalf of Michael B. Yeats and Macmillan London Ltd for permission to reproduce on p. 122 five lines from W. B. Yeats's 'Vacillation' in *The Collected Poems of W. B. Yeats*.

INTRODUCTION

1 Feeling the Invisibles

I've always known we are surrounded by invisibles. Like most people, I was brought up in a religion which thought so too, but which called the invisibles by remote and confusing names, entirely male: Father, Son and Holy Ghost (the last always referred to as 'He'). The instructions given by this omnipresent being or beings resembled very closely the instructions given by schoolmasters in the classroom, the chief difference being that the invisibles were also thought-police, and could monitor one's inmost thoughts.

Yet, despite this, the most compelling invisibilities somehow came through women. My mother – who has now joined the invisibles herself – carried me invisibly for nine months; and, before that, where was I? She used to talk to her invisible, secret sharer in the womb, and on one holiday by the seaside took him swimming with her in tall and fast-breaking waves. As she swam into them (to my father's great concern) she shouted out aloud, but to me inside, 'You must be brave if you can, and learn to ride the waves.' Naturally I do not remember these instructions to herself and to me, but I must have known this sea through her body which, though it surrounded me like a castle, was still invisible to its small inhabitant, as the waves were.

When twenty years ago I came to live by the sea in Cornwall, her words – which she recounted to me when I was, I suppose, about four – returned to my mind. I had lived in towns until then; now I was exposed directly to what are usually called vaguely 'rhythms of nature'. I had not fully realised until then that I was one of the 30 per cent of the population who are so violently affected by weather changes – another set of invisibles – that it can easily become a clinical problem, either organic or psychiatric.

Weather changes very rapidly in Falmouth, as it lies on a narrow estuary of the sea and projects into the Atlantic. As I write, in mid-February, the sun is shining, there are playful-looking little cottonwool-bud clouds in the sky, which is deep blue, and the air is electrically clear and dry. I woke this morning with my skin tingling, and gave my body a full delicious stretch. The weather had appetite in it, and there were springs of joy in me, like the mouth watering in anticipation of the day's events. It has been so all day, and the air is full of vitality.

Yet yesterday I woke racked with pain, my skin clogged and dull, catarrh clicking in my ears and my thoughts profoundly sluggish and depressed, to a day in which the cloud-cover had sealed itself over the estuary and an evil and pearly mist drained all life like a supernatural fog. I was surrounded by invisible potions and tides which changed me, omnipresent electricities. I was Jekyll and Hyde to the weather.

On another day, when rain balanced with sunshine, I could predict without looking at them the heaviness and almost the shape of the rain-blackened clouds moving above the ceiling over my head and into view in my study window. Before it fell, I would dream the early-morning hail like castles of grey flint cobbles which were also masses of pain floating in the air. My experience was like the poet George Herbert's when he wrote:

> Who would have thought my shrivel'd heart
> Could have recover'd greennesse? It was gone
> Quite under ground; as flowers depart
> To see their mother-root, when they have blown . . .
> Killing and quickning, bringing down to hell
> And up to heaven in an houre . . .
> After so many deaths I live and write;
> I once more smell the dew and rain,
> And relish versing . . .

I must in these eddying extremities – which many people also suffer – have remembered my mother's words to me about the waves: 'Learn to ride them.' I tried to be brave. At these times of inspiration I would record the events, and I would find images for them. I would investigate my resources. I would strengthen my mind and my body as far as I was able so as not to fall into actual sickness, actual madness.

Were there studies that would help me in this? I went to the doctor, and he insisted I take tranquillisers. I refused to do this. He took a blood-test, to see whether I had contracted the undulant blood-fever brucellosis. I remember watching the weather over the sea clear to fine blue sky, and sunshine flood into his surgery window as he took the syringeful of blood. He was too busy to notice the wonderful weather change, and I thought how ill and frail he looked.

No medical man at any time asked me whether I felt the effects of the weather. Later on, when I had unearthed some of the facts in *The Black Goddess and the Sixth Sense*, I rang up a big teaching hospital near by, and asked them whether they had any information on medical climatology or biometeorology. They said, 'Biometeo-what?' At that moment I wondered at the thousands of people who were being treated for anxiety and depression, or one of the very serious illnesses that may be induced by weather changes (described in Chapter Two), when they were in fact 'communing with nature', and were not given images by our society to celebrate or express this communion.

Very early on in this quest, I was lucky enough to meet a great and widely known analyst, John Layard, who had retired to Cornwall, and I became his pupil. One of his principal dicta was *Depression is withheld knowledge*. What information was I missing, or ignoring?

Layard was a striking man, in his late seventies when I met him. He had snow-white hair that was worn long and flowed over his collar like steam boiling from a pot. His face in repose had a profound listening quality, and he was very tall. In the centre of his forehead, just above the eyebrows, was a small, round, skin-covered hole in the bone, like a third eye-socket. It was a bullet-hole, from when he had once tried to commit suicide, and you could tell if you had managed to interest him because it would beat with a pulse like a drum. When he knew you well, he would take out his denture for comfort, and then you could see that when he was absorbed in what you were saying he would salivate copiously. Sometimes he seemed not to hear very well, but the deafness went away if you kept to the point.

I did not start off very well with him. Here was this magical man, with a string of degrees and important books to his name, yet matters of bodiless intellect repelled him. If what you were saying did not in some manner reverberate through his whole body, he took it as a lie or a clever evasion, and his face returned a bland, bored, deaf and closed expression. I told him about my dreams, and my opinions of them. 'Stop trying to be so damned clever, Peter,' he would say. 'I see,' I said. 'No, you don't. Stop trying to see. Just tell me the dream. With feeling.' So I would go over it again and again. If I saw colours, that would please him, and he would tell me about Goethe, for whom colours were the deeds and sufferings of light, and arose from the struggle between black and white. But if I heard words or music in a dream, and especially if I smelled, tasted or touched, then his forehead-drum would begin to beat and his mouth water and his wonderful interpretations flowed; and this was especially so when I received a gift in a dream, or had sexual intercourse with a dream figure. Later on, he was able to predict or guide me into the dream I was going to have. He told me he was a *sin-eater*, and that was why his mouth watered. I protested in the name of common sense; he replied, 'We've had enough of that. What we need is uncommon sense.'

Using the intellectualised terms he disliked, one could say that this was part of his technique for dealing with the Oedipus complex which, because of the patriarchal structure of our society, is almost universal. Oedipus is the damnably clever hero who is unconscious of the forces that move him towards his doom. He accidentally and ignorantly kills his father in a fit of rage. Although he becomes a hero by freeing Thebes from one of its plagues (a Sphinx that asks travellers a riddle and eats them if they can't reply), when he settles there by marrying its queen every other kind of famine and pestilence descends on the city. The culprit turns out to be Oedipus himself, who has compounded his crime of father-murder by marrying his mother and having children by her without knowing what he was doing. For Layard, Oedipus' crime was ignorance, ignore-ance. If Oedipus had been aware of the duty he owed to forces greater than himself, the·tragedy would not have occurred and the city would have been free of pestilence. But then he would have been the priest-king of an earlier rule. The ignorance of Oedipus ushered in the plagues of our superbly empty-clever modern age, full of disasters unconsciously invited. In the end, Oedipus had to blind himself, to see.

If, as Freud believed, this pattern, or something like it, was reproduced in every Western individual, then I shared in it. But what were the unconscious forces I was ignoring? Layard patiently began teaching me. I had ignored dreams because they were not scientific; I had been too clever. Now I had to submit to these invisible masters who taught by night. Weather sensitivity was only the starting-point. Nor could I be a mere observer, like a cinema audience. I had to step forward into the picture, with all my senses alight. And it was the non-visual senses – touch, smell, taste, hearing and maybe others that I had not heard of – which took precedence as *touchstones* of truth. The mood-swings continued, and when I complained of them, Layard said, 'It's a battlefield.'

He also warned me that once the process had started, nothing would stop it. If I did not go with it, then I would be in worse trouble than if I had never begun. It did continue, long after Layard left Cornwall, long after he had died. I gradually realised that it was what the Sphinx knew that I had chiefly ignored; she was a representative of the contrary invisibles (how this can be so, I describe later in this Introduction). I realised that, when the 'Bell Jar' descended – that horrible shallow look as of scenery painted on glass – and overlaid everything, it was because I was fighting off the invisibles, the ultra- and infra-happenings, everything I could not see but which affected the way I saw. I had been schooled to distrust all emotional colouring of unknown origin, as if I were only an eye hanging in front of a brain, like a mirror on a grey wall. The weather changes had been eating me up, as the Sphinx ate the travellers on their way to Thebes, because I did not believe in them, they were not in science. But were they? I began to burrow, and discovered that after all there was a perfectly reputable science of biometeorology that helped explain how human beings were so profoundly changed by the weather, both consciously and unconsciously. Why then were its conclusions ignored by the majority? It must be because Oedipus hated the invisibles, even such obvious ones. All of these findings are in Chapter Two.

I wondered whether there was any study besides my dream-study that would alter the way my body responded to these influences, so that I could get more information directly. The air carried a lot of invisible data; obviously not smoking was a first step; I began to practise yoga and yoga-breathing assiduously. Soon there were differences. I found that if, like the Arabs in Chapter Two, I allowed the atmosphere of people to play on me, including the breath, I could often detect the fact that their smell changed according to what they were saying, especially if they were excited. It was more a natural perfume than a 'smell', and I noticed a strange communication or feeling gap when people were obviously using artificial deodorants. Sex had always been powerfully synaesthetic, but touching, smelling and tasting were enhanced by experiments new to me, particularly in oral sex. I also found new dimensions of the erotic in everyday life, and this went into my poetry and novels. I remember noticing for the first time since childhood how in the bath every touch and movement of the water naturally makes a light as well as a sound, and it is as though when we bathe we are enclosed in a wonderful fluid bell of music. Relaxing in the bath is one of the times, known to everyone, when the senses are most balanced and open one to the other; sexual reverie is another; and there is also deliberate relaxation technique. I give an outline of my own practices in the last chapter of this book.

I mentioned the familiar non-visual senses and 'maybe others that I had not heard of'. I realised that I had an electrical sense when I bought a negative ioniser to help me sustain the weather changes, and when I took a 'Field Mill' sensitive to electrical gradients into the attic when the wind was blowing and saw the needle fluctuating to and fro with each gust. I learnt something about homoeopathy, which knows all about weather changes. I found that when a homoeopathic remedy or even ordinary aspirin relieved the rheumatism-like pains that came with weather changes, they were replaced with a soothing sleep and vivid and significant dreams. I had continued the dream-studies I learnt with Layard both on my own account and with other people.

The figure which was to symbolise all these changes had already entered my life without my knowing it. I had become interested in magical practice, as a putative science of the invisibles, and I was writing my first novel, a piece of prose-poetry called *In the Country of the Skin*.[1] Halfway through my second draft I suddenly understood that *my heroine was as black as she was magical*. That is, she stood for all those things that are invisible yet real, the Night-Side of Nature in one human figure.

Her name was Teresa. The novel told how after certain struggles she became open to magical forces that were also natural ones. It was shortly before this that I had begun my dream-studies with Penelope Shuttle which led to our factual book *The Wise Wound*.[2] In it we showed how the rhythms of the female body could, after a struggle with the Oedipal-patriarchal prejudices of our culture, be rediscovered and re-experienced. The figure of the Black Goddess, the Shekhina, the Shulamite of the Song of Solomon, threaded its way through that book; she was its adviser, for the reason that the powerful magic of the menstrual process had until then been exiled and made invisible and turned into illness, just as the mental and physical magic of those weather changes had.

It is thus that the special problems tackled in *The Wise Wound* turn out to be no more than a particular instance of a much more general problem that we all share. We are surrounded by invisibles, yet we ignore what is invisible, real, potent, natural.

Anybody who has performed conjuring tricks for an audience of children, or for that matter led hypnotism or meditation groups, knows that an altered state of consciousness is announced by a quite palpable change of atmosphere. The leader or performer usually notices this before the audience does, and it is his or her business to feed it back to them. That is why they came.

At the very least there is a tingle in the skin which means that you have got them (and they have got you), an impression maybe of an elastic fragrance that has begun to fill out and define the contours of the room, and perhaps an enhancement of light and colour so that what you are doing and the people you are doing it with become vivid and everything seems larger and the show, whatever kind it is, begins to go right.

The orthodox scientist scoffs at such 'feelings', but everybody knows they exist, and, if they are wise, uses them. *The Black Goddess and the Sixth Sense* shows, among other matters, why and how such 'feelings' are to be trusted, and treated as perceptions of actuality, equivalent and maybe superior to the conventionally acknowledged senses. In fact, when we fall in love, make friends, influence people, give Tarot readings, feel compassion, do magic, make prophecies and even converse with the gods, we are exercising a sensory capability that has been concealed by the paradigms of science and by a misunderstanding of religious experience. 'Intuition', 'feelings', 'vibes', psychic and healing powers, are different in quality but not in kind, and a kind of prophecy of what could come about when humankind puts off its intellectual arrogance, condescends to learn from nature, and develops its 'unconscious senses'. I hope that *The Black Goddess and the Sixth Sense* will help to prove this, or at least get people thinking and feeling about it.

The plan of the book is very simple. The case for the limitations and influence of Oedipal man has been argued before, so I condense it in the next section of this Introduction. I say that the Sphinx is more important to us than the man who exasperated her into mock-suicide, and that science can heal the wounds it has long inflicted on magic and romance.

In Chapter One I show how the animals know the invisibles, in a wonderful communion and continuum which joins the whole world. Humans appear to be exiled from these wonders, but are they? I answer this by showing in Chapter Two how humans in truth participate in these marvels, but *unconsciously*, and what we call the unconscious mind is a living organ of perception.

In Chapter Three I assemble evidence to demonstrate that the active images of psychology, religion and magic are the symbolised perceptions of the marvellous unconscious senses, and how they are tending in the present world crisis towards a new evolution.

In the last chapter I try to suggest some working principles for personal research – including how mothers may help rescue their unborn children from some of the worst effects of ignore-ance.

2   The Perfumed Sphinx

Freud was a genius; geniuses are bright but not necessarily right. What they do do, right or wrong, is to provide images that guide, or compel, the lives of the rest of us. If we are not careful we may accept the inevitability of these images. It seems that great men offer us a portion of reality and, because of their greatness, we take it for the whole. Freud's ideas have been profoundly influential and have seemed like a watershed in human thought. He regarded the Oedipus complex as a universal phenomenon, built into the germ-plasm.

Freud formed this theory during his self-analysis, possibly during a period of 'cold turkey' withdrawal from cocaine addiction. He had discovered that the use of cocaine sharpened the intellect, or so it seemed, and might be a cure for neurosis in his patients. Unfortunately it is addictive. It is also anaesthetising and, by the use of cocaine nose-drops and heavy tobacco smoking, Freud had effectually locked, bolted and barred that gateway of intuition, the olfactory sense. Dreams are stimulated by withdrawal of the drug, and this may have given him privileged access to unconscious mechanisms. At any rate the result was the great *The Interpretation of Dreams* in which the Oedipus complex was first proposed.[3]

The image of Oedipus and his cursed nature and the plagues visited on his world by his apparently innocent actions corresponds to the way modern Western humanity sees itself: clever, proud, full of good intentions and yet inescapably doomed. 'What goes on in the minds of these people? They are smart at doing stupid things,' was the comment of a Marshallese woman in the Dennis O'Rourke film *Half Life*. The Marshall Islands took the full brunt of the US Atomic Energy Commission's playing about with the Bikini fall-out. The island people were destroyed, slowly, by the bomb, and the USAEC watched. Richard Scover's apt term for Industrial Revolution man in his book of that title is the 'Clever Moron'.

Alternatively you could say that our planet is haunted by 'creatures from the Id', as in the parable-film *Forbidden Planet*, called by Pauline Kael 'the best of the science fiction interstellar productions of the fifties' and awarded two stars in Halliwell's *Film Guide*.

In it a rescue team of young astronauts, headed by Leslie Nielsen, travels to the planet Altair IV to rescue Dr Morbius (Walter Pidgeon) and his daughter Altaira, the only survivors of a previous expedition. Members of the team are slaughtered by an invisible and almost unstoppable Sphinx-monster, revealed in the light of their neutron beams (which are powerless to disintegrate it) as a bipedal combination of lion, human and eagle.

Morbius has discovered a series of immense machines of no apparent use buried beneath the planet's crust. Twenty cubic miles in size, they are self-repairing, self-servicing, and apparently quiescent, except that the running of deer and the migration of birds show sometimes in light upon their dials. They were left there by a previous super-race, the Krell, and their function was to create an earthly paradise of thought-forms. Unfortunately the benevolent Krell had forgotten their own dark sides, which had long been repressed in the name of civilised life. When the machines were turned on, these unconscious energies stalked abroad in nightmare form, and destroyed their world. Millennia later, history repeats itself. Morbius learns to use the machines, at a fraction of their capacity. They expand his mind, but also amplify his unconscious resentment against the young astronauts, rivals for his daughter's love. The consequence is that creatures from his personal Id wreak vengeance. We shall see that something like these machines actually exists in nature, though not for vengeance, and Dr Morbius moves among them, unconscious of their splendour.

Drug-induced or not, Freud's paradigm seems undoubedly *there*. King Oedipus and the mad scientist Dr Morbius walk among us.

One can ask, however, not only if it is true, but if it is the whole of the truth. One can treat the legend, and the play of Sophocles, as though it were a dream, redreamed in a drug-duelling self-analysis by the twentieth-century genius. Dreams, including collective ones, are meant to be questioned; they are like the riddles of the Sphinx. We may interrogate this ancient legend, so powerful that Lowell Edmunds says, 'The literatures of England and of most of the countries of Western Europe have their Oedipuses, and often a country's Oedipus forms a whole chapter in the history of its literature.'[4] If the story of Oedipus has been implicated in the rise of the modern world, has somehow provided patterns and excuses for a kind of behaviour or mistake that has contributed to the planet-threatening nature of our society, then we may find in it clues to collective errors, and even hints of reparation. Such is the nature of dreams. *Oedipus the King* may be one of the great concealing stories or potent half-truths, so we must look not only at what it contains, but at what it leaves out. We may find that Oedipus' approach to his problems exemplifies a collective approach to the problems of life that imbues our present world, disastrously.

Although he has been such an exemplary and influential hero, nobody can decide whether Oedipus was clever or stupid, or stupid in his cleverness. Lowell Edmunds has usefully compiled twentieth-century opinions.[5] Simply because he solved the alleged riddle, Oedipus was a hero of the intellect to both Hegel and Nietzsche. The classicists Bernard Knox and E. R. Dodds saw the same quality; to the latter 'personally Oedipus is a kind of symbol of human intelligence which cannot rest until it has solved all the riddles'. Oedipus thus becomes a symbol of the questing, visualising modern scientific intelligence. Why then should he blind himself in the end? By no means everybody thought well of him. Gilbert Murray wrote to Yeats about Oedipus' 'mere loss of temper'. Ezra Pound thought the Oedipus story 'a damn silly lot of buncombe'.

Oedipus' tale may yield more beneficent magic if we look at it with the kind of mind, albeit romantic, which maintains a belief in the evolutionary prospects of our species. Whereas Freud, as a representative of our time, profoundly distrusted sexuality – particularly infant sexuality – and saw in this the explanation of Oedipus' self-blindings ('Like Oedipus we live in ignorance of these wishes . . . and after their revelation we may all of us seek to close our eyes to the scenes of our childhood'),[6] we may find another kind of understanding in the words of Gide's Oedipus: 'Only since my eyes of flesh were torn with my own hand from the world of appearances have I begun, it seems to me, to see clearly,'[7] or Shakespeare's words of the blinded Gloucester: 'I stumbled when I saw'.[8] As Bettelheim remarks, Oedipus 'destroyed his eyes in punishment for not having seen what he was doing . . .'[9] Goethe's Faust also experiences his greatest insight after his blinding, and, to the Renaissance Neoplatonists, blindness was the precondition for seeing God.[10] To them, Love himself was blind.

This is not to diminish the power of Freud's diagnosis. The psychologist George Frankl attributes class structure and conflict and most of the ills of society to the sexual class war based on the Oedipal pattern; that is, murderous phallic conflict between males for the favour of the women, those favours being defined by the men themselves. This system is, as it were, only haunted by women, who cannot in it achieve expression or contribute to society anything of their true nature, and are regarded as a kind of castrated man. 'God does not speak to her, only to man . . . she ceases to believe in the spontaneity of her sexual urges . . . for that would make her a being in her own right . . . *female cultural symbols will emerge* . . . Women would again develop their divinities, their principles and ideas in a recognisable manner as distinct cultural entities, and it is high time this should happen if we are to be saved from the aggressive mania of the male gods . . . The Oedipus complex causes us to be in awe of authority, compelling us to adopt submissive and sacrificial or aggressive attitudes . . . The most important project of the sexual and social revolution must therefore be the abolition of the Oedipus complex . . . its abolition means the abolition of patriarchy [my italics].'[11]

Norman O. Brown argues that despite appearances we have a profoundly non-sensuous culture, and nature is concealed and indeed destroyed by masculine idealisms and sublimations arising from the flight from reality inherent in the Oedipus complex. He speaks of the recovery, indeed resurrection, of neglected faculties and functions of the body, and a state in which the human function will be, in Henry Miller's words, 'not to possess power but radiate it'. Brown speaks of a mysticism of the senses which does not fly from the actual world. He quotes Thoreau: 'Our present senses are but rudiments of what they are destined to become,' and how the human being may one day 'delight in that full life of the body which it now fears', and in consciousness 'which does not negate any more'. Brown says that it is and was the poets and philosophers of the Romantic movements who are the real discoverers of the unconscious, and that we must cease to condescend to that which the poets and mystics have directly experienced, for art and poetry 'have always been altering our ways of sensing and feeling – that is to say, altering the human body'.[12] As Whitehead insisted, 'The body is the organism whose states regulate our cognisance of the world',[13] and the essence of the 'Romantic reaction' is 'a revulsion against abstraction (in psychoanalytical terms, sublimation) in favour of the concrete sensual organism . . .'

We shall see how science has favoured abstractions and sublimations in the interests of industrialisation and the Oedipal class war and how this treason of the clerks has operated against the realisation of the Romantic dream. Charles Davy speaks of a 'transition from a participating mode of consciousness to the onlooker mode'; I. A. Richards of 'the Neutralisation of Nature'. Whitehead, like the Romantics, is calling for a science 'based on an erotic sense of reality, rather than an aggressive dominating attitude towards reality',[14] the latter being the Oedipal attitude. In the second Theban play, old blind Oedipus at Colonus learnt how his body, source of sin and pollution, could become a magical talisman – and he himself a magic man. Lowell Edmunds says Freud never read this play.

In short we are moving (like Oedipus) from patriarchy towards something else. It is not surprising if this transition is haunted by those 'female cultural symbols' that were hitherto excluded. They are present in the undertow of the Oedipus story. And the meaning of the blinding of Oedipus? It is that to achieve our transformation we shall need something more than eyes.

Many commentators have noted the story's strong female undertow. According to Vladimir Propp, M. P. Nilsson, Bachofen, Robert Graves, Barbara Walker and others, the Oedipus legend shows indications of a transition from a matriarchal to a patriarchal organisation of society. It is because of this passage that the supreme modern masculine cultural symbol of Oedipus arose: a symbol which shows, as Freud found in his complex, the uneasy source of the energy of the evolution of Western society. It is uneasy because it is a usurpation, and because it is based on the repression of what is represented in the story by the Sphinx, and by what is signified by the acts of incest and blinding.

It is for these reasons that, with our own transition from a patriarchy to whatever may be in front of us, two of the elements present as undertow in the old legend – illumined darkness or blindness and the questioning Sphinx – have fused into a 'new' cultural symbol. This is the Black Goddess, or Lilith, the Dark Girl of the Eastern Love-Books, the Goddess of the Night and the Interior of the Earth, the Kore. In Christian myth she emerges as that counterpart to the Virgin Mary who is called Mary Magdalene, Mary of Bethany, the sensuous lover of Jesus.

Oedipus was blind before ever he blinded himself. The self-blinding was an admission of this. The riddle of the Sphinx – the initiatory question – was asked. Oedipus gave an answer that caused the Sphinx to destroy her visible appearance and to cease instructing him. It was behind this visible appearance that the true riddle lay.

The *explicit* and famous riddle never appears in Sophocles' play. It occurs in various forms in the different sources. One variant form is given by Robert Graves: 'What being, with only one voice, has sometimes two feet, sometimes three, sometimes four, and is weakest when it has the most?' Graves says that Oedipus answered the riddle fresh from the murder of Laius: 'Man, because he crawls on all fours as an infant, stands firmly on his two feet in his youth, and leans upon a staff in his old age.'[15] The riddle was said to have been taught to Oedipus by the Three Muses; that is, it had to do with what we nowadays call inspiration.

It is quite possible, then, that the Sphinx removed the vision of herself from the road to Thebes because of the *wrongness* of the answer. Man? Do not women age also? But that is only part of the answer. Graves says that the whole story is a 'deliberate perversion' of the meaning of a set of sacred icons. The Sphinx herself was, he says, the winged moon-goddess of Thebes, and her composite body was an astronomical calendar-picture of the Theban year: a lion for the waxing part and a serpent for the waning part. However, as she was a moon-goddess, this would reflect the moon-cycle also. The riddle referred to a picture of 'an infant, a warrior and an old man, all worshipping the triple-goddess: each pays his respects to a different person of the triad'.[16]

'Pays his respects' does not bring out the full significance of such a picture. The icon more directly means that the masculine life is a reflection of the goddess's changeability in her aspects of maiden, mother and crone; or, if you like, the god reflects the goddess. Since she is a nature-goddess, this alteration in human beings corresponds to alterations in nature, earth-nature, moon-nature and sun-nature: weather, climate and season. And because both the sun and moon are reborn from darkness, the answer to the riddle also has to do with rebirth; either a promise of rebirth after death, as in the Egyptian religion, or of rebirth in this life, as in the recovery of inspiration; in George Herbert's words 'I once more smell the dew and rain / And relish versing.' This is in fact what goddess-worship means: transformation and rebirth.

Oedipus, then, belongs to that long line of mythical tricksters who in the legends subvert the gods' promise of immortality, or get the message wrong. In these stories the Creator says of the new creation, humanity, that they will die and cast their skins and be reborn as the moon is reborn; the message is relayed by a tricky messenger who says, 'Human beings will *not* be reborn as the moon is reborn,' and because the humans believe this, so death comes into the world, and rebirth remains a fable.

So it is also with climate and season. Neumann, for example, associates the crowned Sphinx on the tenth trump or enigma of the Tarot pack, 'The Wheel of Fortune', with three-headed Time 'whose wings are the months' in the Wheel of Mother Nature of the Western Middle Ages.[17] The riddle thus survives, although we shall see how in the so-called Enlightenment of the eighteenth century the movement towards scientific control and industrialisation deliberately ignored such influences of cyclical time, particularly in respect of the weather. As it was uncontrollable, the science of that time found reasons to argue that the weather should not, and consequently did not, have any profound influence on the minds or bodies of human beings. It was also undemocratic to suppose that people differed in their gifts according to where they were born. There was in this, alas, another subverted message; the vision of nature and humanity as a continuum was denied. The result as always has been a haunting by the very thing denied, as grave as the Theban haunting, and exactly parallel with it. Our clinics and hospitals and psychiatric units are plagued with diseases and illnesses that are weather-caused and weather-controlled. We shall return to this in Chapter Two.

We should visualise the scene. Oedipus staggers blood-crazed on the road to Thebes. He has just killed Laius' attendant with his spear, flung his father Laius on to the road entangled in his chariot's reins, and has whipped up the horses so his victim is flayed to death by being dragged along the ground. He is like St Paul on the road to Damascus, blood-crazed by his persecution of the Christians, caught up to the third heaven and blinded by his vision. Oedipus has performed these cruel acts in a battle-rage inherited from his patriarchal forebears, the power in him raised by the smell of human blood-sacrifices. As in the practice of blood-magic, he sees a vision of the forces that preside over life, a riddle called the Sphinx, with her woman's head, lion's body, serpent's tail and eagle's wings. He sees an aspect of the Wheel of Time, a vision of the tenth trump, the turning wheel of Mother Nature (the world-goddess herself), with its message of death and renewal, its knowledge of invisible things, its promise of the shamanistic mastery of the two worlds of life and death, and the worlds of past and future, a knowledge which Tiresias the blind Seer had attained. It asks its question, in a woman's voice; in effect, 'What dies?' Oedipus answers, 'Man dies.' 'Then I die,' answers the immortal Sphinx, and throws herself off her mountain. Oedipus himself now becomes the riddle, which is 'What is causing these plagues in Thebes?'

The great pre-Romantic Goethe caused his magician Faust to approach the same vision. Faust called up the Earth-Spirit, recoiled at its 'ugliness', then repelled it with his arrogance: 'I am Faust, in everything thy equal!'[18] Goethe himself, however, believed in and practised 'erotic science' and the consciousness which 'does not negate any more'. Idris Parry shows movingly how Goethe used his 'feeling eye', the look 'which seems to become part of a physical field of energy, denying the existence of empty space; it touches and embraces and behaves like an investigating organ, fusing into other senses.' He composes poetry in his lover's embrace in the *Roman Elegies* ('And gently fingered the beat of hexameters on her back'); the buildings and marbles of classical Rome spring into life because he learns in bed to 'see with a feeling eye, feel with a seeing hand'.[19] Faust goes on to transformation and redemption, visits the mysterious Earth-Mothers who are underground, returns with a magical incense, and is saved at the instant he is blinded by Care.

One can argue that Goethe was of, or was aware of, a masculine lineage distinct from that of Oedipus, a lineage represented by

Tiresias, Faust, the English Merlin: the reborn magician in league with the 'dark' feminine powers, with the animals, possessing enlarged and clairvoyant senses. Goethe proceeded in his redemptive drama to show Faust, after his bad start, in continued dialogue with the powers that he had called up. This is the non-Oedipal solution, to proceed in dialogue with your visions; the magical, or Romantic solution. All Romantics have followed it, or attempted to, even though it has led them to the darkest regions and to facing up to the hauntings created by Oedipal repression.

C. G. Jung also took the riddle of the Sphinx in the non-Oedipal sense, but then he was a great Romantic and followed the magical solution of practising dialogue with images of the unknown – not merely to reason about inner events, but actually to converse with the figures of dream and vision in a state of 'active imagination'. This is the basic procedure of all magic and all art, and also of Jung's therapy.

Jung remarks how tragically Oedipus was misled by his own cleverness. The riddle 'was, in fact, the trap which the Sphinx laid for the unwary wanderer. Overestimating his intellect in a typically masculine way, Oedipus walked right into it, and all unknowingly committed the crime of incest. The riddle of the Sphinx was *herself* . . . '[20] It was the dual nature of the Sphinx that he should have contemplated, for according to Jung it is an aspect of the anima, the deep feminine image who 'plays the role of the mediatrix between the unconscious and the conscious, a dual figure like the Sphinx, compounded of animal instinct (the body) and specifically human qualities (the head). In her body lie the forces that determine man's fate, in her head the power to modify them intelligently.'[21] This is the 'great nocturnal goddess, the veiled Sphinx'.

On that hot road, after the reek and smoke of spilt blood, the murderer Oedipus smelling like a butcher, in the mingled perfumes of woman, warm-blooded beast, cool serpent, winged eagle, the riddle appears. Barbara Walker says that the answer to the explicit riddle was either man or God.[22] Oedipus' answer – the former – affronted by the vision's contradictions, hewed it down: how can a thing be both A and not A? Such a vision combines opposing categories, man–woman, life–death, beast–human. It is like those famous 'counter-changing' figures, such as one sees in high form in Picasso's portraits. An elementary example is the Rubin double profile, in which the eye sees first a person kissing from the left, then another kissing from the right. Only if the eye relaxes profoundly can it see the two people united in a kiss. It was not Oedipus' habit to be relaxed; a man of blood cannot afford to be so; besides, his inherited short temper is against it. He is what contemporary medicine calls a type A personality, an over-achiever, a workaholic, never relaxing, driven by some energetic ignorance to an unknown goal, liable to blinding strokes and massive heart attacks. Oedipus' intelligent eye would not give the answer, cause or reason why this monstrous apparition threatening to throttle him straddled the road. Such hot-tempered men hate the body, it is a nuisance; thus Oedipal men are killers: their own bodies pollute their world.

Another kind of man, more relaxed or sensuous, might have offered the Sphinx the ancient Egyptian compliment known as *senta*;[23] that is, of smelling or kissing the earth where she had walked, a compliment reserved for royalty. It is a custom of the present Pope to kiss the ground when visiting foreign soil; this Pope is known also to have a special devotion to the black madonnas of his native country, Poland. But the ordinary gesture of prayer will assist our meditations on the dark goddess here and now. Let us pay nature the compliment which is also used in prayer, of joining our two hands in touch and smelling the warm vapour that rises from them. Thus we join opposites and simultaneously consult two of the non-visual senses, escaping the eye's tyranny. It is a way of making the counter-changing pictures hold still. It is a synaesthesia. It is the sixth sense.

For the Egyptians, the Sphinx was a vision of nature in which opposites united. Gerald Massey says that the orthodox Sphinx is masculine in front (with the reigning pharaoh's face) and feminine behind. Like the gods the pharaohs 'included the dual totality of Being in one person, born of the Mother, but of both sexes as the child'.[24] Tiresias the blind Seer, who in Sophocles' play instantly knew Oedipus' secrets, also knew what it was like to be both man and woman. It is said that on Mount Cyllene he had seen two serpents coupling and, when they attacked him, he killed the female. Instantly he was turned into a woman, and became a famous harlot. Seven years passed in this way; then he returned to the same sight at the same spot, but this time killed the male serpent, and regained his manhood.

The ancient Greeks had an all-embracing theory of the normally invisible natural forces that act upon us, which seems very close to the contemporary information I shall describe in Chapters One and Two. The Keres were ghosts or spirits responsible for famine, pestilence, madness and nightmare.

At the lowest level the Keres were a kind of 'personified bacillus'. Some were harmless, and simply haunted graves, but there is an ancient picture of no less a hero than Hercules overcoming a baleful Ker, 'a tiny winged figure with shrivelled body and distorted ugly face', which he has by the throat.

The ancient Greeks described an illness called Hepialos, which was a shivering flu and 'a daimon that comes upon those that are asleep'. It is caused by a Ker, a ghost-pest, a 'nightmare bacillus'. So was blindness: 'Blindness and madness, blindness of body and spirit are scarcely distinguished, as in the blindness of Oedipus'; both were caused by Keres. They are a swarm of 'unknown evils hovering about men'. They are in the weather, and magicians are possessed by them, or use them. They are wind-demons and harpies. They cause old age and death, 'they are the Snatchers, winged woman-demons, hurrying along like the storm-wind'.

Yet in the upper range of their function they are Fate itself. They are the Gorgons too, those terrifying snake-haired masks whose function it is '"to make an ugly face" *at* you if you are doing wrong . . . *for* you if you are doing right'. At this upper end of the scale, the Sphinx was a Ker, and she was seen as 'the soothsayer', because she answered riddles as well as asked them. The Ker in this form became 'the symbol of oracular divinity' and was accompanied by snakes, 'the oracular beast of the earth-oracle'. There is a vase-painting of Oedipus sitting meditating in front of the earth-oracle, which is the Sphinx on her column. She is 'a very human monster, she has her lion-body . . . ' but she is also 'a lovely attentive maiden'.

We shall see in Chapter Three that the Ker is very close to the conception of the Black Goddess, Lilith, who, rejected, is the origin of the plagues of humankind, but, accepted, is 'the soul of every living creature that creepeth' and also the 'rungs of the ladder of prophecy'. [25]

The Romantic or magical vision has supposedly not had the support of modern science as it is generally understood – although there is a kind of remote romanticism attached to quantum theory, the data of which is not within most people's observation. The reason that this support has not been forthcoming, and we therefore do not live in a society open to the Romantic vision, is that the Oedipal preoccupation and structure of modern science, its remoteness, its propensity to abstractions, 'sublimations and libidinal displacements', its emphasis on instrumentation that amplifies the capacity of the eye rather than studying the data of the experience of the whole body, blinds society to obvious facts and creates monstrous omissions. It is easy to be clever if you leave something important out. Thus Einstein's theories avoid all subjective experience whatsoever; and Freud in effect forbids our acquiring direct knowledge from adult sexuality; he forbids 'carnal knowledge'.

The Romantic movement among other things was concerned to bring back into permitted human experience occasions when the *invisible but real world* was of paramount importance, when the non-visual or dark senses were operating as organs of knowledge. As nowadays we can use the image of the wave-pattern hologram to understand quantum effects, the nineteenth-century Romantics used that of the Aeolian lyre: a frame of strings held in a window-casement that played aleatory music to the changes of breeze and weather – a wind-harp. Thus to Shelley the Romantic human gained accurate poetic knowledge by pondering relaxed sensory impressions which were like 'the alterations of an ever-changing wind over an Aeolian lyre, which move it by their motion to ever-changing melody'. In Coleridge's 'Dejection: An Ode' the wind-harp foretells a storm that when it breaks will restore his former inspiration to him. Wordsworth writes:

> *For I, methought, while the sweet breath of Heaven*
> *Was blowing on my body, felt within*
> *A corresponding mild creative breeze,*
> *A vital breeze which travell'd gently on*
> *O'er things which it had made . . .* [26]

What the science of the time denied was ratification, and therefore development, of these bodily or carnal feelings – indeed 'feeling' is a word derided by science, although science itself is full of territorial aggressive feelings, and is highly masculinised. Nevertheless, in science it is possible to say definitely (and the reasons will be given for this later) that there is a profound physiological response, and therefore a finely calibrated mental and poetic response, to weather changes and to electrical patterns in wind and season, that the air carries deep messages in organic form from all the growing things of the world, as, again, Wordsworth knew:

> Oh there is blessing in this gentle breeze
> That blows from the green fields and from the clouds
> And from the sky . . .

and that all nature is in an intimate communion through these and other mutual influences which will later be described in this book. The Romantics were right to affirm that their feeling-perceptions led to an actual communion with nature and a vision of its unity, and were correct in their high estimation of the imagination, which was to Coleridge 'the organ of the supersensuous', the vehicle of understanding of such perceptions, detected by the neglected, repressed, unconscious, non-visual, carnal or dark senses – and it was this vision that was violently and short-temperedly struck down on the road to Thebes. Freud's words are as follows: '*The deepest root of the sexual repression which advances along with civilisation is the organic defence of the new form of life achieved with man's erect gait against his earlier animal existence* [my italics].'[27] We shall find that civilisation has not expunged or extinguished that 'animal existence' but has instead rendered it unconscious, and that it still operates in our lives as both curse and blessing. Moreover, the unconscious mind is no mere lumber-room of childhood errors and traumata but a living, breathing, sensing, perfumed, luminous Sphinx.

Perhaps if we go to its hale and healthy side, science may at last make amends – if we sidestep its concealed motivations and jealousies. That is to say, in the words of the great Romantic nature-philosopher Novalis, that the process of renewal begins *when the spirit of poetry solves the riddle of the Sphinx.*

Peter Redgrove
February 1987

ONE
THE FALLEN DAUGHTER

'... the white moth had begun to flutter beneath the bushes the black snail was out upon the grass and the frog was leaping across the rabbit tracks on his evening journeys and the little mice was nimbling about and twittering their little earpiercing song with the hedge cricket whispering the hour of waking spirits was at hand.'[1]

'The Animal Soul is that which perceives and feels, without it he may not perceive or feel the Joys of the Universe. Despised as the Fallen Daughter, it is our greatest Treasure, for it is the Kingdom of Heaven on Earth.'[2]

'For the animal shall not be measured by man. In a world older and more complete than ours they move finished and complete, gifted with extensions of the senses we have lost or never attained.'[3]

1   Visible Spirits

The German nature-philosopher Ritter (1776–1810) formulated a central Romantic idea: nature is a cosmic animal (*All-Tier*). This idea recurs; one form of it which has become very popular, and is supported by the findings of contemporary science, is James Lovelock's Gaia. In truth it is an immemorially ancient notion – that the earth is a goddess. Ritter, like Lovelock, came to his conclusions as a result of painstaking scientific research and experiment, and, like Mesmer, decided that there was a galvanic force in all nature by means of which its separate parts communicated. He found evidence of the force in crystals, metals, plants and animals and in the human body: '... animals, plants, metals and stones? – Are they not all parts of *Nature's cosmic animal*?'[4]

The Romantic position at that time was that electricity was the spark of life itself. One remembers that lightning was the father of Mary Shelley's monster. For Novalis the galvanic current was 'a higher consciousness of Nature – of the soul of Nature'. It was an 'inner light', and the use and understanding of electricity, which pervaded the universe, would bring back the Golden age. Schelling, the Romantic nature-philosopher, identified the principle of life with an etherial and electrical fluid. 'How,' he asks, 'is it possible to explain why animals take fright when the atmosphere is charged with electricity, or why experiments with animal electricity meet with greater success during thunderstorms, without assuming the existence of an invisible fluid that permeates both the organic world and inorganic matter and fuses them into one living whole?'[5] This universal fluid to him was the soul of nature and the creative ether. Life was seen by the German Romantics 'as a sort of cosmic circuit in which individual organisms interrupt the current and intensify it . . .'[6]

Not to prejudge the case for galvanic force or 'magic stuff', it is nevertheless true that the animal creation participates in a web of consciousness quite inconceivable to Oedipal onlooker consciousness. We must look at the evidence for this in some detail, as the animal is one of the terms in the Sphinx's riddle. We may also find 'magic stuff' there after all, in nature's continuum.

Humankind has understood from the earliest times that animals respond to and express forces apparently invisible to ourselves. We seem to be exiles from their world, but we have expressed a kind of nostalgia for Freud's 'phase of development that has been surmounted' by creating animal gods. All the religious apparatus, from totemism itself to the animal-headed gods and goddesses of ancient Egypt, shows that humans yearn 'for the lost good' which theologian Paul Tillich tries to tell us is the source also of animal anguish since the Fall.[7]

Gerald Massey, the nineteenth-century poet and mythographer (he is not as well known as Robert Graves, but surpasses him in the latter role), tells us that because animals possessed sharper and more extensive senses than our own, as seers of the invisible, the first gods were given animal form. He reminds us of what everybody has observed: that if you show your cat its reflection in a mirror, 'So far as sight and appearance went, this might have been another cat. But she proceeded to apply the comparative process and test one sense by another, deliberately smelling at the likeness to find out if any cat was there.' Her sense of smell told her there was no other cat present, 'therefore she was not to be misled by a false appearance, in which she took no further interest'. Massey's parable concludes that it was so with primitive humans, who were truly humble, and 'would find no human likeness behind the phenomena of external nature . . .' because the powers first perceived 'were not only unlike the human; they were very emphatically and distinctly more than human, and therefore could not be adequately expressed by features recognisable as merely human . . . which were also necessarily superior to the human and were not the human faculties indefinitely magnified'. He says (and we shall find that contemporary animal researchers have reached similar conclusions about themselves) that the theoreticians of his time had so magnified their merely human faculties that their mental operations were completely dissimilar to those of early humans in contact with nature who, he says, '*thought in things* and almost apprehended with the physical sense alone. [The moderns] overlook the fact that *imaging* by means of object-pictures preceded the *imagining* so often ascribed to primitive man.'[8]

This sign-language would include body-language in all its forms – ritual, gesture, dance, tattoo, ornamentation, and song incorporating animal cries as hunter's calls – and would be projected also as non-phonetic cave-drawings or as hieroglyphs. Massey hints that the origin of speech could have been partly in the high articulation and excitement of animal mating calls, and in the corresponding human cries in the sexual act. Such calls, ritualised for fertility magic, would be very potent on the mind and senses. The animals that had 'demonstrated the possession of superhuman faculties and powers' would become the charged images of those powers, and become the point of contact for the humans who wished to participate in them. This would of course include the bounty of the food-animal, who knew how to live and to multiply in places where humans, without that bounty, could not.

Massey's three great books[9] are crammed with vivid examples, well backed-up by documents and linguistic analysis demonstrating the comparative poverty of our own unparticipatory speech. As an introductory example in his *Ancient Egypt* he offers the figure of the cat which, since it sees by night, was adopted as the living type of the moon on earth in the hieroglyphs, but also shared the fate of the witches in the European persecutions. As the witches were seers and foreseers, 'Whenever they were persecuted and hounded to death the cat suffered with them, because she had been the type and symbol of preterhuman sight.'

Similarly, frog-headed Hekat was also the 'Seer by Night in the Moon, as well as the crier for the waters and foreteller of their coming' because the frog by its croaking heralded rain, and also prophesied the all-important Nile inundation: 'From her, as Seer in the dark, we may derive the names of the Witch as the Hexe, the

3

Hag, the Hagedisse; and also that of the dark goddess Hecate, the sender of dreams.'

In Africa, the frog, because of its startling transformation from the tadpole, was and is frequently a sign-word for the menarche of puberty. A missionary's wife called to the native girl to take charge of the baby. The reply came: 'Nchafuleni is not there; she is turned into a frog.' Massey says that she could not come for a reason of taboo, but said so not in our terms but in the language of animal types. 'She had made that transformation which first occurs when the young girl turns into a woman. She might have said she was a serpent or a lizard or that she was in flower . . .' but that was not her totem.

Juvenal asks: 'Who does not know what kind of monsters Egypt insanely worships?' and Massey's rejoinder is that 'having seen or heard of the long-tailed Ape in an Egyptian temple, the satirist assumed without question that the animal was set up as an object of worship.' Juvenal did not know that 'the Ape itself was the worshipper, as an image in Sign-Language and as the Saluter of the Gods . . . The Ape or Cynocephalus with its paws uplifted is the typical worshipper as Saluter of the Light . . .'[10] for, as modern information agrees, when the moon wanes and then becomes dark, the monkeys around the Equator, which are in menstrual synchrony, begin their cycles with the bleeding and call out in the darkness.[11] The remarkable atmosphere produced by this event in the temple was probably used to induce menstrual synchrony in the women or the priestesses there. The animals themselves were the celebrants, leaders or priests.

Can we see what practices remain in modern times, equivalent to the witch's familiar or the ape with its dramatic response to the moon's phases, and how they correspond simultaneously with the Romantic and scientific view of life? There may be a clue in the universal figure of the serpent, for Charles Whibley remarks that Romanticism was 'born in the Garden of Eden . . . the Serpent was the first Romantic . . .'[12] We recall the Greek staff of the physician Aesculapius, with its twining serpents. 'Paint Two Snakes, the place is then sacred,' says the poet Perseus. The double snake pointed directly to the bleeding-healing rhythm of the woman, and appeared on the Uraeus snake-crown of Maternity, worn by the Egyptian Queen as Goddess, and signified the complete moon-cycle of ovulation and menstruation, body and soul intertwined. It was the healing moon-cycle of death of light into dark, and rebirth from darkness, as the snake, and the moon, as it were, sloughs successive skins: a type again, of transformation, and of *flow*.[13] The direct experience of rhythmic containment and flow is known to all women. Shuttle and I have attempted to recover the meaningfulness of this in *The Wise Wound*, and women are now adopting practices that image the cycle, as the Uraeus did. Few, however, keep snakes, although the snake-woman Lilith appears widely in dreams and art.[14]

The serpent was also reputed to be the great mesmerist of the animal world, in that it could hold its prey spellbound, and therefore it became the living example and evoker of similar mesmeric powers in the human world. Here we link up with the healing powers of the 'relaxation response', which have recently been rediscovered in contemporary medicine.[15] The temples for healing by dream-incubation were originally haunted by snakes, and we shall see that this, as in the case of the temple monkey, might have been because of the snake's sensitivity to its environment. The 'relaxation response' is the first stage of that state of relaxed yet alert imagination we call 'hypnosis', in which the initiations of the mystery-religions were conducted.[16] The ritual objects, the 'things seen', are comprehended only in this state of romantic reverie, which Novalis held to be the clue to the understanding of the world by 'amorous science', as did Ritter, and Goethe with his 'exact sensorial fantasy'. It is the poetic state. One 'thinks in things' for this kind of direct understanding, or gnosis, to 'See with a feeling eye, feel with a seeing hand' and 'Vision occurs when the eye becomes an optic hand' or, as Wordsworth says, with 'an eye practised like a blind man's touch'. The German nature-philosopher G. H. Schubert wrote in the early nineteenth century in his *Night-side of the Natural Sciences*, 'Somnambulism has nothing which is not related to the customary characteristics of living and wakeful people: it is simply that these appear in a quite wonderful manner magnified and refined . . .'[17]

In modern times, Freud, Jung, Ernest Jones and many others have attributed to animal dreams the power of getting in touch with one's libido, one's 'animal self'. A modern neo-Jungian says: ' . . . by recovering his animal nature, man becomes God',[18] and Jesus in the Oxyrhynchus Sayings declares, 'The fowls of the heaven, and of the beasts whatever is beneath the earth, or upon the earth, and the fishes of the sea, these are they that draw you unto God . . .'[19] Some 70 per cent of all dreams in children are animal dreams. Animal dreams in women seem to cluster round the period, and in some cultures the period is seen as a special opportunity for integration with one's animal nature.[20] Freud says, 'Wild beasts are used to represent the libido, a force dreaded by the ego and combated by repression.'[21]

In waking life it has been shown that if a dog comes into a room where there are humans, their blood-pressure goes down.[22] Owning a dog can have a permanently beneficial effect on blood-pressure. Keeping any pet will help you live longer: even the presence of the small body of a budgie will console and heal physically as well as mentally.

Animals induce healing relaxation. Some think there may be chemical and electrical feedback mechanisms as well – we will return to this. The animal's life draws one's attention from one's own, and the natural healing energies can operate unconsciously. If you watch tropical fish, the flickering and the slow dance of the living things induces a light trance, which is healing and beneficial. Skin resistance will increase, and so will the slow alpha-rhythm in the brain. A creative reverie may result. The strange but efficient organic forms appearing and disappearing resemble visions before sleep, when the two worlds touch between sleeping and waking. This is the reverie referred to by Novalis. Problems can be deliberated half-consciously in this mood, and answers like waking dreams given by unconscious mechanisms.[23]

Everybody knows television can do this too, if you turn the sound off and watch the patterns. The purpose of television, however, is not to soothe people and return them to themselves, but to excite, stimulate and frustrate, so that the viewer will feel a desperate need to buy some commodity. Animals and nature, in contrast, induce the relaxation response: 'The movement of brightly coloured fish in a tank or unconfined above a tropical reef, the passing of birds through a forest, the pattern of clouds, all have this dual property of having points of instantaneous beauty that attract our gaze but lapse without notice into an essential constancy . . .'[24] This is not, however, a purely visual response, otherwise television would do as well. When one watches three-dimensional *flow*, as in the complex snaky surface of a body of water, responsive to every breeze (which in its turn communicates the action of the entire environment), there is a deep massage of the ciliary muscles of the eye in their attempt to focus every motion: this can also occur in watching hologram patterns, which have been used to strengthen the eyesight and as advertising in opticians' windows. And the flow of animals described in the quotation would express every environmental factor perceived by their 'numerous and enlarged senses', distilled into the patterns within a tropical fish tank.

One of the first things noticed in such a state of relaxation is that senses other than the visual begin to wake. Relaxation brings a sense of warmth in the skin, and a feeling of pleasant touch and weight in the way one sits and the clothes one has on – if they are comfortable; if they are not, they are doubly unpleasant until any constriction is loosened. Hearing becomes more subtle, so that quiet noises or music can convey exquisite and extended meanings; they can even, if the eyes have closed, give rise to vivid mental pictures or analogies. A trill on the piano may in the very relaxed or 'hypnagogic' state become a flash of vividly coloured tropical birds in a deep green tropical rain-forest, or a shiver feathering over the skin. The sense of smell also subtilises, and one takes increased pleasure in ordinary natural aromas. Any of the senses may speak to any other: the pleasant smell of fresh air combines with its touch into a meaningful caress to which the whole body responds, as we saw Wordsworth's did. There is a healing synaesthesia in this meeting of the senses and, if words are gently spoken accompanied by touch, it can seem we enter a different world. Everybody knows this is lovers' craft. But it is also witchcraft, what witches do in their magic circle, a synaesthetic event. And it is the method and practice of hypnotic trance-formation to conjure into a subject's mind sensations from the senses he or she least uses – a predominantly visual person will be induced into trance by suggestions of touch or smell.[25] As we saw with Massey's cat, no animal will separate its visual sense from the others in testing out its reality. And, spoken into such a trance, a single word becomes a living hieroglyph, and a gentle command, 'Sleep now, and wake renewed', becomes a reality.

There is a tale in an essay by the German Romantic dramatist Heinrich von Kleist (1777–1810) about a fencer whose skill angered his expert opponent. The latter declared that he had met his master but that there was a further master for everyone and everything. He took his rival to a shed in which there was a trained bear and urged him to attack it with his rapier. As soon as he did so, the bear made a slight movement which turned the blade aside; then the man feinted to deceive the animal, but it did not move. The bear parried his thrusts like an expert, but always when he feinted made no movement. No human fencer could equal him: 'He stood upright, his paw raised ready for battle, his eye fixed on mine as if he could read my soul there, and when my thrusts were not meant seriously he did not move.'

For Kleist this is an illustration of how 'in the organic world, as thought grows dimmer and weaker, grace emerges more brilliantly and decisively'.[26] For him, intuition needs intellect, but is higher than intellect. Indeed a recent book on computer 'artificial intelligence' argues that participating intuition is more characteristically human than computer-simulated analytical intelligence, but only in the 'innocence beyond experience' of the expert.[27]

However, despite the behaviourist, contemporary work shows we should not be too cocksure that animals are without conscious awareness. Donald R. Griffin, for example, argues a strong case that the principle of evolutionary kinship and continuity between humans and animals suggests that if an animal communicates with us then it also may be aware of doing so. Indeed animals appear to enjoy communicating, and it could be that it is in the very act of communication that they become consciously aware. This is certainly the case with humans: that communication increases enjoyment of life, and that we are most aware when using some medium such as language in its poetic form, comparable to animal play and birdsong. Griffin says that the hypothesis that some animals are aware of what they do, and form internal images that affect their behaviour, 'simplifies our view of the universe by removing the need to maintain an unparsimonious assumption that our species is qualitatively unique in this important attribute'. He says that inasmuch as human thinking and consciousness is closely linked to language, and in so far as animal communication 'shares basic properties of human language, the employment of versatile communications system by animals becomes evidence that they have mental experiences and communicate with conscious intent. The contrary view is supported only by negative evidence, which justifies, at the most, an agnostic position.'[28] We should no longer automatically suppose that animals are Cartesian clockwork, and we the only ones with souls.

We shall see that animals have communication and sensory systems that appear to surpass the human consciousness. But we shall also see that humans appear to have cut themselves off from this world, not as a result of organic evolution, as Freud supposed, but by social compulsion and individual acquiescence. It is as Oedipus Rex believed: by killing the Sphinx he had solved all riddles and needed no oracles.

Contact with this world, even through the domestic animal, brings healing. Paul Tillich quotes the German nature-philosopher Schelling on the veil of sadness which is spread 'over all nature, a deep, unappeasable melancholy over life . . . manifest through the traces of suffering in the face of all nature, especially in the faces of the animals', and says, 'The tragedy of nature is bound to the tragedy of man, as the salvation of nature is dependent on the salvation of man.'[29] But perhaps that sadness is the sadness of the alienated onlooker consciousness projected outwards on to those animals. Then again it could be that humans, having cruelly separated themselves as a species from the remainder of creation, have denied that creation forms of consciousness which by participation with the human it would otherwise have possessed. A new animal-human partnership may be the next phase of evolution, if we are lucky – for the animals are closer to Gaia than ourselves.

There is an amazing scene, lasting only a few seconds, in Cassavetes's film *Lovestreams* (1984). The hero is a philanderer who has become clumsy in his approaches to his amatory prospects, and is rejected by them. His disturbed and bossy sister makes matters worse and imposes on him by filling his house with pet animals. Late at night he is sitting at his table in despair. Suddenly, sitting opposite him, he sees a wise-looking bearded middle-aged man, who nods at him encouragingly with a friendly power. The next moment he is alone in the room – except for the dog, who has climbed up and put his forepaws on the table. This is the story's turning-point; new energy comes into the lives of both brother and sister after this vision. There is also a wonderful case-history in Laing[30] of a woman who experienced being a dog before she could become a person. I have myself had parallel experiences, and in psychological work encountered many people who have recovered and integrated features of their animal nature and acquired new life and gifts thereby.

This non-Oedipal vision of the integration of human and animal (the vision of the Sphinx) is common to societies that do not prize the onlooker consciousness above other forms of awareness. Joseph Campbell's world atlas *The Way of the Animal Powers* (1984) shows how widespread this vision is even now. Gerald Massey shows its roots in language, fable and custom. There is little doubt that many societies owe their survival and continuity to animal shamanism, and by addressing the animal powers gain seasonal and weather information, essential to hunting and agriculture, medical and spiritual guidance and a sustaining conviction of the unity of all being on this earth: a Romantic vision in short. The statement of a chief of the Duwamist tribe is typical of the native American Indian view: 'What is man without animals? If all the animals were gone, men would die from great loneliness of spirit, for whatever happens to the beast also happens to man . . . '[31]

There are already many studies in contemporary medicine of how companionship with an animal will heal mental illness (which may as I have suggested by definition be the loss or imbalance in a person of their animal powers). Dogs are the most familiar catalysts in 'animal-facilitated therapy' because of ' . . . their ability to offer love and tactile assurance without criticism . . . ' They become a social catalyst also; they promote a 'widening circle of warmth . . . a positive affective state'.[32] There are wonderful accounts of dolphins healing neurologically impaired children.[33] 'For the animal shall not be measured by man. In a world older and more complete than ours they move finished and complete, gifted with extensions of the senses we have lost or never attained, living by voices we shall never hear . . . ' Thus it is possible that we, humans, are the little brothers, not yet grown up.

Even in so obvious an observation, supported absolutely by statistical figures, that people who are married live longer than people who are not, we have no idea of the underlying mechanisms. We have 'little idea about how the transactions of everyday life, or the objects of everyday life influence our health'.[34] Could it be by a kind of continued alchemical interaction between the conscious state and the unconscious animal sides of the two partners, as Jung suggests? The immune system is affected by a bad marriage, and the white cell-count becomes depressed.[35]

There is no doubt that such an alchemy occurs between people and people, and people and animals. Aaron Katcher says that this belief was forced on him when he observed 'that patients with coronary disease who had a pet enjoyed a better life expectancy than similar patients without pets'.[36]

People also talk to their pets, and confide in them, shamefacedly. This contrasts with the full-blooded shamanistic dialogues which Michael Harner – a white initiate of American Indian shamans – has relearnt for himself and his students. He says: 'Shamans have long believed their powers were the powers of the animals, of the plants, of the sun, of the basic energies of the universe. In the garden earth they have drawn upon their assumed powers to help save other humans from illness and death, to provide strength in daily life, to commune with their fellow creatures, and to live a joyful existence in harmony with the totality of Nature.'

There is often a guardian spirit called the *power animal*, and it can appear in human form, as in Cassavetes's vision, for to the shaman humans and animals are part of the same family. It is not just the highly trained magicians who can draw on guardian powers: 'In many primitive cultures, anyone with a guardian spirit may use dancing as a means of evoking his alter ego,' and this spirit may appear in multiple forms in the process of unification. It may manifest itself, for example, as a possession; or consider the experiences of Laing's patient. 'The dancer's spirit finds its dramatised expression in dance steps, tempo, movements, miens and gestures: in the sneaking pace, then flying leaps of the ferociously yelling "warrior", or in the swaying trot of the plump, sadly weeping "bear mother"; in the rubber-like reptilian writhing of the "double-headed serpent" . . . in the "lizard" who sheds tears over his devoured offspring or in the mighty "whale" who grabs smaller fish.' It is a system of cure and psychological fitness only so far glimpsed in our own culture. 'Paragnostic' powers are claimed: knowledge obtained by other than ordinary means.[37] Michael Harner's book gives instructions for achieving such experiences; for example, how to contact your 'power animal'.

Nevertheless, people who merely confide in their pets already know something of the shaman's experience. The pet, as empathic listener responsive to undertones of speech, body-language and odour which run deeper than ordinary communication, can resemble and act through its body-language as a counsellor or psychotherapist. The dog, for example, is 'non-directive, non-judgmental, and sensitive to the speaker's emotion', and in this situation, as with the silent Freudian analyst (who may be putting out more communication than he realises within his silence), the healing associations flow and the 'talking cure' takes place without an audible word being uttered by the 'therapist'.

It is more than talk, though, because 'people caress their animals when talking to them, and the dialogue with the animal is an alternation or superimposition of talk and touch. When we think about the definition of intimacy, one of its hallmarks is the combination of talk and soft touch.'[38] We shall see how important chemical communication is among animals – indeed Edmund Wilson of *Sociobiology* fame says it is the dominant means in many animal species, perhaps even in most – and how far-reaching is the evidence that it operates in humans, but unconsciously. The dialogue with the pet must then be suffused by the pleasure-smells emitted by the animal's skin and breath as the fur is caressed; and in feedback reinforcement the human will send human smells of pain or sorrow and then, increasingly, pleasure to their partner in the dialogue, the animal consoling, and the two linked into one therapeutic pleasure-unit. This is almost an 'amorous science', and the study of human-animal interaction 'permits the study of intimacy without sex in the same way that the procedures of Masters and Johnson permitted the study of sex without intimacy'. Can we, though, consider the animal energies involved to be wholly distinct from loving human sex? Surely it is a continuum, and the animals come to teach us the elements of intimacy without shame. The dog never shows shame and this is part of his power: 'He remains . . . in the condition of Adam and Eve before the Fall . . . ' Like the original human couple, 'The animal is permitted to display his anus and genitals without shame . . . '[39] He is naturally free of the sublimations and libidinal displacements which we considered in our discussion of the Oedipal dilemma in the Introduction. In our intimacy with the animal we are again in that state of relaxation, the healing relaxation-response, in which a kind of pre-Adamic synaesthesia is commonly glimpsed. This 'grace is not uncommon between people and animals'. And between people and people? This Kleist tells us we must achieve: 'As the image in a concave mirror turns up again right in front of us after dwindling into the distance, so grace itself returns when knowledge has as it were gone through an infinity.' His interlocutor exclaims: 'Does that mean . . . we must eat again of the tree of knowledge in order to return to the state of innocence?' 'Of course,' is the reply, 'but that's the final chapter in the history of the world.'[40]

Scientist Aaron Katcher goes further, and argues that the healing power of the guardian pet is not limited to its individuality. The characteristic constancy of an animal is 'the constancy of cyclical time, life in the cycles of day, month, season, lifetime' and of course weather; all animals respond visibly to the weather – from the house-cat to cows who lie under hedges when storms are coming. The domestic animal restores a sense of natural time in a culture dedicated to 'improvement, to hierarchical progress, to getting ahead, to accomplishment'. The animal generates a feeling of continuity and constancy spanning the sudden changes to which human life is subject: bereavement, job-loss, divorce, house-moving, the birth of a child; these are the occasions on which, statistically, we are most prone to illness, and, 'We would expect, therefore, that pets should protect against the pathogenic effects of life-change.' There is also something supernal about animal loyalty; Katcher points out 'a quality of love that exceeds the capacity of mere humans' and it is like the love of a god, for animals are, he says, both 'mortal and immortal. An animal's blood flowed like human blood, but its species was undying.'[41] Everybody knows how a guide-dog can give eyes to the blind. Now there are guide-dogs for the deaf.

There is also a sacred element in the quality of animal play, the spontaneous intimacy of it. It is said that the Psalmist was mistranslated when he said, 'Be still and know I am God.' This is apparently better rendered as, 'Be playful and know I am God.'[42] It teaches us to pay attention not only to the dreams and visions that come from the unconscious mind, but also to the bodily movements and feelings in response to that invisible world which in full playful waking consciousness are unpremeditated: the actions which Arnold Mindell in his book of that name calls 'Dreambody', and Jung calls the somatic unconscious. Mindell shows us how many illnesses can be traced to the frustration of this 'Dreambody' when it is not allowed full expression; full bodily expression is one of the lessons that playing with an animal teaches us.

Animals can act as twenty-four-hour-a-day nurses' aides, especially with the bedridden chronically ill. They can be taught to react and give the alarm to changes in breathing, heart-rate, unusual perspiration, or excessive fever. The medium of this communion is still a mystery to science: not only does the human blood-pressure go down when an animal is present, but when a human approaches an animal its heart and respiration rate goes up, and it is soothed by stroking. The great American physiologist W. Horsley Gantt hoped by studying these effects to eliminate all possible known stimuli and uncover a special kind of animal energy. 'Is the effect of a person transmitted by the known sense, or is it transmitted through radiation or some kind of as yet unmeasured waves with unknown laws of transmission?'[43] Animal magnetism, in effect.

It is significant that the movements of yoga and tai-chi and the postures for intercourse in the love-books are all named after animals and the actions of animals. As Jung remarked, 'Civilised man must heal the animal in himself and make it his friend . . .' but it is more a question of healing that 'civilised man'.[44]

> With all their eyes at once the creatures gaze
> Into the Open, but our eyes are turned back
> And set like white blind traps to catch
> Tree, animal and child before they know they're free.
> Only from the dark animal gaze do we really know
> What's out there, since we snatch the young child
> And wrench it round so all it sees is objects and not
> Subjects, and never the Open which is the deepness
> In animals' faces. Only we can see death; the free
> Animal has God in front and death a long
> Way behind, so when it moves, like a fountain
> Already in eternity it moves, a fountain.[45]

Meanwhile, we must not trap our children in the merely human, as Rilke counsels. Who can doubt that there is a natural and healthy communion between a boy playing with his dog or a girl riding a horse: the awareness between the two can be *seen* – but it is a multi-media event! At the Macomber Farm Project in the USA children are taught to sense as the animals do. There are scent-mazes to explore. There are special glasses to put on and see as sheep or horses. There is a platform that simulates an animal stride for, as in yoga, posture retunes the senses.[46]

2 Closer to Gaia

We must now look at what is known of the extent of the animal senses, and the versatility of animal communication, to see what organic life is capable of. We shall glimpse the world from which the human being seems to be excluded. After that we shall study the range of the human unconscious or subliminal senses, and argue that this exclusion appears to an extent to be more by choice than necessity, which is a kind of original sin. For the sources of the following information, please see note 47.

The ways animals communicate with their environment has turned out to be a much fuller and richer series of transactions than any scientist anticipated, and several unsuspected and new senses apparently not shared by humans have been discovered in animals since the 1950s. In the 1930s the idea that birds might orient themselves by means of the sun or stars was thought a romantic notion – as indeed it is. It was believed that animals could only navigate towards or away from, or at an angle to, a fixed source of light. It was an impossibility that they should be able to find their way without using navigation tables and almanacs, as humans do, against the constantly changing background of sun and stars. It was not until the 1950s that it was shown that they were quite capable of making the necessary flight-compensations. By 1975 it was undoubted that birds practised 'time-compensated sun- and star-orientation'. Indeed, some birds seem to have an inherited knowledge of the night sky. Much was learned by observing the flight of blackcaps under artificial skies in the Bremen planetarium.

Moreover, birds are now known to have a magnetic sense also and find their way on immensely long migrations by means of the geomagnetic field. Fromme showed conclusively that robins could find their migratory direction in cages in the laboratory, but in a steel chamber this did not happen. When he switched on artificial magnetic currents, the birds responded to those. Homing pigeons are similarly endowed. When a pigeon claps its wings and rises in flight it is sending out a radio-blare from the feathers in its wings, which are made of piezoelectric keratin ('piezoelectric' means that the protein keratin is one of many substances which turn movement or pressure into electrical currents – see page 34 below). This electrical transmission orients the bird to its place in the geomagnetic field. Birds are also sensitive to the Coriolis force produced by the rotation of the earth. The geography of the earth has its sound-map too, which is used by navigating animals. 'Infra sound' produced at low frequencies by individual geophysical features has its own tone, and can be recognised at a distance of thousands of kilometres.

The pioneer in much of the work on magnetism was Frank Brown at the Marine Biological Laboratory in Woods Hole, Massachusetts. In 1960 he showed that the mud snail 'could actually distinguish between various magnetic intensities and was also aware of the direction at which magnetic lines of force passed through its body'. The magnetic sense has now been proved for termites, June bugs, pond snails, weevils, crickets, locusts, wasps, flies, some beetles, fruit flies, several kinds of fish and whales; possibly it will eventually be concluded that the entire animal kingdom is sensitive to the geomagnetic field. Although special magnetic sense-organs have been found in some animals – pigeons, for example, which have magnetic particles of iron oxide in their retinas – it is probable that the whole body is the receptor, as we will show in the next chapter. If this is the case, then animals live immersed in their medium, which penetrates them through and through. It may be a kind of 'unlimited mutual penetration of oceanic imagery' that animals experience, only focused for particular needs, like feeding or communication. Anton Ehrenzweig shows that in humans this is the nature of the creative state, the 'oceanic de-differentiation', the place in which we find all our scattered elements in play, and from the experience of which we can assemble them in new wholes.[48] Similarly, Jung declares: 'The unconscious is nature, which never deceives.'

Ultrasonic sounds are emitted by bats fairly continuously, but it was not until the late 1950s that it was proved that these animals used sounds beyond the range of human hearing in a system of echo location so sophisticated that it not only provided the bat with the means of flying without collisions through the blackest night and the darkest of caverns, but also enabled it to catch the tiny night-flying insects on which it fed. It was also shown that certain moths had not only developed hearing sensitive enough to warn them when the bats were flying, but had also developed the ability to generate jamming frequencies of ultrasonic sound themselves, making them invisible to the predatory bats. It is likely that moths also use the moon and the stars as navigation guides.

Whales, porpoises and dolphins also use echo-location sonar – for finding their way and for catching prey. This ultrasonic sense makes light of the blackest places. The dolphin generates its sonar through horn-shaped transmitters on each side of the nasal passages, and the sound-waves are concentrated by reflectors into twin beams. The vibrations are produced by the rapid filling and emptying of internal sacs fitted with valves – a kind of internal wind instrument like a French horn. The songs of whales and dolphins in the ocean spaces probably produce musical waves of great complexity, like architecture, which extend through the entire resonant space. According to *The Times* (10 November 1986), dolphin sonar can ease human childbirth.

The sea is full of signals and counter-signals. The spawning of the croaker fish in 1942 set off the American undersea defence system in Chesapeake Bay, and detonated its mines. Gurnards grunt; the pistol-shrimp can shatter glass with a noise from its pointed claw; toad-fish roar. In fact, most fish make some communication by sound, and receive sound messages. Herrings chirp at various rates which carry messages such as, 'Change course, beware predators, gather into a school.' Many fish sounds are produced by percussion of the swim-bladder, or a banjo effect of moving ligaments stretched over hollow spaces. Some, such as moon-fish and soldier fish, grind their incisors.

You could call all hearing, including ultra-hearing like this, one of the *feeling* senses, like touch. These animals would therefore have *touch like sight*. It would be a projected sense; they would send their touch ahead of them in the form of these vibrations, and the returning echoes would touch them back. Although dolphins have special receptor organs in the head, it is probable that this touch of sound (like Wordsworth's caress of breeze) is felt over the whole body, and within the body too, as the sonics and ultrasonics penetrate a certain distance within. Most fish 'hear' through the touch organs of their lateral line. The carp has developed a special 'ear' out of these organs.

This is inner touch; and if we can conclude with Donald Griffin above that animals are aware (and it is parsimonious to posit otherwise) in ways which resemble our own consciousness, and this touch being the supremely erotic sense (through which a person, according to Blake, may pass out into eternity at what time he pleases), dolphin communication then resembles erotic play, felt sight, the optic hand. Perhaps their great talent is play ('Be playful and know I am God') and this accounts for their extraordinary brain development, for they have larger brains than human beings.

The sense of touch in fish is extraordinary; they can seemingly 'feel' the entire length of the stream in which they live, from source to mouth, or throughout a body of water like a lake. Such sensitivity is almost unimaginable to us, except through metaphor.

Also in the late 1950s a wholly unsuspected sensory modality was discovered which, like the magnetic sense, has the profoundest implications for the argument of this book: the electric sense. It was shown that the electric ray and the electric eel perceive by electrifying their environment. They create, by means of electric batteries in their musculature, a tremendous electric field which (as in the echo location) is distorted by the objects around: it is radar rather than sonar. This class of fish swims through the water electrifying it by rapid pulses from their living battery. All objects which are better conductors than water draw the lines of force of the field together, and all poor conductors force them apart, so a picture is formed, much in the way the field of electromagnetic radiation we call visible light conveys by reflection and diffraction the visible world to us. The charge, however, is so strong that it can stun prey, and fishermen as well.

Not all fish generate large currents, and it is probable that most of them that do not are still sensitive to modulations of the earth's electrical field. One of these is the dogfish, which by this means dowses out its prey fish even when it is buried in the sand. The sense organs that do this, called the *ampullae lorenzini*, are widely distributed on the body surface. Sharks also use this kind of passive radar system.

Another type of fish generates weaker currents than the electric eel, but uses them with considerable sophistication. An example is *Gymnarchus*, which sends out both spaced electric pulses and a regularly oscillating electric field. The latter is used in electro-location, the former in social communication with other fish of the same species. The electrolocation field can be modified so as to avoid interfering with fields being used by their fellows, much in the same way as radio stations avoid interfering with each other by choosing different wavelengths and frequencies. Recently, the amphibian duck-billed platypus has been added to the list of animals known to be electro-sensitive.

Yet another unsuspected sensory modality was discovered among honey-bees. Bees, like birds, not only orient themselves by the changing position of the sun, but by means of the polarisation patterns of the blue sky. It has now been shown that nearly every animal is sensitive to polarised light, while human beings are almost blind to it. Thus you can get a glimpse of part of the visual subtlety that animals by the water enjoy on a sunny day by slipping on your Polaroid sunglasses. Immediately the world is full of detail, and the water no longer dazzles, but allows the sight to penetrate it.

Animals using these previously unsuspected sensory channels are of course building up a cognitive map of the environment, and it is here when we are questioning animal awareness that 'problems of spatial position, of orientation and of direction finding . . . lead us naturally to the problem of conscious self-awareness'. We should not fall into Ouspensky's error of attempting to demonstrate that animals are necessarily and vastly our inferiors, by removing from them, as he does, the richness of all sensory modalities other than the visual surface, and then comparing theirs with the human performance. This is to show that chalk is not good cheese. (Later in the same book, however, he affirms: 'Animals often give the mystical sensation of nature to men.')[49] We should consider too the problem of pain in animals. We all believe that warm-blooded animals feel pain, but insects also on injury release pain-hormones into their blood; caged bees show panic reactions; and recordings from microelectrodes in insect brains show extreme electrical reaction to injury, as one would expect.

Apart from these recently discovered unsuspected senses, which must alter our attitude of habitual condescension to the powers of animals, other senses similar to extensions of our own have long been known and studied in them. We can only hint at the richness of material here.

Many animals can see without eyes, at least to an elementary degree, and so have 'dermo-optical perception'. Eels and lungfish have light-sensitive tails, and so do blind cave-fish. Clams have light-sensitivity in their soft parts. Hydras and sea-anemones have light-sensitive skins. In amoebae and most protozoa the whole substance of the protoplasm responds to light.

Many animals can see far into the ultraviolet, which is invisible to us. The whites of roses, morning glories and apple blossoms are all different colours to the bee, because of the differing amounts of ultraviolet they reflect. If we could look through a bee's eye we would 'be surprised to discover more than twice as many blooms as our ultraviolet blind eye can see, with ornaments never registered before,' says Karl von Frisch. There are flowers in the tropics which are pure red but reflect no ultraviolet, and bees ignore these, but the humming-bird is 'red-sighted' and feeds on the nectar. Moths see ultraviolet, and the horseshoe-crab has a special set of ultraviolet eyes. There are more than seventy octaves of electromagnetic radiation, and the human being acknowledges the visibility of less than one octave, our sight being cramped, as it were, between the red and the violet: the colour of our arterial and our venous blood.

Many animals can also see into the infra-red; they can see heat-radiation. Mosquitoes and body-lice find their way to juicy places by infra-red. The rattlesnake has a special infra-red sensory organ. Moths have sophisticated antennae for infra-red detection; fish have elaborate temperature senses; and certain animals, such as the incubator bird, have an *absolute* sense of temperature exactly set for the hatching of their eggs.

The marvels of smell in dogs are well known. They are capable of perceiving the 'odour fingerprint' that is the perception of individuality in each living thing, and which is linked to the nucleo-protein 'gene-markers' that make each cell in each piece of tissue entirely individual, and this pattern is part of the immune system too, which defends that individuality against damaging intrusion. Thus we have the equation: individual odour equals hereditary make-up, and this can be perceived by the chemical senses of such animals. They can detect actualities and details of smell to an incredible extent. They are sniffing right down into the gene, into the hereditary material. In the laboratory it has been shown that dogs are able to choose correctly from among a set of clean glass slides the one that was touched by a single fingerprint as much as six weeks earlier, sometimes if the slide has been exposed to the elements for some days; but not even a bloodhound can tell the difference between the odour fingerprint of identical twins, for the reason that the hereditary material is identical between them. To the enhanced animal senses the sub-microscopic world of genetic material is thus continuous with the world of behaviour and natural scents. The rabbinical legend of Adam is that God gave him both microscopic and telescopic senses, so that he could name all the creatures. Either the rabbis got it back to front, or else the creatures still live in Eden.

The olfactory area in a human nose measures only 5 square centimetres, but in a German sheepdog covers 150; there are 5 million olfactory sensory cells in humans as opposed to 220 million or so in this kind of dog. However, the moth's olfaction is as superior to the dog's as the dog's is to ours. Starfish smell out clams through many layers of sand. Ichneumon flies smell out through tree-trunks the wood-boring creatures beneath whose skins they lay their eggs. The salmon finds its way through thousands of kilometres of ocean water to spawn in the river where it was hatched. It does this by taking its bearings 'from the scent of its native streams and following a characteristic trace of scent upstream like dogs following the scent of a track'. Electrical orientation is probably involved too.

Eels have comparable abilities. Harold Teichmann showed that eels could detect synthetic rose-scent diluted by a proportion of one thimbleful to fifty-eight times the quantity of water in Lake Constance. The salmon and the eel are able, then, to detect the entirely individual odour of a particular body of water, and scent it out from halfway across the world.

Minnows smell with their skin, and are so sensitive that the equivalent in a human being would be their being able to tell by touching a door-handle the names of the people who had touched it during the course of a day. Yet animals are not overwhelmed by this sensory input: Lewis Thomas tells us that fish in a shoal live and respond to their environment as one creature, yet each has its individual and distinct 'odour fingerprint'.

Chemical communication by scent, as we said above, is possibly the most important mode of communication in the animal world. Many warm-blooded animals, as is well known, use scent-marking to establish territories in elaborate patterns. Wolves are typical, for the whole of a region occupied by them is laid out with intelligence posts or signal posts at a couple of kilometres' distance from each other. Any newly arrived wolf can obtain from these scent-marked posts – stones, trees, mounds, skulls or any suitable objects are used – the information he needs to keep alive. They will speak to him of friends, foes, hunger, a possible mate, hunters, sick or well beasts, potential companions.

The variety of animals who use such a system is enormous, and includes deer, cats, martens, badgers, hedgehogs, rhinoceroses, etc., but all mammals seem to possess scent glands, and they are found too in fish, reptiles, amphibians, and also in insects and other invertebrates. It is likely then that a sophisticated language of smell and scent marking is used throughout the animal kingdom. Insects that live in communities, such as ants, bees, wasps and termites, circulate in their hives and nests chemical messengers called 'phero-mones' which, in contrast to hormones circulating *within* the blood-stream, circulate outside the body and 'join two or more individuals into a higher unit', such as a termite nest working like a single organism regulated by its queen's pheromones.

Some animal scents change body-structure radically, as when the locust is pheromone-changed from a harmless grasshopper into a creature with a 15-centimetre wingspan capable of eating up crops as if by fire in marauding hordes of 6 billion or so individuals.

The exception to the scent rule seems to be birds. Although birds can smell quite well (and some water-birds smell with their legs), birds have no scent glands, and there is no indication that smell is important in their social life.

An aura or penumbra of smell surrounds most mammals, how-ever, and it is one of the chief forces in their social personas, including the way they mark their territories. White rhinos tread in their faeces to potentiate their footprints. Some antelopes and Brazilian giant otters create a riverside quagmire, in which they defecate, urinate and ejaculate, and then wallow. Lionesses paddle in their urine.

We have discussed above some examples of the exquisitely sensi-tive touch or hearing responses in sea-dwellers; this sensitivity runs through the animal kingdom, whatever the environment. The web of the spider is a kind of telephone exchange of vibration. When a male garden spider wants to attract his mate, he fastens a thread to her web and plucks it in a certain rhythm. The difference between this and vibrations made by captured and struggling food is clearly registered by the female. With the funnel spider, the female will wrap the food in its web and call the young by another special rhythm when it is safely dead and wrapped up.

Here is a description of the perceptual world of that Sphinx-like highwaywoman, the tick: 'After mating, the female climbs to the tip of a twig on some bush. There she clings at such a height that she can drop upon small mammals that may run under her, or be brushed off by larger animals. The eyeless tick is directed to this watchtower by a general photosensitivity of her skin. The approaching prey is re-vealed to the blind and deaf highwaywoman by her sense of smell. The odour of butyric acid, that emanates from the skin glands of all mammals, acts on the tick as a signal to leave her watchtower and hurl herself downwards. If, in doing so, she lands on something warm – a fine sense of temperature betrays this to her – she has reached her prey, the warm-blooded creature.'[50]

There is very fine discrimination. The tree is like the spider's web to the bird. Birds will sit all night in a tree that is vibrating to the wind, but will awake instantly if a marten is climbing towards them. Their touch-hearing lives along the whole tree, along similar lines to Pope's description of the spider: 'The spider's touch how exquisitely fine!/ Feels at each thread, and lives along the line.' Bluebottles and blueflies have pressure-gauges in their antenna-joints which are efficient wind-speed indicators when they are flying. They can 'see the wind' as magicians and shamans are reputed to. The gigantic sea-jellyfish, the Portuguese man-of-war, fills the water round it for hundreds of cubic metres with its touch- and vibration-sensitive tendrils. Fish below the size of a mackerel may safely swim there, but if the jellyfish feels a larger fish intruding it fires its stinging batteries, and gathers the stunned prey into its digestive aperture.

Communication signals *between* animals have been shown during the past thirty years to be complex, diverse and versatile, beyond what was previously expected. In investigations that range through the animal phyla and many species, from fiddler crabs to chimpanzees, the *minimum* communication has been shown to include an announcement 'that the sender is of a given species, sex and appropriate age, and is in one of a relatively few basic behavioural states, such as readiness for fighting, fleeing, or mating', on an intensity scale from weak to strong. This is the minimum capacity observed. There is often – perhaps always – a 'finer grain' in animal language. Birds and mammals recognise their individual companions of the same species: the signalling behaviour is flexible and interrelated, and 'fairly complex sequences are performed, with each step depending on an appropriate signal or response from the partner'. One could say as much or as little after watching human beings with the 'onlooker' mind.

Recent work on bees has shown extraordinary richness. Had a comparable language system been discovered in monkeys, 'What an impact such a finding would have had on theories about human language!' Yet this takes place in an insect with a brain weighing only a few milligrams. They use the 'waggle-dance' to indicate to other forager bees the exact position in relation to the sun, or the polarisation of light on a cloudy day, of food supplies outside the hive, and what type of food is to be found. Sometimes returning foragers do not dance, and then the odours from one bee to another give the necessary communication, regurgitated or carried on the limbs or body. The dance can indicate food, water, or desirable resinous material from plants. When the hive is about to swarm, waggle-dances are performed over the whole mass of bees, and these indicate the position of alternative new homes for the swarm, such as different cavities in trees. The sounds the bees make also add to the information and communicate the excitement of a forager bee at a rich discovery of food. Tones of body-sound are vital also in the duel between the young queen and old queen ('hooting and croaking') or if the hive is disturbed by an intruder. As the hive is dark, these 'complex jostlings' will be perceived by the tactile and vibration sense organs. In finding a new home for the swarm, the worker bees *compare* information as to which will be the best site: the bees 'speak' and 'listen' to each other, confer and reach a decision through these dances of touch, odour and sound-vibration. There are other rituals, such as the 'buzzing run', which carries the message of 'Let's go!' after the scouts have agreed the location of the new hive. It is very probable that there is much more still to learn about the communication systems of bees.

There are equally astonishing discoveries about communication in chimpanzees – one young female chimpanzee named Washoe was trained to communicate with human companions in American Sign Language for the Deaf and acquired roughly 130 signs, invented some herself, and used them in conversation with humans. Chimpanzee communication in the wild is likely to be far less basic. Great spotted woodpeckers can learn to communicate different food needs to humans by means of a telegraphic drumming code; but in the wild the grammar of birdsong has been shown to be extremely versatile and flexible. The long call of laughing gulls has a 'finer grain' in which it communicates various messages under different circumstances. It conveys not only identity, but 'I am your parent – come and get fed' or 'I am your mate – let me sit on the eggs' or 'I am the occupier – get out' or other messages; it is 'semantically and practically open'.[51]

To summarise what cannot be doubted about the sensory channels of social communication between animals: chemical communication, including pheromones, is widespread, and is particularly important in insects, flying phalangers, rodents, cats and

monkeys; sounds are important in both vertebrates and invertebrates (it has recently been demonstrated that the cat can hear right
down to the minimum subatomic quantum noise-level);[52] aquatic
insects use surface waves; tactile communication is frequent, as is
electrical orientation and signalling in many groups of fishes; visual
signals have widespread use, especially gestural ones – a particularly
striking example is the courting of some fireflies, which signal sexual
readiness by exchanging light flashes. But it is also clear that research
has only scratched the surface; and, if the honey-bee is any example
and is also, as is presumed, low down on the evolutionary scale, we
cannot estimate what marvels of communication may be revealed
when humans rid themselves of their arrogance and consent to learn
from animals more closely related to us. It is all very well praising a
young female chimpanzee for being able to converse in deaf-and-
dumb language with human beings, but why should she learn our
language? Should we not try somehow to learn hers? No anthropologist would set out to study the behaviour of a tribe by demanding
that the tribe first learnt English. Donald Griffin, in proposing a
pattern of future research, insists that two-way communication is
essential in any definitive study. You cannot be sure that animals are
talking to you unless you can talk to them. It must be a participatory
investigation, like Jane Goodall's acceptance without disguise by
wild chimpanzees, which was pioneering work. An alternative
approach would be direct impersonation of, say, the chimpanzee by
a disguised experimenter using chimp sounds and gestures and
drenched in chimp pheromones, and this would be pure shamanism,
an animal dance in an animal mask among the animal powers. We
might very well find that communication among animals is as rich as
or richer than our own, through sensory channels that we have
forgotten and could relearn: through touch and gesture, through
smell, through animal warmth and magnetism. It is the feedback
from the animal so exquisitely responsive to its sensory world that
brings about the animal cures with which we began this chapter. The
reverence shown by the shamans to their power animal is a type of
'participatory investigation' by direct impersonation. The shaman
becomes the animal in his dances, and conveys his healing as the
animal itself would, as the dog by his presence heals his hypertensive
master, sick with civilisation's coronaries.

If animals are by their senses so immersed in the continuum of nature, it is not surprising that they can convey otherwise invisible information to us, as if by magic. Shamans are known to be able to predict animal food supply and weather changes from their trances in which they communicate with their power animal: as has been suggested above, the trance is a method of relaxed concentration with guided imagery in which more is discerned of its subject than in the ordinary tense and contracted mind. Shamans or no, it has long been known that animals respond to weather changes and earthquakes when no sign is visible to the ordinary human who cannot perceive anything but the coarsest changes in the continuum.

Animal indications of earthquake or hurricane[53] include insects starting to fly close to the ground and near water, earthworms coming out of their holes, ants leaving their hills, deer and other game departing from the woods and becoming less shy, cattle and pigs refusing their stalls, chickens crying constantly and birds giving their special weather or rain calls, snakes leaving their lairs, bears quitting their winter quarters prematurely, dogs howling in unison, and many wild animals appearing suddenly tame. Tributsch gives the title *When the Snakes Awake* to his remarkable book, thus acknowledging the environmental sensitivity which makes them such potent cultural symbols.

In the case of an earthquake, it is suggested that animals respond to subsonics created by the grinding of rocks, to the electrostatic charges built up by mechanical pressure, and to charged aerosols released from the ground. The Chinese have an advanced system of earthquake warning based on the observation of animals; in the West we prefer to disregard this valuable source of information.

At about 10 a.m. on 20 February 1885 sea birds in screaming swarms darkened the sky above the town of Concepción on Chile's Pacific coast. The dogs fled out of the houses at 11.30. At 11.45 an earthquake destroyed the town. The research ship *Beagle*, with Charles Darwin on board, was lying at anchor off the coast. Unfortunately, he slept through the quake. Had Darwin himself recorded the animals' behaviour, earthquake premonition might now be in the mainstream of science. To this day the villagers on the slopes of Mount Etna all keep cats. If they rush out of the houses, the humans follow. Because of the flood of information pressing on the senses, it is very difficult for humans to keep their mental or even physical balance during an earthquake. One seismologist reported that he did not know during the main quake in the town of Valdivia whether he had been able to stay on his feet or whether he had several times been thrown to the ground. Among the information to which human beings ordinarily do not pay attention, but which is increased so as to overwhelm consciousness in an earthquake, are the subsonic vibrations, changes of electrical charge in the air, magnetic storms and very high barometric pressure. Incipient or very mild earthquakes in places such as England, on the other hand, tend to give rise to folklore. Disorientation possibly from this cause occurs in Cornwall, and is attributed to earth-spirits or 'pixilation'. '"They say it's the little folk. Tourists rather enjoy it, I think, being overcome and left vague for a moment because the landscape seems to shift and alter and you can't remember where you were and what it looked like a moment ago." "I think it is the spirits of Nature, which we call changes of the weather, the vast electrical cliffs, slipping down in the sky, avalanches of invisible lightning. And I think there is weather travelling under our feet too."'[54]

Geo-electrical phenomena may be the explanation of the strange phenomenon referred to in Sylvia Plath's poem, 'The Great Carbuncle', in which on high moorland at evening people's hands and faces become luminous for half an hour or so. Visions of flying saucers have been attributed to charged aerosols rising from the ground in semi-earthquake regions and producing a form of trance. It should be recalled that the Delphic oracle, which gave all that bad news to Oedipus, was pronounced by a priestess, who inhaled trance-inducing and prophetic vapours from a deep cleft in the ground. She took the name of an earthquake-sensitive animal: the Pythoness.

There is recent scientific work which is full of astonishing suggestions as to the almost inconceivable extent of the natural continuum of communication between non-human creatures. It has been shown not only that trees control their insect populations by means of pheromones which they secrete on their leaves and barks, *but that they actually communicate with each other by means of chemicals carried on the wind*. Thus, if a certain tree in a grove of *several species* is attacked by insects, then its secretions carried by the air will stimulate insect-resistant secretions in its companions. Add to this the likely interactions between weather, forests and their population, and you have an astonishing picture of a continuum between plants and animals, and of the trees as presiding and senior influences. One remembers too that all such chemicals enter the natural water-cycle of the clouds and the rain. Thus nature has its chemical 'moods'.[55]

Some of the most astonishing and accessible ideas concerning the natural continuum are found in the writings and work of a physician and scientist, Lewis Thomas, particularly in his *Lives of a Cell*. Here the continuity of nature is more accessibly evoked on the basis of a strict scientific discipline than it is in some more famous books, such as James Lovelock's *Gaia*, which contains ideas, as Lovelock acknowledges, anticipated by others, such as James Hutton and Vladimir Vernadsky.

Thomas appears to equate the unconscious mind, leading down to the depths of the self, with the subcellular details of the body; moreover this is a *collective* unconscious, since *certain of these details are almost identical in all creatures*. Our metabolic energy is provided by minute cell-inclusions called 'mitochondria'. These, together with the centrioles, basal bodies and certain other structural features, appear to have originated as a kind of bacteria that swam into the original primitive cell and stayed there without changing throughout evolution. These germs that infected the primitive cell to its benefit are called 'prokaryocytes'. Thomas speaks of these essential constituents of the human cellular structure as those 'other little animals . . . sorting and balancing me, clustering me together . . .'[56]

Moreover, it is because these protoplasmic constituents are so closely related, whatever the species, that the basic substances created by them and used in communication in the plant and animal worlds can cross boundaries between phyla and species, so that creatures of very unlike kinds can communicate with one another in constant natural adjustments, as we saw above with the trees, who 'understand' each other. The chemical constitutions of animal and plant hormones, sex pheromones and messenger systems in plants and animals, are all closely similar. This is why, for instance, the pig responds to the truffle – the latter emits a sex odour-chemical almost identical to the pig's own; and why you find human insulin in a common bacterium. Aspirin may be a plant growth hormone.[57]

Thomas sees individuality as the fragile thing. He says he is 'grateful for differentiation and speciation, but I cannot feel as separate an entity as I did a few years ago, before I was told these things, nor, I should think, can anyone else'.[58] The continuum of earth's life is to him the astonishing thing. To Thomas, nature is less like a single organism than a single cell. In the flux of this continuum it is as though humans with their onlooker science select only the bad news, for our medicine takes notice only of the harmful nucleoprotein substances or viruses. In truth, there are passed in every way through every creature continuous streams of nucleoprotein, which is the kind of molecule that carries information, whether as gamete nucleus or virus: it is the library of life, continually rewritten and added to.

Thus 'we live in a dancing matrix of viruses . . . ' Virus diseases, so much of the province of medicine, 'may be looked on as an accident, something dropped'. That we are so preoccupied with antisepsis and death and disease seems like 'human chauvinism'. 'Devouring nature' as an idea is, then, the wrong way round, for the majority of associations between living beings are 'essentially co-operative' and when creatures seem to be adversaries Thomas sees that in the overall picture as a kind of 'stand-off relation . . . It takes long intimacy, long and familiar living, before one kind of creature can cause illness in another.'

We isolate microbes in the medical laboratory but, in truth, comparatively few of them can be suitably cultivated alone, for 'they live together in dense, interdependent communities, feeding and supporting the environment for each other, regulating the balance of populations between different species by a complex system of chemical signals . . . Disease usually results from inconclusive negotiations for symbiosis, an overstepping of the line by one side or another, a biologic misinterpretation of borders.'[59] Lewis Thomas is the same scientist who led the group of researchers who were able to identify the 'gene-marker' with the absolutely distinct and individual 'odour fingerprint' that each creature possesses.

There is a much earlier experiment that would also have overturned the 'onlooker' paradigms of biology if it had been widely known and correctly understood. Some people have warts so badly that their entire body surface is painfully affected by them. A group of such patients was induced into hypnotic trance, and the suggestion was that the warts on *one side of the subjects' bodies* would heal and disappear. This is indeed what happened – a perfect experiment, with each person their own control, and half their warts gone.[60]

The seminal point here is that the development of warts, like that of cancer, involves the immune system, in that tissues stimulated by an invading virus are not rejected by that system. However, *by word of mouth* the complex molecular key-and-lock system by which the gene-markers and the antibodies operate was altered. By verbal command, the proteins were adjusted in their structure. The scale of size here is that as the molecule is to the whole body, so a golf-ball is to the size of the earth. Not only, then, can genetic make-up be smelled in the 'odour fingerprint' but human language can also alter nucleoprotein structure. If this is the case, as is suggested by Stephen Black's admirable study,[61] then we had better be careful how we use words. Words can be the source of blessings, or plagues. Each night at about nine o'clock most of the population sits down in front of the hypnotically flickering television for a trance-induction session in which we are given a deliberate selection of the bad news from all over the globe. Of course there is bad news; but can we ever estimate what viruses and psychological plagues may be created by this negative feedback? These are the plagues of Thebes, the monsters from the Id. We would be better off, maybe, with a balance of good news, for that exists too, as this book hopes to continue to show.

3   Magic Stuff

'It was a memorable night! I will name it the night of the Great Peacock.' We are in the laboratory and home of the great French naturalist, J. H. Fabre, called the 'insects' Homer'.

The Peacock is a big moth, the largest among the European species, with 'its livery of chestnut velvet and its collar of white fur'. The wings are grey and brown, zig-zagged across with a paler colour and bordered with white, and 'in the centre of each wing is a round spot, a great eye with a black pupil and variegated iris', of concentric black, white, chestnut and purple-red.

On a May morning a female Great Peacock clambered out of its cocoon in Fabre's study, and was put in a gauze cage. That evening there was a cry from Fabre's little son, who was rushing to and fro dancing and stamping: 'Come quick! . . . come and see these butterflies! Big as birds! The room's full of them!' The whole house, in fact, fluttered with the male moths. Father and son entered the study, candle in hand. 'What we saw is unforgettable. With a soft *flic flac* the great night-moths were flying round the wire-gauze cover, alighting, taking flight, returning, mounting to the ceiling, redescending. They rushed at the candle and extinguished it with a flap of the wing; they fluttered on our shoulders, clung to our clothing, grazed our faces. My study had become the cave of a necromancer, the darkness alive with creatures of the night!' Magic indeed! – the darkness alive.

This magic was repeated for eight nights in succession, but how did the visiting moths find their way, and what attracted them? They arrived in the perfect darkness of a heavily clouded night, through grounds protected from the mistral by densely planted cypress and pines. The house itself was hidden by plane trees and was reached by an alley thickly bordered with lilacs and rose trees, and thicketed with evergreens. Fabre was convinced that neither sight nor sound could account for the nuptial visitors.

Smell remained as a possibility: ' . . . Are there effluvia analogous to what we call odour: effluvia of extreme subtlety, yet capable of stimulating a sense-organ far more sensitive than our own?' Fabre had already discovered, unfortunately by brutal mutilations, that, whatever the sensitivity was, it resided in the gloriously plumed antennae. He tried to mask possible odours by sprinkling naphthalene (moth-balls are made of it) around the study. It did not trouble the male visitors. He changed the position of the cage; the visitors still came. However, when he replaced the transparent gauze with tin boxes, wood, cardboard, a bell-jar, hermetically closed, then no males arrived. He changed the species, and experimented with the Lesser Peacock moth. The results agreed. Then an awkward fact made itself plain. The male visitors came *with the wind*. If the attractant was a perfume, that would be impossible!

He repeated his experiments with the Oak Eggar moth. Still the males would not come to a hermetically sealed container; and still they reacted to the female in a room full of the worst scents that could be devised. But they seemed to linger around the objects which the female had touched; it was a 'love philtre' exuded by her body and exquisitely tuned to her own species. It appeared to be a perfume that lingered on objects made of glass, or on cloth. The male moths would pay these objects attention instead of the female. The female might be in the same room, but the males would pay her no attention until her 'female alembic' began to operate.[62]

The attractant did seem to be a perfume most exquisitely and minutely perceived, and no other explanation fitted; but how did the male moths detect this perfume when they were flying *with* a strong wind? It should have blown away the subtle structures and concentrations of perfume that they would need to find her out in her constantly changed containers and rooms.

In order to explain this mystery of the animal senses we must establish the nature of another factor in the natural continuum, and that is electromagnetic radiation. We shall create a model from the available information which will show (begging the question of animal awareness for the moment) that certain animals not only 'see the wind' as magicians are rumoured to do, but see perfume and electricity too, in a kind of synaesthetic 'cloud of glory' or 'magic stuff' that is everywhere, like Mesmer's aethyr, or animal magnetism.

It is perhaps not realised how full the world is of invisible colours. It is clear enough in our usual world how the narrow band of electromagnetic (EM) radiation we call light shining from the sun is altered in its pitch, wavelength or colour by falling upon all the contents of that world, and is absorbed or re-radiated, and this creates all the colours, hues and tones which we enjoy. Goethe called this 'the Deeds and Sufferings of Light'.

A substance can be completely transparent to radiation, as glass is to visible light, and allow that radiation to pass without changing its pitch, colour or wavelength. It can also alter the colour of that light by bouncing it about within itself, thus creating many colours, as an oil-film on water does.

However, not just light, but any radiation, from fast gamma waves to the slow long Schumann waves proceeding through the atmosphere at the resonant frequency of the earth, is bounced off, around and variously within all the matter of the world, altering its character and effect as it does so. We are surrounded by these 'Deeds and Sufferings' of radiation, extending through the whole seventy-plus known octaves of EM beyond the single octave that we can see.

Nature abhors categories. There are no single entities such as 'wave', 'particle' or 'field' in nature; on the contrary, they are all capable of turning into one another, like an extraordinary conjuror's show. The reason why radiation is called 'electromagnetic' is because it is both electrical and magnetic at once, and capable of immediately becoming either.

Everybody knows about the field round a magnet, that which

makes an iron fragment jump to the attractor. There is a similar field round anything which is electrically charged. It can be static, or vary in strength. When it varies, it radiates electromagnetically. An electromagnetic wave is created, which consists of oscillating electric and magnetic fields at right-angles both to each other and to the direction in which the wave is travelling.

The wave can turn itself back into pure electricity. Thus, if you spark high-tension electricity from an electric coil, you will create electromagnetic radio waves. If you have a similar spark gap adjusted in the next room, that will pick up the broadcast, and turn it into sparks. These sparks will also broadcast radio waves in their turn, and create a strong intermittent magnetic field. Indeed, it is thought that an EM wave propagates by turning very rapidly first into electricity, then magnetism, then back again into electricity.

You can turn the magnetism into electricity by moving a conducting wire in its field; this is what happens when you spin a coil of wire between the electromagnets of a generator. Also, if you erect a wire of the right length on your roof, out of all the EM waves which surround us constantly all the time it will pick out a pulse related to its own length, and turn it into a varying electric current, the imposed modulations of which our sets translate into television pictures.

It is important to know that this kind of transaction is occurring round us everywhere, not only in the man-made world of electronics, but much more so in the world of nature, where it all began. EM waves are being turned into electric currents within conductors like copper wire or iron ore deep in the earth, and these currents as they flow in turn create magnetic fields, which in their turn will charge moving conductors with a current, which will send out an electromagnetic wave, to be absorbed or re-radiated, changed in its pitch, wavelength or colour, everywhere.

EM is also held as fields or standing waves on the surfaces of non-conductors like plastic film or insect wings and, when these move, they regenerate altered EM. It should be realised that 'conductors' and 'non-conductors' are comparative terms: all things have degrees of conduction and resistance. 'Semiconductors' (of which the transistor is such a one) turn out to be very important in the living organism – this was hardly understood until their use in electronics transformed technology. In living tissue, the movements of clouds of electrons through protein lattice-structures are highly sensitive to environmental fields and currents, and provide an alternative communications network to the nervous sytem.

There are also substances called 'electrets', which are comparative non-conductors, like birds' feathers, insects' carapaces or human skin and hair, which, when they stretch or flex, generate currents. Alternatively, electrets will hold an electric field as a magnet holds a magnetic one. These organic electrets show a type of 'piezoelectricity', which is a property shared by many crystals, including crystalline rocks. When these crystals are pressed, they generate current; or, alternatively, if a current is passed through such a crystal, it vibrates. Thus EM can be turned, or transduced, into audio vibration, and vice versa. Piezoelectric crystals are thus used in the manufacture of both microphones and gramophone pick-ups.

This transduction is the clue to the maser and the laser, which rely on a type of stored fluorescence in a crystal or a vapour. In museums you often see mineral specimens in a dark showcase radiating a variety of weird colours. A lamp behind the scenes will be bathing them in invisible ultraviolet light, and they are turning the invisible light into various vividly visible colours. This happens when radiation falls on a substance which absorbs it. The electrons become charged up or excited, and re-radiate the energy at a different frequency or colour which will be characteristic of the re-radiating specimen.

Everybody knows the fluorescent electric tube. Here an invisible current is passed through a gas, which re-radiates visible light. It might just as well, depending on the gas, re-radiate an invisible colour, like ultraviolet. Moreover, gases do not need a tube to re-radiate; free-flowing gases in nature will fluoresce, but often in colours we cannot see.

Gases containing free-floating organic materials, like pheromones, are especially voracious of infra-red microwaves, and the organic molecules will re-radiate this energy that is poured into them, although it will be transformed by the vibratory system of the particular molecule.

A gas (or a crystal) may absorb a lot of radiation before re-radiating on its own frequency. This charged gas then becomes very sensitive and selective towards additional radiation. Suddenly the right wavelength (the one you want amplifying) will cause it to produce its accumulated fluorescence all at once, like an uncoiled spring. This is the basis of the maser (Microwave Amplification by

Stimulated Emission) and of the laser which is a similar system producing visible light. Both maser and laser produce *coherent* radiation; that is, the electromagnetic waves they produce march all together, as it were, in step. Since the emissions are not scattered, they do not blur with each other, but combine into a single-minded pulse. In man-made lasers or masers, this coherent pulse is further amplified within a resonant reflecting chamber, like a hall of mirrors. However, free-floating masers exist anywhere, in nature or out of it, where there are the right conditions of radiation, constitution and proportion of emitting to non-emitting substance. For example, a rain-cloud full of organic molecules transduces in many ways the radiation that plays upon it from the sun, and it is possible that it not only amplifies into coherent pulse a particular component of the radiation it receives, but that as it alters its dimensions it becomes for a while a resonant chamber which by internal reflection amplifies this pulse further. We are all familiar with the strong 'moods' the clouds possess. It is already known that a cloud, like a combination of cathedral bell and electrostatic machine hanging in the sky, will pick up audio subsonics generated by storm-action far out at sea, and act as a kind of satellite echo chamber, re-transmitting them, and causing a type of storm-sickness in coastal towns. The compression wave audio will itself change the electrostatic and electromagnetic qualities of the cloud, and vice versa. It may form re-radiating 'phonon masers'.[63]

Everything echoes with EM in its Deeds and Sufferings. It is worth looking at a drop of oil spreading on water. First the oil spreads in rainbows of all colours, but as the film thins the colour rises in frequency from red to yellow to green to blue to violet and finally disappears into the ultraviolet. This is because the light is resonating in the decreasing space between the oil surfaces; the iridescence results from the interference between the light rays reflected from the upper and lower surfaces of the oil-film, which is like an echo chamber or resonant space. Technically, a phase disparity is created which summates to variously changing frequencies – if the light were audible sound you might hear the red buzzing higher and higher in pitch with the changing colours until it faded away into ultraviolet inaudibility.

This rainbowing of surfaces, this resonance and echoing, is taking place with all substances at all times; EM is being bounced about everywhere, and transduced not only into different modes of itself but also into the palpable audio-touch vibration spectrum. An electrical storm may make rocks buzz or railway lines twang; this is an audio component of the EM. Air, under varying pressure, like a note sung, will have varying electrical properties. In outer space there are EM waves so low in frequency and so long that when they hit the earth they can be heard and are called 'whistlers'.[64] A strong magnetic field will twist polarised light – this is called the Faraday effect – and thereby alter the quality of what you see; that is, if you put your Polaroid spectacles on. Humans are not ordinarily sensitive to the marvellous subtleties of polarised light in nature. However, some of the freshness of the world after a shower is due to increased polarisation.[65] EM, like audio, is being bounced about everywhere, in varying degrees of diffraction, coherence and polarisation. Indeed, one view of atomic structure is that matter itself is like an interference pattern between waves – you can say that matter is a particular form of electromagnetism. Guy Murchie uses these words about the 'full scope' of the radiation spectrum: 'If in a long view of the ocean, say, one could regard the tides as nothing but extremely long, low ocean waves of a super order and very slow period, so might the end waves of radiation be conceptually extended into other orders of space and time: down into the deep infra-bass frequencies of slow-flashing variable stars and whole gyrating galaxies, and – why not? – up into the still less understood ultra-altissimo frequencies that quite possibly vibrate somewhere far inside the inmost hearts of atomic nuclei.'[66]

One can grasp all this quite easily by watching the surface of a pond when pebbles are thrown in (except that EM waves are not compression waves, as those in water or air are; the *patterning* is, however, entirely analogous). The initial waves bounce and ripple everywhere, reflect, cancel each other out, echo from the banks, scatter into incoherence, augment each other in coherent patterns, die away, receive the complexities of a sudden rain-shower, distributing them within its space. Everything echoes with EM; every current that flows creates an EM wave; and when an EM wave meets a shape that tunes to it, an electric current flows. These inaudible effects can be compared with the echoing of sound in every substance of a cathedral when the organ is played, the organ here standing for the sun, moon, planets and stars as sources of different tones of direct and reflected radiation. The acoustic space of the building will already have been designed to be very sensitive. For example, Basil Spence in re-designing Coventry cathedral took great pains to re-create the original acoustic atmosphere. He felt 'that a cathedral should not only look like a cathedral but should sound like one too . . . ' He tested literally hundreds of samples of plaster until he found one that had all the desired acoustic qualities – a resonant chamber.[67] But the audible compression waves, pulsed by the echoing, focusing nave, the vibrations of the music, will also light up with minute electric currents, and consequently broadcast, the piezoelectric stones of which the cathedral is built. The stones will begin to live. The energy of the organ pulse and the singing will also accumulate in the free-floating masers of incense and candle-flame, human breath and perspiration, until they can hold it no longer, when it will discharge in a flickering subvisible fluorescence, also pumped up by the strong infra-red radiated by the human metabolism. We will call the totality of this the 'spell' or 'atmosphere' of the place, which has been expressly designed to create just such a magic.

The cathedral space if left empty of people and music will still resonate in a daily beat as it is warmed by the rising of the sun and cooled by its setting. The musical interludes of the services, in their rhythm, are like the regular passage of cargo-ships over the larger and slower beat of the sun- and moon-tide in an estuary. Bodies of water, confined with their own resonant space of bank and shore, show their local movements, and these play over the slower, continual tidal resonance of the water to the moon's and the sun's gravity passing overhead. All is penetrated and immersed in the wave-complex of visible and invisible light. What we see is determined as much by the invisible as the visible, for the quality of the visible light cannot be separated from the Deeds and Sufferings of invisible radiation, or the look of a place from its sound, or the smell of it from the look, for, as we shall see, wherever there is a fragrance there is likely to be a subvisible radiance, charging the light with its underglow.

Goethe knew this, for in his 'Deeds and Sufferings of Light', darkness – the invisible – was a contributory power, just as the Chinese Yin always accompanies the bright Yang. This is in contrast with Newton's theory, which has been favoured by our European visual 'onlooker' consciousness, and holds that only visible light is concerned in the generation of colour.

The Chinese call the radiant continuum *feng shui*, which means 'wind and water'. It corresponds exactly to Anton Mesmer's hypothetical fluid. Its medium is called *ch'i*, which is both cosmic breath and creaturely energy. Humanity's place in nature is described as 'a drop in a flowing stream'. It is said that 'while all things – hills, streams, trees, humans, stones – inhale *ch'i*, they also exhale it, thus affecting each other', and '*ch'i* is not just a signal telling us to move – *ch'i* actually moves us'. The Chinese say that we possess many senses, not just the five common ones: 'People possess more than one hundred "senses", most of which are latent.'

Feng shui is the science of perceiving 'nature's moods' and acting on that information to build houses and cities. It is presided over by the dragon-force, *ch'i*, which resembles our Western Sphinx; only more so, since it has 'the head of a camel, the horns of a stag, the eyes of a demon, the ears of a cow, the neck of a snake, the belly of a carp, the claws of an eagle and the soles of a tiger', and it can either be the size of a mountain range or it can shrink to that of a maggot. It is embodied in nature; it is nature's energy. Human beings, standing outside nature, those onlookers, can sometimes discern it: 'There is a touch of magic light . . . the sky has a new light: another world . . . Upon coming into its presence, one's eyes are opened; if one sits or lies, one's heart is joyful . . . Here *ch'i* gathers, and the essence collects. Light shines in the middle, and magic goes out on all sides.'[68]

Or, as Coleridge in 1800 asked himself: 'N.B. What is it that makes the silent *bright* of the morning vale so different from that other silence and bright gleams of late evening? Is it in the mind or is there any physical cause . . .'[69]

Living things certainly fluoresce visibly. Under particular weather conditions immensely strong atmospheric electric fields are created, which can pull electrons away from conducting fluids, such as the body fluids of an insect. A cascade of these electrons can then excite atmospheric gas molecules to fluoresce visible light. This apparently happens with migratory flights of the Spruce Budworm moth, which gather in clouds as big as 100 kilometres wide. In the right weather conditions, these flying cities of moths fluoresce in clouds of glory, and are said to account for some UFO sightings of luminous flying saucers.[70]

To return to Fabre's laboratory: the darkness of the night and the direction of the wind might turn out not to be material in the enigma of the male moths. Infra-red light (that is, heat-light, which is normally invisible to us) is absorbed and re-radiated strongly by most substances. To those animals which can see by infra-red, the night is brilliantly lit by the moon, *even if it is behind clouds*, as there is an infra-red 'window' in water-molecules.

The female substance, the pheromone, emitted by the female moth is intensely fluorescent in infra-red: it forms a maser-cloud as it evaporates into the air. This rapidly diffusing chemical substance, in itself an attractant, would also be fluorescing its particular signal-light (invisible to us) in the night-time infra-red, and exuding from windows or any other opening. The female would be secreting light, and filling the house and beyond with her pulsing coherent broadcast, picked up by the aerial-like antennae of the males. The house would seem stuffed and surrounded with a cloud of enticing and changing light, like a laser light-show in a disco, and the male moths would fly into it just as they did into the smaller candles and lamp within the house.

There, in the laboratory, the female moth will have been flapping its wings, though not flying, as its feminine alembic gets going. This vibration will modulate the pheromone fluorescence, altering its 'colour' with each beat, and the wing-shadows cast in the luminous mist will act as a direction-finder: clearly the beat alters according to which angle you approach it from, and will be lop-sided unless you steer at it head on. Such principles are used in flying aircraft by visible light or radar. This whole picture relies on Philip S. Callahan's model, of which more later.

Thus, there is an uncanny pulse from the female wing-beat, twisting or becoming more symmetrical and satisfying as the visitor gets closer. The darkness does not hinder, the radiating perfume diffuses to an unknown extent past and through the foliage, and is visible to the males flying even with the wind, the luminous house is sheltered in its foliage (which would also in its own scented clouds of organic molecules fluoresce under the moonlight and in the re-radiated infra-red from the soil).

Moths are known to make ultra-sounds, and these would also modulate and re-radiate in the cloud as the wing-beats do; the minute sounds and motions of the female concealed within the laboratory being immensely amplified in the cloud, like a Brocken Spectre cast on a mountain mist, and like an astronaut's twisting navigational tunnel, focusing right down not on a runway but on the tiny powerful emitting source of the female. Everybody has seen those videos in which the slightest movement of the pop-singer leaves a trace or a twinkling spectrum of colours; the moths achieved this long before the video-men, and, as we so often find, our artificial devices are copies of unconscious processes subliminally observed in the outer world or in our own bodies.

Philip S. Callahan is a hard-headed entomologist working in US Government Insect Control, a field in which, in order to be funded, his science must work, and be seen to work. But both his success in practical science and the beauty of his ideas are due to the quality of his imagination, which is able to compare the world we live in with the environment of the insects he studies, a world so largely but not entirely unsensed by us: he wants us to see more of the *likeness* between our means of sensing rather than the *difference*.

Callahan draws attention to that strangely neglected portion of the EM spectrum, the infra-red. We have already pointed out that humans see only one octave of the spectrum – the infra-red contains seventeen octaves, yet little is known about it. Perhaps it has been avoided by the 'onlooker' consciousness precisely because it is one of the chief domains of non-human life.

Infra-red is 'the one portion of the electromagnetic railroad track that is best termed *natural radiation*'. The sun emits enormous amounts of infra-red (IR) and so does the moon, and only a comparatively small proportion of this radiation is stopped by clouds, for these are completely transparent to a range of IR wavelengths and translucent to others. Callahan says, 'Natural night light is just as important to our bodies and to all living things as is daylight, for . . . night-time – as well as daytime – is primarily an infra-red environment.'[71]

How interesting, then, it becomes that the colour that humans have used to represent life-energy, from the scarlet-stained bones of buried prehistoric man to the warning-to-life red of a traffic light, should be the visible end of this important part of the spectrum. In the Bible, in the Book of Revelation, red stands for 'fiery might and energy' and was the colour reserved for kings, who might be supposed to be radiating an especial amount of this energy. In Africa, the king was 'the only man entitled to wear fabrics dyed in the colour of the liquid that carries life': the blood.

Moreover, the stars radiate IR (over 3,500 known stars radiate nothing else, so are invisible to the human eye) and so does the planet

Venus. Thus the night landscape is bathed in bright infra-red. The Jonases remark: 'Many odorous solutions strongly absorb waves from both the infra-red and the ultraviolet portions of the spectrum, and perhaps it is significant that there is a connection between odours and the part of the spectrum that is invisible to us.'[72]

Callahan, in pointing out *likenesses*, lessens the boundaries between the visible and the invisible parts of the spectrum, and thereby helps diminish human insularity. The lens of an eye is strictly comparable to any other EM aerial, except that it collects visible EM. It is a dish-antenna. Insect eyes operate as aerials or antennae in the ultraviolet; insect spines 'see' in the infra-red. The plumes of the antennae of the Peacock moth which Fabre so cruelly mutilated would have, literally, microwave antennae very similar in structure to those devised by electronics engineers. This is because 'in the infra-red portion of the spectrum, the study of antenna engineering and the physics of optics overlap . . .'

Beyond the infra-red we have the horn antennae and long metal bars that resonate to, collect and guide the microwave and radio frequencies, which include our televisions. We have extended our perceptions by using these conscious, artificial means of seeing into the invisible, as by the use of X-ray microscopes at one end of the spectrum and radio telescopes at the other, but unconsciously we have avoided the infra-red, where insects could be our exemplars, seeing more than we see, or choose to see, in a radiation mode which affects us most strongly.

Callahan worked in electronic guidance systems during the Second World War, and noticed how moths were attracted to the glow from the gaseous rectifier tubes. He saw that their antennae vibrated continuously in that glow, and how accurately the moths' feathery structures resembled radio antennae. Looking back on those days, he realised that the molecules in the air around the moths were being made to oscillate by the shortwave radiations emitted by the tube. Surrounding the tube ' . . . there is an aura of invisible infra-red emissions of many, many wavelengths, depending on what molecules are in the air . . . The same may be said for the aurora of the IR frequencies rising from a cotton or corn field, or encircling the mammalian body. Over and around such fields and living bodies are vapours of scent molecules stimulated to oscillate as little transmitting "tuned circuits" by the energies of sun and night-sky light.' A charged cloud, an aura, an unseen glory has been created.

The molecules resonate in the same manner as an artificial circuit of coil and condenser puts out oscillations which are long radio waves, in step and with 'coherence'. They are little tuned circuits which sound, as it were, an E M 'note' when battered by the scattered E M source, just as a bell will ring wherever you strike it or whatever you strike it with. This is Callahan's account of a free-floating maser.

The Japanese use the word *Ukiyo* to denote a feeling for the minute and transitory detail of the world, and for things felt by intuition rather than seen through the eyes. Callahan translates this *ukiyo* as 'the fleeting-floating world' and compares it to the invisible energy-structures among which the insects studied by him live.

He watched the little flies dancing in the aura of a rock on Dartmoor; to him the warm tor-top or the radiation of a candle was not simply heat or visible light. Rather, it was that both are 'generators of tremendous amounts of infra-red energy – a sort of invisible fleeting-floating energy world that we barely understand – a world where mists of molecules from the candle, or above the hot rock, glow like various colours of fluorescent neon lights'. They are an 'invisible St Elmo's Fire'. When the atmosphere is at a high tension of electricity, a pointed object like a church steeple or the mast of a ship focuses the electric energy and causes the air molecules round it to break up into ions, to glow and to emit visible light, to fluoresce, like an uncontained manifestation of neon lighting – this is St Elmo's Fire.

Even small electric potentials in the atmosphere will cause the molecules round almost any object to glow in the infra-red. We cannot see it, because the lenses of our eyes have neither the correct shape nor material. If we could see in the I R, a field of corn in the moonlight would look like a vast array of fluorescent lights. Callahan's vision of Dartmoor is of how under the sunshine the scents arise from the ancient rocks, from the heather, the moor grass, the mosses and lichens, the sweat of the moorland ponies and the scents of curlew and lapwing and tor-climbing human being. The sun beats down on the tor and the tor re-reflects its radiant energy back into the brew of vapours, and the molecules in them blend and rotate and vibrate as they absorb the rays. In doing this, they oscillate not in visible colours – blue, red, green – but invisible colours of longer wavelength: 'If we had infra-red eyes, we would give names to these colours – these auras of beautifully psychedelic infra-red frequencies, as easily tuned to by an antenna as are the visible colours by the rods and cones of our eyes.'

A sudden storm swept down upon the traveller Callahan, and he sought the shelter of a Dartmoor inn with its great fireplace and its flickering peat fire. Why, he wondered, did an open fire stir 'such hypnotic longings in the hearts of men' and seem such a living thing? His answer was that although all we can see is the visible light emitted, and all we can consciously detect is the heat, 'The fire is the generator, the transmitter, the oscillator of many thousands of invisible frequencies that we, in our ignorance of nature, lump under the single term of heat.' It is more than heat. Perhaps, he muses, humans have the remnants of the ability to perceive the 'invisible fleeting-floating world'.[73]

And we, ourselves? Our bodies too are a living fire, for the molecular body scents and gases that surround us are irradiated by our own warm-blooded infra-red emission; they too are stimulated to emit such invisible colours, and this changing aura of invisible colours is affected in its multiplicity by the atmospheric electric tension and its ionisation. Given this vision by an intuitive and accurate scientist, we are now in a position to study more deeply the unconscious senses of humans, which may, with the information I have sketched, appear less mysterious, more feasible to the sceptic, and none the less marvellous. We also have Ritter's or Coleridge's Romantic continuum, or one of them: radiant matter, 'magic stuff', the veritable and verifiable magnetic fluid.

TWO
EXTRA-SENSUOUS PERCEPTION

'For thou shalt undirstond that the soule hath two maner of felinges: one withouten of the fyue bodili wittes, another withinne of the gostly wittes . . .'[1]

'Supposing that developed human consciousness had not one pole (that by which we made contact with the outside world, of which touch is the final arbiter) but two: an outer sense of touch and an inner sense which was in direct communication with the inner life-forces of the universe.'[2]

1 Blindsight and the Black Rainbow

The God Heimdal in Scandinavian myth was the guardian of the bridge of the gods, Bifrost, the rainbow. Heimdal could hear the grass growing on the ground and the wool growing on the backs of sheep. He could see what was happening 100 miles away, and the note of his horn, Gjallar, could be heard through the whole universe.

In other mythologies the rainbow is the 'great snake of the underneath' (Yoruba), the 'dead people's road' (Catawba), the great Rainbow Serpent which women create by dancing during their menstruation, and which swallows them up and takes them to Heaven (Australian Aboriginal). In local tradition in Austria and Germany the dead who have died in a state of grace pass safely over the rainbow, but the wicked fall through it into the raging fire which we see as the red band in the spectrum; it is their hell, and they stand there burning in it. Blake thought Hell was misunderstood: 'I was walking among the fires of Hell, delighted with the enjoyments of Genius; which to Angels look like torment and insanity . . .'

It is possible not only to see the red in a rainbow, but paradoxically to glimpse also some of the infra-red beyond sight. It appears as a perceptibly darker band of sky between the red outer arc of a primary rainbow and the red inner arc of a secondary rainbow. You normally see a bow at 42 degrees above the anti-solar point (marked by the shadow of your head), because raindrops refract most of the light at this angle. But there may be a larger, fainter secondary bow formed at 51 degrees, and this bow reverses the colours. Robert Greenler photographed the infra-red bow in 1966, and remarked, 'I saw for the first time an infra-red rainbow that had hung in the sky, undetected, since before the presence of people on this planet.' The visible darkness was, however, described by Alexander of Aphrodisias 1,800 years ago.[3]

It is not difficult to experience what looks like ESP by infra-red 'dermo-optical perception', or 'seeing by the skin'. Cut out identical squares of variously coloured paper, and get somebody else to lay them on a table so you do not know the positions of the coloured squares. Now devise a blindfold you can't peer down, which is difficult, or, better, use some sort of covering over the table, under which you can slip your hands. Now, *feel with your hands for the colour of the paper*. Call out the colour you feel, and see whether the square you pull out is this colour.

You will not be right every time, and some people are much better at this than others. You have to learn the feeling in the hands that changes as you pass them over the squares. Some people eventually get it right every time. It is best to begin by rubbing the hands briskly together, as a masseur will.

This experiment seems to work, when it does, by means of that old animal magic, infra-red, which is emitted by the skin of the hands. The different colours absorb varying amounts of infra-red and reflect back the rest, which is picked up subliminally by the temperature-receptors in the skin.[4] One has to *guess*, which is a way of getting at what the unconscious senses tell one. The guess is a kind of act of attention towards the very slight feelings one senses in the skin; with practice these become more definite.

I headed this chapter Extra-Sensuous Perception because the word 'sensuous' (as opposed to the word 'sensory') implies a certain gusto. The people who do best at this kind of experiment (and Rhine found this with his famous card-experiments on ESP) are the enthusiasts and those who can create an atmosphere of enthusiasm. People who can be taken up into the fantasy that it is possible to see through the skin find it comes true. Who knows what subliminal information the gambler, caught up in his dream of sudden wealth, may gather through his fingers while shuffling or dealing the cards? It is by no means impossible that the gifted player, who can feel further than most into the infra-red with his animal senses, may be able to read the thermogram of his opponents' faces as they examine their concealed cards. The play of their emotions will vary the pattern of their bodily heat, and this will show subliminally in the infra-red. A series of *expressions under the skin* is created by the expansion and contraction of blood-vessels and these will shine invisibly through the opponent's poker-face to be picked up as *feel* by the skin or sensitised eye. In these casinos, despite their trappings of sophisticated high life, it is pure animal 'grace' or luck, the combination of spontaneity and concentration, the romantic 'don't care' of high stakes and the excitement of the risks taken, which create an almost supernatural atmosphere. Such a place will be alive with free-floating maser sub-fluorescence too, for the excitement will arouse the volatile human scents, which will be charged or excited by the beating hearts, the infra-red of the body, the bright lights and pulsing, subdued music. No one can say for certain what actual information this charged atmosphere may bring the gifted gambler, simply by smell of opponent and spectators. Data that comes subliminally and is acted upon will look like luck or inspiration.

So it is with premonitions of death. The living human body behaves as what is called a 'black body', that is a perfect emitter and absorber of radiation. Moving pictures of the details of body temperature behind the skin can now be taken by thermography. Many big science museums have thermograph video displays.[5] You can walk on to the TV screen as a wonderful rainbow-coloured patchwork man with brightly hot eyes and flashing colours playing over your face and clothes. You can hold your breath so that the big vein in your forehead glows, spreading up and out from a point between your eyebrows like a fan.

Thermography will show the heat emitted by a breast cancer, or by the cerebral hemispheres. There is a chilling picture in Jon Darius's book. It is the self-portrait of a thermographer, R. Bowling Barnes, who died in 1981.[6] A dark shadow over his face, particularly above the right eyebrow, shows what is now recognised as a clear warning sign of an impending stroke. His son says: 'A sinister capability, we discovered very soon about the thermograph, is its ability to reveal this "mark" on the face of the unsuspecting victims of arterial disease. I recall many unhappy moments when a casual "snapshot" taken of a visitor or friend showed what our eyes could never have seen about the individual's future.' Such a mark predicting death 'felt' by those sensitive to infra-red would constitute a kind of clairvoyant premonition.

Another category of people who are good at the dermo-optical perception game is that pair of extra-sensuous enthusiasts, to wit, people who have just been making love. The skin is so alive with mutual caresses that lovers, for a while anyway, may seem to 'live' in the whole of it; and the 'afterglow' of an orgasm is the ideal state in which to respond even to the faintest feelings. Love-play is also the perfect entry to other forms of play, such as ESP party-games. In a state of sexual or erotic excitement it is not uncommon to feel one *sees* the shape of a lingering caress, even the shape of one's partner's hand laid on the skin of one's back. People become more easily suggestible or persuasible if they are touched and stroked. This of course means that they can be wheedled into believing a falsehood, but it also means that they can be caressed into understanding a truth or another way of seeing over-familiar matters. The erotic state – again, a mixture of concentration and spontaneity – is a hypnoidal state, probably the most powerful kind that we are capable of experiencing, and it is in this condition that unexpected regions of the self are revealed, as the majority of people know from experience. The 'lover's finger-light' in *Romeo and Juliet* now no longer looks so fanciful: 'Lovers can see to do their amorous rites / By their own beauties . . .'

Children too can strike a lucky vein of dermo-optical perception in our game. Most of the time a child is in a state of quick enthusiasms and high fantasy. There is a very beautiful 'found' poem in D. M. Thomas's *Logan Stone*. Thomas was only half-listening at the breakfast-table one morning when he suddenly realised that his six-year-old son Sean was talking poetry, so he began taking down the spontaneous poem. Sean was telling the tale of how the day before at school he had kissed one of the little girls. She was called 'Eve' so the poem is appropriately called 'Eden'.

As soon as Sean kisses the little girl, the world transforms: 'When I kiss Eve / all the clothes dance . . .' Everything becomes magic, and begins to work by itself. It is because 'When I kiss Eve / magic stuff comes / out through our mouths . . .' Clothes dance about and hang themselves away tidily, the dinner lays itself on the table and washes up after itself, the pictures draw themselves with the crayons, the school remodels itself into a church, the mud grows apple trees and cherry trees and the piano plays itself. This is the famous Romantic 'elective moment' if ever there was one!

We have already shown that 'magic stuff' is really there for animals, immersed as they are in their natural continuum of hearing-touch, extended vision, EM senses, profound olfactory sensitivity and such synaesthesias as the free-floating pheromone maser. We shall show that it is there for humans also. Recent research proves that when humans kiss semi-hormonal 'semiochemicals' are exchanged whose effect is so powerful as to be almost psychedelic and also somewhat addictive.[7] Clearly this kind of arousal, whatever its chemical stimulus, opened the world to Sean.

It seemed to Gide's Oedipus that only since his eyes of flesh were torn from the world of appearances had he begun to see clearly. This clear-seeing (we shall understand that it can be called 'clairvoyance') is the recovery of the subliminal or animal senses. For Blake, the senses were originally diffused over the entire being, as in the relaxation or hypnoidal experience. To him all the senses except touch had been turned rigid, unable to expand or contract as they did once in Eden (and seem still to do, albeit unconsciously, in the kaleidoscope of the thermogram and also in the electrical patterning in the skin). This rigidity was due to the kindly meant religious impositions of Urizen, Blake's Oedipus-Laius figure.

The Sphinx in the legend stands for the knowledge in us which is both human and animal at once, and which we first gain in our relations with the pre-Oedipal mother, from the womb onwards. This living knowledge is so precious that the loss of it was by Freud equated to castration. The child becomes aware of the angry presence of a father in whom this knowledge has been lost by the very same processes that the child is about to undergo. This may culminate at five years old or thereabouts, when the child comes into the full Oedipal conflict, and is also sent to school to learn the visual-intellectual ways of the Oedipal culture, which are in themselves 'castrating'. The strain of the contradictory feelings of love, hate and fear has enforced a repression, which is accompanied by a withdrawal of the erotic, animal or non-visual senses which were so much engaged with the younger child's sense of life. In Freudian terms, the 'shock of threatened castration' leads to the development of the superego, the patriarchal conscience; and this is reinforced by schooling which invariably includes 'religious instruction' embedded in a patriarchal myth. It is the time of the famous 'latency', the pause until puberty in psycho-sexual development in which an ability to form abstract visualisations is favoured over direct expression through the body.

In our society it is probable that the full range of the erotic senses –

the senses-in-the-feelings – seldom recovers from this latency. That light in the skin goes out for most people much of the time, during which contemporary humans are actually, though not physically, blind. Our culture wishes us to see with nothing but the eye, lest we might truly enjoy, and become content. Nobody could pretend that physical blindness of the eyes is fun, but there is still much to be learned from gifted blind people about the subliminal senses and the abilities that must be latent in all of us.

One of the most famous blind men of all time was Saul of Tarsus; Paul as he became. Hot with his persecution of the Christians, hot, maybe, as Oedipus on the way to Thebes, Saul was struck blind on the road to Damascus with a vision that he could not describe, for it was too great for the eyes. Later on, as Paul the Apostle, he used blindness as a magical riposte to those who would not see his point of view; the sorcerer Barjesus, for example, whom he struck blind. In this he took a leaf from the book of his great religious opponent of the time, the Goddess Isis, who was often depicted as a Sphinx, or a black woman. Isis had the initiatory power to 'blind men who provoked her wrath and *afterwards restore to them their sight*'. They could not have remained unchanged by this experience, any more than Paul did. The Isiac religion also practised oneiromancy, when the goddess would impart divine vision in that other 'blindness', sleep.[8] Paul, like Oedipus, came out of the other side of blindness with enhanced vision, yet the religion he founded is masculinist, and will not officially consult the paradoxical visionary darkness, 'in a glass darkly'.

We have already mentioned Tiresias the blind seer, who saw with his inner senses to the heart of Oedipus' mystery and gave away the secret of male erotic inferiority. Hera's initiatory punishment was blindness, as if to compel him to attend to the body-light of touch in bed, and thereby improve his performance. A different story says that he was blinded by seeing the glory of Athene's bathing, another vision that could not be sustained by the eyes alone.

A third famous blind man is fictional. Max Carrados, the blind detective, appears to have supernatural powers. He is blind, yet he arrives at a complete solution to a mystery merely by touching, weighing and tasting with his tongue a Greek coin. He is not happy in his blindness, but he finds it has compensations he does not expect: ' . . . a new world to explore, new experiences, new powers

awakening; strange new perceptions; life in the fourth dimension.'[9]
The author, Ernest Bramah, explains that this part of the fiction is
fact, and refers us to a remarkable book *Biography of the Blind*,
compiled by James Wilson (blind from his infancy), in which we can
see the latent human abilities fully at work.[10] It is an old book, but
not for that reason to be disbelieved, and its stories are matched by
more recent accounts (please see, for example, the Appendix).

A Dr Abercrombie in this *Biography of the Blind* comments on
how the loss of one sense can be followed by an increase in others *by
an act of attention*, 'by an increased attention to the indications of
the other senses'. In our own day various mechanical sonar systems
have been invented to help the blind, and remarkable work has been
done in teaching people to read through the skin of their back –
camera images are translated into patterns of pressure within a kind
of harness. There is evidence that normal hearing takes place by
creating sonar holograms dolphin-fashion. The blind person has
always used the tapping of a stick as a sonar; 'facial vision' is
reported;[11] and it is wonderful to be with somebody who although
they cannot see none the less knows the moon has risen, by the
feeling in the skin, and can point to its place in the sky. Abercrombie
gives us stories from his own time of a wonderful enhancement of
touch in the blind: 'in some cases, it is said, to the extent of
distinguishing colours'. This is more easily believable after our small
ESP experiment. It appears that non-sighted people have been
especially esteemed as judges of horses: there is a particular relationship with animals, as with the guide-dog, when human and
animal become a syzygy. One blind man detected the blindness of a
horse, which sighted judges had failed to do. When he was asked how
he knew, he said, 'It was by the *sound* of the horse's step in walking.'
Another knew that a horse was blind in one eye because 'he *felt* the
one eye to be colder than the other'. There were also two young men,
brothers, who 'knew when they approached a post in walking across
a street, by a peculiar sound, which the ground under their feet
emitted in the neighbourhood of the post and they could tell the
names of a number of tame pigeons, with which they amused
themselves in a little garden, by only hearing them fly over their
heads'.

Another man, a wine-dealer, had a fight with his brother and was
able to land his blows as if he were sighted, by his hearing, and in fact
knocked his brother out. When he was asked, 'What are eyes?' he

replied, 'Eyes are organs on which the air has the same effect as my stick has on my hand . . . ' He defined 'a looking-glass' as 'a machine that gives things an existence, far from themselves, if placed conveniently relative to them. "Just as my hand," said he, "which I need not place near an object in order to feel it."'

Blind Dr Rumph of Hanau was able to identify plants for his herbarium by tasting and feeling them. Although Nicholas Saunderson, LLD, FRS, lost his sight at twelve months, he went on to become a mathematician and geometer, and was able to 'lecture on the prismatic spectrum, and on the theory of the rainbow, and acquired his ability in exact geometry with its diagrams by touch solely'. Moreover, when observations were being made on the sun, 'He has been seen in a garden . . . to take notice of every cloud that interrupted the observation, almost as justly as others could see it.' I have met a sighted man who was so weather sensitive (like myself, only more so) that he could tell the exact shapes of clouds without looking at them as they passed over. His sensitivity changed to illness in bad or strongly electrical weather, and we shall return to this.

Saunderson could also tell 'when anything was held near his face, or when he passed by a tree at no great distance, merely by the different impulse of the air on his face'. He could judge by his ear 'the size of a room, and his distance from the wall. And if he ever walked over a pavement in courts or piazzas which reflected sound, and was afterwards conducted thither again, he could tell in what part of the walk he had stood, merely by the note it sounded.'

A tailor called Macguire was able after blindness to continue his trade, and this was making tartan dress; he could, it appeared, distinguish all the colours of the tartan by touch.

Bramah's own examples include Margaret M'Avoy, who could distinguish by touch the colours of silk, cloth and stained glass, and Wilette Huggins (reported in the *Daily Telegraph*, 29 April 1922), who discerned colours by their odour, and attended lectures and concerts, though totally deaf as well as blind, 'and [heard] by holding a thin sheet of paper between her fingers directed broadside towards the volume of sound' as an amplifying device. Remarkable examples recently in the news include a blind painter who was able to smell the colour of the different pigments she used, presumably beneath the odours of turpentine or other solvents; and an accomplished deaf musician who passed out of the Royal College of Music top of her year and became a virtuoso percussionist.[12]

One of the best documented of all famous blind people was Helen Keller, who lost not only sight but hearing, and as a consequence of that, speech too, when she was less than two years old. She learnt to live by touch, by the manual alphabet and the sensation of what it referred to, and 'by the devotion and intelligence of her teacher'.

'As the cold water gushed forth, filling the mug, I spelled w-a-t-e-r in Helen's free hand,' and this was how the blind girl learnt the name of things, by touch. She seemed, however, to have access to many other abilities. She could tell when her brother was near, and could name people she met while walking or riding, as if she could see them. Part of this seemed to be because she could read the muscular tensions, by touch, of her sighted companion, to a degree of fineness which could distinguish the way she stood or held herself in the presence of different persons, so it amounted to a name written by her body, like a hieroglyph. She appeared to be able to 'hear' too, but only when she held her companion's hand: this might have been touch or vibration, or perhaps, like thought-reading, a response to sub-vocalisations.

On one occasion Helen Keller was told that a little girl called Florence was buried under a stone in the graveyard. She dropped on to the ground as though looking for Florence with touch, and asked where she was, and who had put her in the earth. It happened that she had been given some of the dead girl's toys, without knowing to whom they belonged. 'On her return to the house after her visit to the cemetery, she ran to the closet where these toys were kept, and carried them to my friend, saying, "They are poor little Florence's." This was true, although we were at a loss to understand how she guessed it.'

All began for Helen Keller with touch, the sexual sense, the Fifth Window through which (according to Blake) one may pass out to eternity whatever time one pleases. Helen Keller had no alternative. With *touch*, there was the animal affinity as well as the optic hand. 'I have just touched my dog. He was rolling on the grass with pleasure in every muscle and limb. I wanted to catch a picture of him in my fingers, and I touched him lightly as I would cobwebs . . . He pressed close to me as if he were fain to crowd himself into my hand . . . If he could speak, I believe he would say with me that paradise is attained by touch.' Her sight and hearing ligatured, other senses rose in compensation: 'I sense the rush of ethereal rains . . . I possess the light which shall give me vision a thousandfold when death sets me free.' Smell was vital also: 'Suddenly a change passed over the tree. All the sun's warmth left the air. I knew the sky was black, because all the heat which meant light to me had disappeared. A strange smell came up from the earth. I knew it. It was the smell that always comes before thunderstorms.'

Extraordinary though her access to her non-visual senses was in waking life, it was even more remarkable in sleep. Her dreams synthesised them into a glory, greater than ordinary sight uninstructed by them. In her old age she wrote: 'I dream of sensations, colours, odours, ideas, and things I cannot remember.' A 'wonderful' light reached her in sleep: '– and what a flash of glory it is! In sleep I never grope but walk a crowded street freely. I see all the things that are in the subconscious mind of the race.' She insisted that the blindsight she possessed was actually spiritual vision, for 'I know my friends not by their physical appearance but by their spirit.'[13]

The psychologist F. L. Marcuse believes that great reserves of potential reside in many of our senses. He experimented as if he were blind. Blindfolded, at first he could hardly manage, but within a month he was able to feel or 'sense' the presence of objects. He could not tell how, at first, but it turned out that he was subliminally processing sound reflections.[14] An act of attention enforced by a secure blindfold had opened up a dimension nearing the animal in his sense of hearing. Marcuse is one of those psychologists who believe that the improved sensory ability reported in hypnotic sessions is there anyway, and elicited because it is required, or attended to, rather than because mysterious new nerves are grown. This suggests again that these abilities exist and operate unconsciously, but we ignore them by ignorance.

Similarly, though the blind are admirable sources of information on radiant heat sensitivity, they do not distinguish this from their other sensitivities unless their attention is drawn to thermal sensations. Blindsight is a non-visual multi-media event. Edward T. Hall and Warren Brody conducted interviews with the blind during which the importance to them emerged of currents of cool air round windows in navigating a room and retaining a sense of the outside. Also a 'brick wall on the north side of a given street was identified as a landmark to the blind because it radiated heat over the total width of the sidewalk'.[15] It was thus more than a heightened sense of hearing that helped the blind to navigate, and probably a simultaneity of this with other non-visual senses.

Remarkable results have been obtained recently in retraining the ear among normal people by listening to certain full ranges of sound frequency on Walkman personal cassette players. The ear becomes so cleansed and responsive that the whole world seems remade in sound. Depression, hypertension and all kinds of stress are thereby relieved. The effect spreads outwards from the sense of hearing to brain-function and the other senses, so the whole quality of life is enhanced.[16]

The senses of animals were compared to those of humans in a series of experiments by the South African naturalist Eugene Marais, who claimed the latter were very much sharpened by hypnosis. Marais recalls Kleist when he tells us how the senses become more 'perfect' as one descends the scale of evolution and how in man 'sense degeneration has reached an extreme point', and echoes Freud too, but differs from him (as I do), when he says, 'Hypnosis proves, however, that this degeneration in man is not organic, or even functional in the generally accepted sense of the term.' The sensitiveness is hindered by the 'high mentality and when this mentality becomes dormant under hypnosis the inhibition is removed'. (Hypnosis was never a part of Freud's developed method. He was said not to be a good hypnotist, and this is why he gave it up. If true, this could have been a consequence of his alleged cocaine habit, as hypnotism involves identifying certain normally subliminal clues. An important one is the 'change of atmosphere' and the establishment of a trance can actually be smelt! However, Freud remarks quite casually how he reset a woman's menstrual cycle like a clock, by hypnosis, and this must have required considerable skill.)[17]

Marais compared the sensitivity of chacma apes with that of hypnotised Boer girls. He alleges that both ape and human girl were able to distinguish by touch alone whether a bar of metal was or was not a magnet. The chacma could detect by taste the presence of one milligram of quinine sulphate in four litres of water, and so could the girl. In a strong light the ape could *see* the drug in a 1:800,000 solution, and the girl could too, but only 60 per cent of the time. In a solution of 1:600,000 she could detect it infallibly.

The ape's powers of vision were almost beyond belief. One young captive male could recognise a human friend from 6 miles away, over a landscape flickering with mirages. The girl could only do this at a distance of 3 miles, and through binoculars, and only when hypnotised. Another girl, hypnotised and then blindfolded, could recognise by smelling small objects taken out of a bag who out of twenty different people had handled them previously. The ape's sense of smell was apparently inferior to the girl's. She was better at hearing tests, too. When hypnotised, she could hear a hiss of constant volume imitating a snake at 230 yards; the average person needed 20–30 yards. The chacmas heard it at 50–65 yards. The human sense of touch under hypnosis was extraordinary also. The girl sensitive to magnetism was tested by using African giant snail shells. Twenty of these virtually identical shells were numbered on the inside and placed in order on a table. The girl, blindfolded, was brought into the room and allowed to touch, but without moving them at all. She was then taken out of the room and the order of the shells was changed. When she came back she was able, still blindfolded, to arrange the shells in their original order without a mistake.

A hypnotised boy's sense of locality was found comparable to that of a bird finding its nest; experienced hunters who were not hypnotised could not match it. Marais believed the boy remembered kinaesthetically and unconsciously all the twists and turns of his body when he was blindfolded and taken on a confusing route far from the nest.[18]

It is a pity that no control experiments were made. The merit of the study in which the warts melted away under hypnosis was that each subject was his own control. Another psychologist, T. X. Barber, did use controls, and found that for 'Enhanced Cognitive Proficiency' no 'state of trance' was needed, merely instructions under experimental conditions. Such conditions are in themselves an act of attention, however. 'A wide range of experiences that have been traditionally associated with a special condition (a "hypnotic trance") are viewed as potentially within the repertoire of most normal individuals.' These include control of pain, amnesia, dreaming, skin temperature, visual acuity, allergic responses, age regression and relaxation, fully supported by experimental data.[19] Jung, as early as the inaugural dissertation for his medical degree in 1902, weighed up the possibility of 'Heightened Unconscious Performance' in occult phenomena. He had been studying the psychology of several spiritualistic mediums, and describes how 'thought-reading' by means of table tremors was not only possible but easy with the right subjects. Somebody starts the tremors in the 'table-turning' and the medium unconsciously returns them in an amplified form. During the sitting, there is an increase of partial hypnosis among the participants, which renders them more mutually sensitive. A simple experiment is to think of the number 'four'. Unconscious tremors will communicate the number to the medium, who will return the pattern with amplified 'tilts'. Jung says this works 'in many cases with unpractised persons'. As the seance continues, further depths of the unconscious open up. (The information-carrying tremors would be similar to Helen Keller's ability to read from the touch of her sighted companion's hand who the latter was talking to.) Jung concluded from his data that there was no choice 'but to assume for the present a receptivity of the unconscious far exceeding that of the conscious mind'. Under the conditions of a seance – the highly symbolic setting and strongly motivated desire to communicate with spirits – the act of attention to these unknown areas would be supported by the mutual suggestion that such things were possible. He mentions Binet's experiments, in which letters, or complicated small objects in relief, were laid on the hypnotically sensitised back of the hand or the neck of subjects whereupon 'the unconscious perceptions were registered by means of signs'. Binet concluded on the basis of these experiments that 'the unconscious sensibility of an hysterical patient is at certain moments *fifty times* more acute than that of a normal person'. I have myself known a woman able to call out the shape of an object held just above her head and otherwise concealed from her.

Jung says that not only hypnotised people, but people in an ordinary state, in simple ESP experiments with numbers 'are able to guess, from tremor movements, quite long trains of thought'. This is like animal hearing-touch. He quotes Leopold Loewenfeld's *Der Hypnotismus* (1901) which suggests that there is not a vast difference between hypnotic induction procedures and the way people commonly get new ideas, for, 'The restriction of associative processes to, and the steady concentration of attention on, a definite field of representation can also lead to the development of new ideas which no effort of will in the waking state would have been able to bring to light.'[20] One of the simplest ways of doing this has already been mentioned: Benson's 'relaxation response'. You simply concentrate on the number 'one' by speaking it silently with each out-breath.

Strangely enough, heightened sensory acuity in hypnosis is a neglected area, as a computer search of the literature tells us.[21] The impressive 'anecdotal' evidence of former times would not satisfy the fantasies of voyeuristic impersonality of the modern Oedipal scientist who prefers to neglect knowledge of this kind. My suggestion is that the unconscious senses are operating all the time, whether we know it or not, that we store this information, and that we get at it through a whole variety of quite natural 'acts of attention' which range in a continuous spectrum of innumerable social and personal devices, from the reverie of the fisherman soothed by the ripple and flow of the river to the frenzy of the gambler and the physical training of the sportsman or the yogi, from the absorbed play of a child with a pet animal or doll, to deep trance 'somnambulism', voodoo, entering the psychologist's black room or lying down in the witch's cradle (a more ancient piece of 'sensory deprivation equipment' than the black room but which still – like blindness – compels one's attention to the 'gostly wittes', as does the hermit's cell); sleeping on a problem overnight or the 'restriction of associative processes to, and the steady concentration on' the sexual embrace itself.

The eminently sober *Oxford Companion to Animal Behaviour*[22] informs us about the all-but-supernatural skills of certain 'primitive' sea-going peoples, who have developed navigation methods based on the analysis of wave-patterns. Such methods, combined with the observation of stars, permit accurate landfalls over vast oceanic distances. The wave-pattern is the result of an immense multitude of interacting waves of different frequency, direction and magnitude, and there are in it important constituent waves that the navigator has learned about during years of training. Carried by the modulations of these waves will be compass directions and the positions of objects that significantly alter the movement of the water, as for example major islands or reefs. It is important than on one hand this pattern is learnt, but on the other, it is recognised that its most important practical aspect is not its visual appearance. It is *felt*. 'A skilled navigator from Puluwat in the Caroline Islands of the south-west Pacific, for example, sits on a special seat in the canoe he is guiding to some tiny distant island, and feels "through the seat of his pants" the pattern of waves in the sea beneath him.'

2 The Osmic Fountain

I am well aware that, with all this talk of invisible radiations beamed at us from each other and from cosmic sources, I am myself displaying the classical schizophrenic fantasy. Yet the 'magic stuff' is there, as we have already seen and shall increasingly understand. There is another possibility, then, that the people we dub schizophrenic, like the shamans, sorcerers, poets and witches who 'can see the wind', are actually sensing further, beyond the Oedipal consensus, than those who are agreed to be sane. What place is there in this society for people who see visions? If they are lucky enough to encounter a belief structure which assures them that what they envision is real or useful, and they find it is so, and can handle it, then they become witches, shamans or poets. But if they encounter a psychiatric doctor who cannot understand these matters except in terms of 'mad' or 'sane' and can see no way of adjusting them to society, then the person surprised by the extension of his senses will be treated as mad, and will accordingly withdraw into the isolation of true madness. Felix Sulman, for instance, speaks of weather changes that affect 30 per cent of the population in an overt reaction and the rest of humanity in an occult response (using the word in its medical sense of 'hidden'). In effect this means that 30 per cent of people are weather sensitive frequently to the point of its being a medical or psychiatric problem, and the rest are not consciously susceptible. Women apparently, due to a different pattern of stress hormone secretion, are more apt to be weather sensitive or susceptible than are men, and so are children. Sulman says of the person susceptible to weather electricity: 'They have a sixth sense that makes them suffer and therefore deserve our help.'[23] We shall return to consider weather in detail.

Harry Wiener takes this sense-extension view of schizophrenia in four remarkable papers published in the 1960s.[24] The extra sense he considered operative is, however, smell. It appears that the schizophrenic, like the artist, is first of all full of the discovery of an ability which seems to add new vistas of knowledge and feeling-tone to the world. If he is then diagnosed as 'mad', he may enter the tragic second phase of withdrawal, which is accompanied by disturbances of metabolism and other physical changes.

There are about half a million schizophrenics in an active phase of the condition in Britain. The cause is still mysterious to orthodox medicine; a popular view is that it is caused by the disordered *internal* secretion of metabolic chemicals: hallucinogens. This is a strange bias of the facts, which in Wiener's opinion show that *external* chemical communication is involved. R. D. Laing is famous for his interpretation of the schizophrenic situation, in which the body-language, the look and the feeling of the people surrounding the schizophrenic contradict what they say with their mouths. The 'mad' person can see the living lie of which the 'sane' family is unconscious; the schizophrenic is susceptible to a greater extent than is convenient to the human weather which surrounds him.

We have seen, however, that there is more to body-language than visual gesture. Wiener's suggestion is that the schizophrenic regresses to a more 'primitive' mode of perception through the subliminal senses, as though Freudian Oedipal man were getting down on all fours again. He makes a very good case, with compelling documentation, for the schizophrenic's ability to respond to smell as a dimension of body-language. His contentions have been very much strengthened by later work on chemical messengers up to the present day.

The feats of people with enhanced olfactory ability challenge the extra-sensuous abilities of blind people. Wiener quotes many cases in the older literature.[25] A. A. Brill treated a patient who claimed to be able to tell people apart by their smells, and to know when his cousin was blocks away by this means. This looks less like a delusion when we consider the famous modern 'dirty T-shirt' experiments in which males and females can detect each other's gender and mothers can recognise each of their children by the smells of their T-shirts.[26] Rau found when he had been working with Saturnid moths (which, like Fabre's insects, use a moth odour as a sexual attractant) that he and members of the family eventually learnt to distinguish the previously imperceptible specific moth smell, and discovered that it formed streaks and small rivers in the atmosphere. His wife once located a stream of odour about 15 feet wide. Rau himself knew a man whose feats of perception by smell would rank him with the insects. Apparently in the wilds of Montana, where wood was used for fuel, this man could smell coal smoke from a train 14 miles away.

The psychoanalytic literature multiplies instances, as Wiener shows. Freud's patient, called by him, significantly, the 'rat man', said he was able as a child to recognise everybody by their scent. Another of Brill's patients was extremely sensitive to the odour of faeces, and could not use the bathroom until an hour after any other member of the family. Another patient was incommoded in the outside air by his sensitivity to odours. He interpreted them as poisons, and would search out the paint-shop or drug store responsible. Eventually this patient made a good adjustment – he became a perfumer! Kalogerakis tells of a boy he observed from the age of two to five, who could tell where his parents had been, and whether they had made love, by their smells. He distinguished the smells emanating from different parts of the body, as sensitive masseurs do.

The word 'ectohormone' (now pheromone) was coined by the famous physiologist Bethe, apparently from his own experience. He could tell people apart by smell, and whether they had exercised, were emotionally excited, whether they were menstruating or ill. He could also distinguish the smells of other people on the person he was with at the time, and thus could tell whom they had met that day. He did not seem aware that his abilities were exceptional, and offered them as an explanation of how ants and bees might communicate.

Laird in 1935 obtained information from 254 distinguished people about their sense of smell. Eight of them proved remarkable in this area. One man knew when any particular person had been in the room, and could tell who they were, by the odour of articles of clothing. A woman doctor aged sixty could locate people by their smell and knew where her husband had been by the smell on his skin or clothing.

Professional perfumers are, of course, prodigious in this area. A paper quoted by Wiener describes the sense of isolation experienced by one such who could smell a world of subtlety undetected by his fellow creatures; this may parallel the withdrawal stage of the odour-sensitive schizophrenic. Wiener himself asked a professional perfumer whether he could distinguish people's moods by their smell, and he replied without hesitation that he could, and seemed surprised that anybody had to enquire about this; it was so natural to him.

I know a lay analyst who during interviews receives quite complex cues from his clients that are like puffs of smell conveying different emotions and thoughts: there is the 'I am about to recall a dream' smell, there is the whiff of panic that it is nearly time to finish, there is the smell of accord over an insight, and the 'ignore me' gas of private disagreement. It is like thought-reading, which in a successful case becomes mutual. External chemical messengers are clearly an important element in intensely emotional communication, such as the transferences of analysis, the rapports of hypnotism and the telepathy of lovers, but such signals are only one of the many involved in communication by the unconscious senses.

Some perfumers can name the country from where a sample of lavender oil comes, and even the farm. This resembles those feats of winemanship when the connoisseur appears to be able to taste the countryside, even to taste the earth itself, in the wine when he can tell what geological strata existed below the vineyard.[27] Perfumers have been used to analyse the complex spectrum of human sex hormones and also the famous 'aura' of schizophrenics.

This is the curious atmosphere that a schizophrenic is alleged to carry about with him, and by which experienced doctors often say they can diagnose the illness. The diagnosis may go thus: I suspect you are schizophrenic because I feel that you are; medical students are taught to take special notice of this feeling. Similarly, policemen are supposed to be able to smell crooks, and vice versa. Rats can be trained to distinguish schizophrenics. An explanation for this 'aura' might be that persons who are odour sensitive respond to other people's smells with an aware smell of their own. If the doctor as a 'normal' member of society prefers to keep smell-language at the subliminal level of 'feel' or 'hunch', then he will reject outright this signal of unexpected awareness and forbidden knowledge, and call the feeling 'mad'. One must always remember what a powerful emotional effect a smell can convey. This smelt rejection might well lead to outbursts of anger or distress on the part of the 'madman' whose uncomfortable awareness is amplified in response to the reaction of the doctor. It is a common delusion among paranoid psychotics that a fearful smell emanates from their bodies, but the cause of this may be other people's fear, escalating.

The paranoid may well feel that he is persecuted by his perceptual system. Blind people are seldom schizophrenic; they understand the dark senses. It is known that schizophrenic patients reflect by their disturbances hidden conflicts between hospital staff. 'The schizophrenic is aware of his own and other people's unconscious . . . '; he has an ability 'to sense unconscious impulses in the psychiatrist', and an 'uncanny knack for nosing out hidden aspects of his personality'.[28] The 'aura' is sometimes called the 'praecox feeling', and it is considered that the patient who makes the doctor feel angry or sick is giving that doctor diagnostic information. One experienced physician remarks as guidance to other doctors: 'Your own reaction to these signs and symptoms should be counted an equal part of the disease picture. If not puzzled or uneasy, or even appalled, you are unlikely to be in the presence of catatonia. You should feel like a man standing before a half-trained tiger. The tiger tries to be good, but watch his eyes and the fibrillations rippling down the coat.'

In one hospital, a sociologist after visiting a manic patient became 'benevolent, gay, elated, and restless'. He then met another manic: 'I had found him wearying but now I talked with him eagerly and felt a great fellow-feeling with him. His incredible ramblings seemed to make more sense than before.' The 'aura' of groups taking LSD is said to make non-users high. There was an ancient belief that the scent of the young had a rejuvenating effect on the old. Francis Bacon speculated that this is what kept teachers young. In the Bible (I Kings I) a young virgin is called in for King David who, after enjoying her body-scent and breath, was renewed. Emperor Rudolf of Habsburg called upon his noblemen to send their wives and daughters to cure his fever by kissing him. The practice is called Shunamism, after the virgins of Shunam, whose exhalations were said to prolong life. It is one of the sexual encratisms which advocate contact without orgasm, like karezza.

Sometimes an *analyst* has to defend himself against charges of olfactory hallucination when it is his animal senses speaking to him. Thus Groddeck had a patient who smelt very bad to him, and his colleagues said this was simply a hysterical conversion enabling Groddeck to pick a hole in his patient. Angrily, he replied: ' . . . But taught by fools and by children, I have been converted from my derision to a belief in psychic smell. I now know that with every disturbance of his being man produces a particular smell, produces it in a moment, and in a moment makes it disappear. I know, in spite of all learned teaching to the contrary, that man is primarily a "nose-animal", and that he only represses his acute sense of smell during childhood because life would otherwise be unbearable.'[29]

You do not have to be mad to observe these things; to associate these abilities with madness alone is to indicate how far we have outlawed them. The dimensions of feeling-tone that the unconscious senses, including the olfactory sense, add without our conscious knowledge to what we culturally suppose is a visual response are immeasurable. There is the famous and tragic case in most medical textbooks of the old man who had lost all his senses except the sight of one eye. When that was closed, he slept like the dead.

It appears that people who lose their sense of smell die or become senile much quicker than people who retain extra-sensuousness. It is as though life loses interest for the non-osmic.[30] Lewis Thomas[31] points out how like the act of thinking smelling is, and this is how it should be since the cells that do the smelling are themselves proper brain cells, the only ones whose fibres carry information first hand from the outer world. 'Immediately, at the very moment of perception, you can feel the mind going to work . . . setting off complex repertoires throughout the brain, polling one centre after another for signs of recognition, old memories, connections. They are also the only brain cells that replicate themselves. There must be wonderful antibiotics in the mucus bathing this exposed surface of the brain, since it seldom becomes infected.' Just as blind people are able by echo detection to distinguish an object that subtends an angle of only 5 degrees, so trained smellers can tell the direction of an odour source that subtends only 7–8 degrees, despite the small distance between the nostrils.[32]

The schizophrenic 'aura' is an intensification of the common experience of one's own 'space', including olfactory space, which can be invaded by others, and is another human-animal thing, as the American anthropologist Edward T. Hall shows us. He says that when schizophrenics are approached too closely, the unfortunate people panic like animals in a zoo and, in describing how they feel, they say that anything that happens within their 'flight distance' seems to take place *inside themselves*. ('Flight distance': how close an animal will let you approach before it flees.) This is like Wordsworth experiencing the 'corresponsive breeze' inside himself, and Rilke feeling the path of a bird flying right through him. The larger animals require more 'flight distance' between themselves and others, the small animals less; the antelope will flee when the intruder is about 500 yards away, but the wall lizard's flight distance is roughly 6 feet. Some species require contact and bundle together, like pigs, hedgehogs and hippopotami; while horses, the cat and the hawk are non-contact species. Non-contact animals surround themselves with a kind of invisible bubble, as Hall calls it, known as 'personal distance'. It is probable that this 'bubble' contains more activity than is usually recognised, at the very least many chemical messages.

The American keeps a small bubble around himself which he considers inviolate even in a public place. Hall, waiting in a hotel lobby, was annoyed because somebody stood so close to him that his vision was crowded and he could also hear the man's breathing. Hall moved his body in a way that should have communicated annoyance, but this only encouraged the intruder, and he moved closer. When the latter's friends arrived, Hall understood that he was an Arab and, discussing the incident later with Arab friends, he found that for Arabs public means public, and there is no concept of, or opportunity for, privacy in public space.

For Arabs, the invisible bubble was meant to be broken and shared. Olfaction is important in Arab life and is 'a vital part of a complex system of behaviour. Arabs consistently breathe on people when they talk . . . To the Arab good smells are pleasing and a way of being involved with each other. To smell one's friend is not only nice but desirable, for to deny him your breath is to act ashamed . . . By stressing olfaction, Arabs do not try to eliminate all the body's odours, only to enhance them and use them in building human relationships.' Here is a clear indication that the loss of the olfactory dimension in Oedipal European man as described by Freud is culturally determined. Arab–American diplomacy founders on this. Americans are trained not to breathe in each other's faces. Who would expect that this would communicate shame to the Arabs, and not courtesy?[33]

The linguist Joos points out how the meaning of words is changed by the heat and odour of an intimate utterance delivered in a whisper close to the skin of the ear. The whisper avoids customary social meanings, and reminds the addressee of meanings and feelings *inside the skin*.[34] This is a characteristic of lovers' language and of magical language also. The postulant to the Osiric mysteries after labyrinthine stumblings was left in the dark and a priest would rush towards him and say in a whisper into his ear the simple initiatory secret that must be felt as well as comprehended: 'Osiris is a dark god.' As Massey says, the mystery religions were instituted in order to protect the marvels of the commonplace from those who would devalue them.

The multi-media or synaesthetic capability needs to be useful and used if it is not to shake the sensitive to pieces. No doubt the Puluwat canoeist with the ability to navigate great distances by the wave-pattern felt through the seat of his pants would fundamentally be fragmented, so to speak, by vibrations of our world, meaningless except in terms of commerce. The use of human-animal senses synaesthetically, as multi-media, is the rule and not the exception in other cultures. How can the Eskimo travel across his apparently undifferentiated white territory? It is by sensitivities strange to us, not by actual 'objects or points, but relationships; relationships between, say, contour, types of snow, wind, salt air, ice crack'. The direction of the wind and its smell, the actual complex texture of the ice beneath his feet, will give the Eskimo the information that enables him to travel hundreds of miles over 'visually undifferentiated waste'. Language is the sensitive mirror to synaesthesia. Hall says that the Aivilik Eskimos have 'at least twelve different terms for various winds. They integrate time and space as one thing and live in acoustic-olfactory space, rather than visual space.'[35]

Even if they are not honoured there, these multi-media events are a part of common experience. Concerning touch, for instance, which Blake calls the Fifth Window, the anthropologist Hall concurs. It is 'the most personally experienced of all sensations. For many people, life's most intimate moments are associated with the changing texture of the skin. The hardened, armour-like resistance to the unwanted touch, or the exciting, ever changing textures of the skin during love-making, and the velvet quality of satisfaction afterwards are messages of one body to another that have universal meanings.' But this is not an event in the medium of touch alone. It is also an event in all the others. There are electrical changes, as we will see, and there are thermal changes also, as we have seen. Hall points out that recent thermographic work indicates that the ability of the skin to detect and to emit radiant heat, or infra-red, is very high, that emotional states are reflected by changes in blood supply to different parts of the body, and therefore human beings are well equipped to send and receive messages of emotion by these invisible means.[36] As the texture changes, so does the IR emission and, with the IR emission, the olfactory emission too: the Dyson theory says that the source of the smell sensation is the *radiation* of the molecules concerned (another theory says it is a lock-and-key mechanism with the olfactory nerve-end chemicals, and therefore is similar to the immune system). The amount of information that can be transmitted from 'inside the skin' is very great indeed. What we might distinguish as a single sexual odour, as Wiener points out, may be composed of at least a hundred identifiable components: 'muskone and its analogues, indoles, branched fatty acids, esters, steroids and pyrimidines'.[37] Modern work puts the constituents of the 'odour fingerprint' as at least 200. These hundreds of odours the olfactory system detects contrast it, in Schneider's opinion, to 'vision where three primary colours are involved, and to taste, where four major categories of stimuli are involved'.[38] We are responding to these subtle influences all the time whether we know it or not, as is shown by their effect on skin-resistance, blood-pressure, respiratory and pulse rates, insulin output, blood sugar level, and many other parameters.[39]

In his youth Hall noticed at dances that while some partners were hot, others were cold and 'the temperature of the same girl changed from time to time'. He says that it was always at the point where he found himself 'establishing a thermal balance and getting interested without really knowing quite why' that the young women would insist on escaping to get some fresh air. He checked on this in later life, and found that women were quite familiar with these thermal changes. One claimed that she could tell the emotional state of her boyfriend from 6 feet away in the dark. Another woman relied on temperature changes in the chest of her partner 'before things went too far'. At the more obvious level, 'perfume or skin lotion can be smelled at a greater distance when skin temperature rises' but there will be an undersong of the pheromones too.[40]

Dress will be a vital link in the multi-media show, and not only visually. It is known that odours change their qualities according to the background radiation. Everybody who uses perfume knows not only that the same scent smells different according to whether a black dress or a white one is worn, but that it has a quite different effect depending on who uses it. A very important area of IR emission is the throat and chest, the neck and the soft parts just above the collar-bone on both sides, where the collar rests and the great arteries run. It must be for that reason that people cover and uncover this part of their bodies not only to regulate their temperature but to alter their feeling of decorum or alternatively their sexual charge. Of course the neckline permitting just that much or this much disclosure, the cleavage of the clothes unfolding on the cleavage of the swelling bosom, is visually teasing to most men, and no doubt reinforced by patterns of breast-feeding customs, but it is also a kind of subliminal convection-fountain of body-perfumes rising on warm air in invisible colours and feelings out of these depths, controlled, as by sluices, by the opening or fastening of the clothes, and beaten upon by the drumming of that most powerful of bodily IR emitters, the heart. These powerful and delightful emanations will affect not only the dancing-partner, who will be emitting them himself (although to a lesser extent as masculine formal dress is very tightly closed), but the emitter also, and maybe she senses whether 'things have gone too far' as much by her own emanations as by his. This rising current of radiant 'aethyr' will be the rainbow bridge between head and body, psyche and soma.

It is part of the 'somatic unconscious' that Jung sparsely mentions in unpublished seminar work, yet which is the physical, genetic basis for his 'collective unconscious', the 'odour fingerprint'. Perhaps the odour is the soul, as was once believed.[41] Let us see, with our invisible eyes, this dance between partners as a true alchemy of radiant living vessels, distilling between them their thoughts which are the same as their feelings in one formal, measured yet intimately uncontrollable act, the projection of which the great psychologist saw remotely in dreams and visions and scarcely at all in actuality, where it also resides.

We may kiss each other in order to consume these elixirs, rediscovered by the modern world and called 'semiochemicals' and described in the popular press[42] as body stimulants 'triggering love and desire'. Indeed, as six-year-old Sean Thomas discovered, a kiss may change the world, and a chemical communication by smell may alter our perceptions completely. This is the Philosopher's Stone; magical ritual intercourse may depend on the conscious production of external chemical messengers by means of visualisations, which when exchanged between partners alter perception and enhance it: in Tantra these are the '*kalas*', present in sweat, breath and urine. This Philosopher's Stone almost rediscovered by the industrial scientists of the modern world has been used in merchandising. Car interiors are made to appear more desirable by spraying the artificial upholstery with a natural leather smell, and, on being presented with two counters of stockings, shoppers have bought only the scented ones. Now that a use has been found for olfactory study in catching criminals by their 'odour fingerprints',[43] it will become less neglected, but I doubt whether it will be used to contribute to the freedom of the individual. It will be misused, unless we ourselves learn that this 'animal' thing is a part of our highest nature and potential, the 'lost daughter' or animal soul who is black because we do not need eyes to see her.

The Black Goddess is also that part of the mother we do not see, but which haunts us all our lives. This is the great pre-Oedipal Sphinx, sitting on her mountain of spices. The riddle is literally under our noses. Perfume does not belong to the fathers; they have a smell, true, and the thunder and lightning over their skin of the IR transmissions of emotion, but they are driven by outside matters. They seldom sink down into the perfumes of themselves, the great galleries of meanings from inside the skin, which all may share who approach her, and which is an extension of that sojourn truly inside the skin, when she was carrying the child who now, without knowing it, remembers that time in an embrace in which the two invisible bodies interpenetrate.

This is the sense in which the woman's house is also her body, an equation known to Freud, who thought it merely a dream. It is full of the verifiable magic of the invisible goddess, this house, and is regulated by the rhythms of her menstrual processes and her pregnancies, processes which are in their turn exquisitely responsive to emotion, good and bad fortune, every change of the weather and sunshine, which in their turn relate to cosmic processes. Through it all threads the tune of the moon-pulse as regulator, if she wishes it. This goddess-house is the temenos – moon-place – in which we may study these matters; it is a device evolved, as zoologists agree, for prolonging the protection and influence of the womb – for the way in which we *differ* from the animals and our closest relatives among the primates is that we are an instance of neoteny. We are born, as it were, too soon, helpless, and half made up (unlike wild animals who can clamber and walk as soon as they are born), so that we may continue to develop, as though we were still womb-creatures, possessed of womb-plasticity, under our mother's influence in the home. This is the sense, and it is a vital one, in which we are, as the Neoplatonists say, a 'special creation'. The model of the depth of our proper relationship to the world, as we shall see, may first have been given us in the womb and consciously understood and recalled in the alchemy of the home. Families create living vessels of alchemy in their homes, distilling human weather from room to room both in the day and in the night, when those visions of approaching knowledge come, the dreams that emanate also their own perfumes under whose auspices we live. These are also carnal knowledge, since dreaming always takes place in a state of sexual excitement – extra-sensuous perception. These are some of the reasons for rituals of the home, the naming of parts of it after the parts of the body, in the complex systems of 'primitive culture', and advanced ones too, as in the Chinese geomancy of the home, *feng shui*. Other reasons will follow. Although we know now that the typical Western house is a shrine of deodorant consumerism and not magic; the only cosmic messages it hears are radio static, and it is plugged into the universe via the TV set.

To say it again, psychoanalysis tells us that the child fantasises the mother's body as a great breaking-open treasure house of all kinds of jewels and golden riches. The fantasy is truth. The treasures are the stored molecules, the incredible and knowing aromas of the mother's metabolism of love, evoked in her by her lover, or by her enjoyment of herself, or by her child's richness of perfume. The greatest art depicts these invisibles, the bounty of the goddess. Rembrandt, it seemed to Adrian Stokes, 'painted the female nude as the sagging repository of jewels and dirt, of fabulous babies and magical faeces . . .'[44]

So it is between lovers. The use of perfumes, the 'sexual attractants of plant, insect, or mammalian origin', precedes recorded history. It may be that the Bible has reversed the story of the Queen of Sheba travelling to learn wisdom from Solomon. The non-biblical legends say that she was black, and came from Abyssinia, 'along the road of spices'. Patai says she was Lilith. She had a cloven foot and hairy legs, so was a kind of Sphinx, and posed difficult riddles to Solomon, some of which he was unable to answer. One of these was so outrageous that he fell off his throne; the question was: 'What is the colour of God?' Another was: 'What is the water that is neither in the air nor in the river, nor in the ocean nor in the rain?' The answer to this is supposed to be 'the sweat of a horse in its mane' but it is a double riddle for 'women's love', or the wetness between the thighs of the Queen of Sheba, with her animal pubic mane. The patriarchal recensions say that Solomon persuaded her to shave. He is said, however, to have given her a child.[45]

The indications beyond patriarchal prejudice are that the phrase 'Solomon's Wisdom' meant his consort, the Queen of Sheba, or Black Goddess of the Perfumed Way, as the Hindus say that his love-partner Shakti is Shiva's 'Wisdom' or 'energy'. Thus in the biblical Proverbs[46] which are attributed to Solomon, we learn that the Lord possessed Wisdom in the very beginning of his way, that she was set up from everlasting, and when he prepared the heavens

Wisdom was there; then she was by him, as one brought up with him, daily his delight, rejoicing always before him; her delights were with the sons of men and he that sinneth against her wrongeth his own soul.

That tantrically perfumed Song of Solomon in the Bible (called the Song of Songs) is haunted by the Black Shulamite who has lost her lover: 'I am black, but comely . . . while the king sitteth at his table, my spikenard sendeth forth the smell thereof. A bundle of myrrh is my well-beloved unto me: he shall lie all night betwixt my breasts . . . Who is this that cometh out of the wilderness like pillars of smoke, perfumed with myrrh and frankincense . . . ?' Later in the poem, the male has profited from this osmic refresher course: 'A garden enclosed is my sister . . . Thy plants are an orchard of pomegranates, with pleasant fruits, camphire, with spikenard, spikenard and saffron: calamus and cinnamon, with all trees of frankincense; myrrh and aloes, with all the chief spices; a fountain of gardens, a well of living waters . . . ' Just snuff up those pheromones![47]

Similarly, in the apocryphal book The Wisdom of Solomon there is a wonderful goddess-hymn (beginning at Chapter VII).[48] Wisdom is radiant, she is traced out from the beginning of creation. Solomon called upon God and the spirit of wisdom came to him, and *he chose to have her rather than light*, because her bright shining is never laid to sleep. In her hands were innumerable riches, and Wisdom was the mother of them. She gave Solomon an unerring knowledge of the things that are: the constitution of the world, the circuits of years and the positions of the stars, the nature of living creatures and the violences of winds, the diversities of plants and the virtues of roots; and she was the artificer of all the things taught. She is more mobile than any motion, and she penetrateth all things, because she is a breath of the power of the Almighty, and an effulgence from everlasting light. *Being compared with light, she is found to be before it, and Solomon sought to take her for his bride*. We shall find how accurate this passage is to the image of the Black Goddess beyond light, and to the sense of reality we desire, mediated through neglected or emergent sensory modalities.

Wiener reviews[49] the intimate relations between smell and the sexual process. Hagen in 1901 compiled extensive information in a book, *Die sexuelle Osphresiologie*, and emphasised the particular odours of menstruation, coition and abstinence. He thought there could easily be sexual antipathy between persons because of incompatible sexual odours; and noted reports by Darwin of sexual excitement in apes caused by the odours of women. (Female bears in Yellowstone Park customarily attack menstruating women.) Daly and White in 1930 thought that human sexual odours were directly comparable to communication in insects. N. D. Fabricant in a review article in 1960 stated: 'The naso-genital relationship, observed and at the same time relatively neglected for more than 2,000 years, is worthy of rescue from the domain of neglect. The entire field of investigation awaits the attention of intrepid investigators.' Freud, at the outset of his career influenced by Fleiss, was such an investigator, but it is possible that his alleged cocaine habit spoilt his feeling for the subject. Fleiss would control painful menstruation by painting the 'genital spots' in the nose with cocaine. Kalogerakis in 1963 suggested, with evidence, that the sense of smell plays 'a crucial role in the evolution of the Oedipus complex', as did Daly in numerous papers, though he attributed the crucial role to the periodic perfumes of the mother's menstruation.

In his *Sexual Selection in Man* Havelock Ellis leaves vision to the last, and deals with touch, smell and hearing first.[50] The section on smell is full of Romantic, evocative and even Gothic imagery. Apparently ravens in Cornwall are attracted to perch on houses where people are dying, by the *odor mortis*. Continent young men have a goatish smell, according to many ancient writers, and the smell of sexual excitement in men comes from the skin and the breath, or both. Sometimes it may smell of chloroform, at other times of rancid butter. Menstruating French girls may give off the smell of leather. The Romans believed that a large nose meant a large penis; this might be paralleled in women by the clitoris size: 'Her nose, which by its length assures me/ Of storms at midnight if I fail to pay her/ The tribute she expects.'

It is certain that there are close interrelations between the sexual system, the pulmonary system and the olfactory. Nose bleeds are often associated with menstruation, or occur instead of a delayed period, or among males in the household before the woman's bleeding starts. Acute nasal congestion and sneezing is associated with an important coital event: 'the bride's cold'. Ruth Winter[51] tells us that with laryngotomy – surgical removal of the vocal cords – the sense of smell is lost for up to eight years afterwards. 'Patients with sex-hormone deficiencies along with olfactory disorders also have impaired pulmonary function,' she says. People training for opera are well known to become sexually excited in the presence of their teacher, and are usually warned tactfully of this. Singing is one of the sciences of extra-sensuous perception like *pranayama* (below).

Ellis notes cases in which patients like to have their necks squeezed and how this heightens olfactory sexual sensation. We saw how important a place the throat was to the osmic dancers. Rudolph Steiner says it is the genitals of the new age, creating by speech. We compared the emanation from it to the rainbow bridge between heaven and earth, mind and body. Breathing is both conscious and unconscious, since we can control our breath or leave it to work by itself. As speech it balances in the throat, and spoken words can be deliberate as well as subconsciously inspired. Thus the importance of the throat in the magic of possession and prophecy. Maenads in Greek art are depicted with throats swelling as in deep orgasm, because they run inspired by Dionysus.

In yoga, the throat is the *Viśuddha chakra*, the place of aether and dreaming; and dream, again, unites conscious and unconscious processes. B. K. S. Iyengar says that Ādi Śesa, the Lord of the Serpents, is the supporter of yoga.[52] In yoga breathing the throat is squeezed by lowering the chin to the breastbone in the *jālandhara bandha*, while the anus (*Mūlādhāra-chakra*, the animal centre of smell) and genitals are contracted in *mūla bandha*. This double inner caress contributes to the energising powers of this *pranayama* or science of breath. It is a technique for enhancing the unconscious senses by close and prolonged attention to the act of breathing and its effects of compression and relaxation on the body's interior. The environment of air is incorporated into oneself, and one gives into it with the absorption of sexual encounter. The entire mucosa of the lung is energised and the olfactory sensoria high in the nose are sensitised, the skin becomes full of energy and its sexuality is diffused through it, able to expand or contract as desired, as Blake said was so in the beginning.

A master of the art will have great presence, for he will have been practising techniques that are favourable to the extension and purification of his breathed 'human atmosphere' or aura, distilled and redistilled, and to the controlled restfulness of his skin radiations. The timbre of his voice, audible and sub-audible, will be a reflection of, literally, his body's constitution, and his awareness of the inner resonance of his chest cavity; the dolphin's sonar is a parallel. There is evidence that the ears project supersonics that enable us to hear partly by echo reflection, as with so many animals. In fact the body radiates on very many levels, to feel out its environment. Speech, sight, hearing and mind were known to the ancient Hindus as 'breaths', as they were to the ancient Greeks. Thus it is said of the 'breathing spirit': 'Speech pours all names in it, with speech it obtains all names; breath pours all odours in it; with breath it obtains all odours; the eye pours all forms in it; with the eye it obtains all forms.'[53]

If this master studies Tantra his enhanced feeling for, and control of, his sexual functions will lead his sexuality, like his breathing and all his enhanced senses, to become an organ of actual knowledge and discovery, a 'breathing spirit'; he is then a master, or she a mistress, of 'extra-sensuous perception'. He will be aware that these are natural gifts, but that it is his duty to himself to carry them over beyond puberty into adult life. He or she will be fit to make a temenos sensitive to all things on their own account, or with a lover, or with pupils or children. We shall see that women are possibly more powerful in these ways by nature, and without special training.

Havelock Ellis describes smell as 'the sense of imagination'. He points out how Shakespeare in various passages 'implicitly places the attraction of odour on at least as high a level as that of vision'. One example is Sonnet 54: 'The rose looks fair, but fairer we it deem/ For that sweet odour which doth in it live . . . / Of their sweet deaths are sweetest odours made.' Ellis quotes Galopin's Le Parfum de la Femme: ' . . . The purest marriage that can be contracted between a man and a woman is that engendered by olfaction and sanctioned by a common assimilation in the brain of the animated molecules due to the secretion and evaporation of two bodies in contact and sympathy.' This again is sexual alchemy: the bodies of Keats's lovers mingle like two perfumes in 'The Eve of St Agnes'. 'Into her dream he melted, as the rose/Blendeth its odour with the violet' – and this moment of spiritual awakening has been compared to the Song of Solomon.[54]

The mysterious 'sympneuma' taught by the Oliphants in the 1880s seems to be the production of a charged electrical 'spiritual body' made of mingled breath between them; a kind of mutual distillation by breathing, which would survive death. There was a more sinister report of a certain Harvard professor of German who allegedly killed his wife to obtain her perfume at the moment of death, which would then be a constant companion-spirit to him. The 'subtle body' and the 'aromal body' are often equated in sexual occultism.[55]

In his *The Origins of European Thought* R. B. Onians has a long study of the breath, breath-soul or spirit, the *thymos* which is the energy of a person's *phrenes* (diaphragm or lungs) which the ancient Greeks thought the seat of one's soul. *Thymos* is vaporous, it is the moist fume of the breath, and it is the soul that escapes at death. Onians's study is full of detail corroborative of the fact that the ancient Greeks thought and spoke in synaesthetic ways and were aware of sensory modalities of which we have become unconscious.[56] Kathleen Raine, in her great *Yeats the Initiate*, remarks: 'The so-called ectoplasm of the seance was known in the ancient world. Porphyry, in his *De Antro Nympharum*, writes that "according to the opinion of some men aerial and celestial bodies are nourished by the vapours of fountains and rivers and other exhalations . . . the souls of the dead . . . condense this watery vehicle like a cloud . . . ".' Yeats himself considered that 'materialised images might have been evoked in the Greek mysteries'.[57]

C. G. Jung compares offering the spirit body to the gods by means of burning sacrifices to the spiritualist belief in the constitution of the spirit world. In Oliver Lodge's book *Raymond*, the great physicist's son returns after being killed in the Great War. They question him about the hereafter. 'From his answers they concluded that what is called matter in the next world consists of molecules exhaled by the stuff on earth. A certain warmth causes movement of the molecules, which are then exhaled into the atmosphere like smells; one can smell a brick, for example, as one can smell a cigar. These molecules are taken up to the thinnest atmosphere, where they are collected by the ghosts, whose houses, built of brick smell, have the same form they had on earth . . . ' Jung uses a similar idea of odorous molecules caught on the surfaces of walls and other surfaces in accounting for his seeing the ghost of an old woman haunting a bedroom where he was staying. He associates the vision with a 'hypnoid' state in which the senses are enhanced. 'If the olfactory organ in man were not so hopelessly degenerate, but as highly developed as a dog's, I would undoubtedly have had a clearer idea of the persons who had lived in the room earlier. Primitive medicine men can not only smell out a thief, they also "smell" spirits or ghosts . . . It is also conceivable that intuition in man has taken the place of the world of smells that were lost to him . . . The effect of intuition on man is indeed very similar to the instant fascination which smells have for animals.'[58]

Ellis quotes a German work which says that many women 'have an intoxicatingly agreeable breath which plays no small part in the love-compelling atmosphere which they spread around them' and artificial perfumes need play no part. Casanova declared: 'There is something in the air of the bedroom of the woman one loves, something so intimate, so balsamic, such voluptuous emanations . . . ' Don Giovanni in Mozart's opera 'smells out' a woman. It is almost the signature of true love to enjoy the atmosphere of the beloved; modern deodorants severely limit this experience. Féré noticed, when living opposite a laundry, that an old woman working there rubbed her hand in her armpit and smelled it as a stimulant to her flagging energies (if your energies are flagging, try it now, because it works). Huysmans followed the fragrance of women gleaners in the country sunshine, and it had something of 'the relish of wild duck cooked with olives and the sharp odour of shallot . . . it united . . . with the formidable odours of the landscape; it was the pure note, completing with the human animals' cry of heat the odorous melody of beasts and woods.'

'*Sight is our most intellectual sense, and we trust ourselves to it with comparative boldness without any undue dread that its messages will hurt us by their personal intimacy*,' says Ellis (my italics). We have noted the common chemical continuum by which the animal and vegetable kingdoms communicate across their boundaries, and smell is a part of this, as Ellis also states. Sometimes passionate people will smell strongly of violets, roses, pineapple, vanilla. He tells us that the *Chenopodium vulvaria*, or stinking goosefoot, is a weed that carries the chemical propylamine, which is found also in the white thorn or mayflower. Propylamine is chemically related to the family of capryl odours that are present in goats' musk, human sweat, the odours of vagina and semen, Herb Robert, the berbery, the henna plant and the chestnut. The spermatic odour of the henna flower is very pronounced; it is used for dyeing the nails and hair and as make-up for other parts of the body. To one of Ellis's correspondents there was an exact resemblance between the scent of semen and that of the pollen of grasses. She thought that this was the explanation of the 'very exciting effect of a field of flowering grasses . . . If I am right, I suppose flower scents should affect women more powerfully than men in a sexual way.' Mantegazza says: 'Make the chastest woman smell the flowers she likes best . . . and she will close her eyes, breathe deeply, and, if very sensitive, tremble all over, presenting an intimate picture which otherwise she never shows, except perhaps to her lover.' 'Saying it with flowers' then, is a most intimate romantic communion asserting a common ground with nature through one of the dark senses.

Contemporary scientific accounts support the older anecdotes. Robert A. Schneider, like Ellis, believes in the power and the incredibly fine tuning of the human olfactory sense. He speaks of odours leading to a general excitation of the whole nervous system (maybe the reader has tested this with his or her own armpit or whatever). He tells us again that though the enormous development of the cerebral hemispheres in humans seems to have overgrown and superseded the primitive olfactory brain, neurologically the olfactory pathways have intimate and potent connections with emotions, behaviour and visceral function. There is a direct connection with the unconscious or semiconscious 'limbic' system in the brain. During sexual excitement 'sensory perception including that for odour is heightened but appears to be ignored, at least on a conscious level, even though these sensations may add to total gratification'.[59] Extra-sensuous perception again (call it ESSP).

Alex Comfort's splendid contribution to a standard scientific work, *Pheromones*, edited by Martin C. Birch, should convince anybody who is doubtful about the 'likelihood of human pheromones'.[60] Dr Comfort is well known as a popular and accurate writer on sex (*The Joy of Sex* and *More Joy of Sex*), and was at one time noted as a poet. His survey is well balanced and admirably documented. He recalls that Groddeck argued that a person is as 'macrosmatic as the dog', but represses the capacity in adult life for psychosexual reasons, and 'even the most learned man has to let his nose decide for him in matters of love'. Comfort says, 'Human beings have a complete set of organs which are traditionally described as non-functional, but which, if seen in any other mammal, would be recognised as part of a pheromone system.' These are the apocrine glands clustered in armpit, chest and nipple, anus, ear, eyelid, lips and pubic region. Broadly speaking, apocrine glands are the odour glands, which argue a pheromone system by their presence. The simple sweat glands are called eccrine (but Wiener says these carry pheromones, or external chemical messengers (ECMs) as well).

Apocrine glands, then, are associated with conspicuous hair, with the foreskin and female labia, and with the production of smegma by foreskin and clitoris. Comfort says that the system seems over elaborate for the apparently minor role of odour in human culture, and, moreover, 'The amputatory assault on these recognisable pheromone-mediating structures (by shaving or deodorant) in many human societies implies an intuitive awareness that their sexual function goes beyond the decorative. A conspicuous and apparently unused antenna array presupposes an unsuspected communications system.' Lewis Thomas tells the story of the scientist who weighed his beard clippings from his electric razor every morning. Normally he lived on an island alone. However, when he went to the mainland and mingled with women, the weight of his collected stubble soared![61]

Alex Comfort tells us that it is not clear 'why odour release should be enhanced at the infertile time of menstruation', thus oddly repeating the usual scientific assumption that sex is only for reproduction. His love-books do not discuss the mental experiences accompanying physical love, but Shuttle and I have argued that, like dreams, they have evolutionary and survival value.[62] He does, however, in The Joy of Sex concede menstruation to be 'often a woman's randiest time'. He concludes his otherwise thorough survey of evidence by predicting that we may see the time when deodorants rate with environmental pollution – 'as they do already among the sexually experienced'. He thinks that aromatherapy may move out of the realm of fringe medicine, since in it only small and non-poisonous quantities of odorous substances are needed to elicit a physiological response, in contrast to the dangers of hormone treatment. Pheromone action 'compared with the use of systemic hormones (some pheromones in insects operate at the single-molecule level) [is] well worthy of examination in a culture which urgently needs all the control over its reproductive processes it can get'.

The upshot of all the information is that human stimuli are reinforced by unconscious effects, a few of which we have so far examined. There can surely be no pretence of 'objective science' where human beings are concerned – the number of variables is just too great. What we chiefly call science, which is that part of science in the service of commercial industrialisation, has ignored the better part of the play of these variables, to our great impoverishment, however much it may have increased the wealth of nations.

3 The Intelligence of his Air

Everybody without exception is consciously acquainted with certain very powerful subliminal influences, and most people spend a good part of the day talking about them. I mean, of course, the influence of the weather on our moods and perceptions. 'It is constantly observed,' said Dr Johnson, 'that when two Englishmen meet, their first talk is of the weather; they are in haste to tell each other, what they must already know, that it is hot or cold, bright or cloudy, windy or calm.'[63] We should begin with the example on which most people's experience agrees: the storm. Ellsworth Huntington argues that a stormy climate is fundamental to the growth of certain kinds of civilisation. Not only will there be the 'growth of a social system in which great stress is laid on the dynamic qualities which are needed to meet such difficulties' but there are direct physiologically determined inner effects too. The extreme contrast of the human mental and physical state before and after a storm may provide interior conviction of the unexplored resources of the psyche – as in the German early Romantic movement *Sturm und Drang* – storm and stress – or lead to religious belief in revelation and transcendence. We shall see that an avatar of the Black Goddess, Lilith, was once a storm demon.

Meteorological changes show that the 'pathetic fallacy' of the Romantics, in which human moods and nature's moods coincide, is no mere fallacy after all, and cannot be explained by some such theory as 'projection'. It must be seen as an interaction with outside forces that reach into our very glands. The adventures among various climates of Wallace Stevens's poetic hero Crispin teach him, in Carolina in spring, 'how much/Of what he saw he never saw at all' and to change his self-assertive, 'Nota: man is the intelligence of his soil' to 'Nota: his soil is man's intelligence.' As a consequence of his deference to the world's inexhaustible reality, Crispin has four daughters, beautiful in different ways, who are the four seasons. Harold Bloom says of him: 'Stevens turns to the idea of the weather precisely as the religious man turns to the idea of God . . .'[64]

People think and behave differently as the air pressure changes. The unpleasant atmosphere before a storm makes one say that the air feels heavy. Actually it is light, as the barometric pressure has gone down. 'It seems heavy because it makes people feel dull or slightly inert. A moderately warm day before a storm may be most delightful, but not at all stimulating . . . ' Then the rain begins, and there is an immediate change of mood with the atmospheric change: 'While the rain is falling one settles earnestly to work. Towards the end of the storm, even though the rain is still falling, the air often changes its quality and has a stimulating effect . . . The exhilarating quality of the weather after a storm is well known. Children and animals show it in their play. Adults walk unusually fast. Physicians have devoted much attention to the way in which sufferers from rheumatism, epilepsy, arthritis and many other diseases feel bad on the approach of a storm but recover and feel unusually well when the storm is over.' The daily deathrates in New York City increase as the warm air masses sweep in. After a storm breaks, the influx of cool air is accompanied by an increase in health. A normal storm introduces weather which tends to kill sick people, but as it passes away this effect is reversed. The 'heavy' feelings of dejection before a storm which may be so harmful are far from imaginary. They are accompanied by measurable physiological 'tides': 'The rates of pulse and breathing, the blood-pressure, the composition of the blood and various other bodily functions all vary systematically with the coming and going of tropical and polar air masses.'[65]

An American neurologist, Weir Mitchell, put this unusually vividly. 'Every storm, as it sweeps across the continent, consists of a vast rain area, at the centre of which is a moving space of greatest barometric depression known as the storm-centre, along which the storm moves like a bead on a thread . . . ' The rain usually precedes the storm centre by 600 miles or so, but beyond and around the rain *lies a belt which may be called the neuralgic margin of the storm*, and which precedes the rain by about 150 miles. This fact is very deceptive, because the sufferer may be on the far edge of the storm basin of barometric depression, and seeing nothing of the rain, yet has pain due to the storm [my italics].' Mitchell summarises this state of affairs as follows: 'A moving area of rain girdled by a neuralgia belt 150 miles wide, within which, as it sweeps along in advance of the storm, prevail in the hurt and maimed limbs of men, and in tender nerves and rheumatic joints, renewed torments called into existence by the stir and perturbation of the elements.' (A millennium ago the law of the Friesians, *Lex Frisonium*, imposed a special fine if an inflicted wound resulted in a weather-sensitive scar.)

Writing in 1877, Mitchell observed not only that 'neuralgic' attacks in his patients were related to storms, but that the 'separate factors of storms, such as lessened pressure, rising temperature, greater humidity, winds, appear as a rule to be incompetent when acting singly to give rise to attacks of pain. Either then it is a combination which works the mischief, or else there is in times of storms some as yet unknown agency productive of evil.'[66] He thought this agency might be either electrical or magnetic. One of the greatest of German nature-philosophers, Alexander von Humboldt, who attempted to give a comprehensive physical description of the universe in his lectures (later printed in the mid-nineteenth century as *Kosmos*), offered this definition of climate, and by implication the 'pathetic fallacy': 'All modifications in the atmosphere which affect our senses markedly, namely, temperature, humidity, changes of the barometric pressure, wind, the amount of electric tension, the purity of the atmosphere or its admixture with more or less noxious gaseous exhalations, finally the degree of habitual transparency and clarity of the sky, which is not only important for the increased radiation of heat by the soil, the organic development of plants and the maturation of fruits, *but also for the feelings of man and his entire mood* [my italics].'[67] Von Humboldt, of course, also made contributions to mainstream science which have survived.

William A. R. Thomson, the medical climatologist, asks why, if health, as it seems to, depends primarily upon weather, and climatology has been the basis of the practice of medicine from time immemorial, as is the case, this branch of medicine is not widely taught. The doctor had to be 'a meteorologist if he was going to do justice to his patients. Yet, how many medical schools today include bioclimatology in their curriculum? Certainly none in the United Kingdom.' He says, 'Physicians are taught to use every treatment from penicillin to the scalpel, except the omnipresent climate and weather – or protection from it . . . man has sinned against nature in two ways. He has not only refused to respect it, he has also tried to develop independent of it.'[68]

What Thomson says is fully borne out by other authorities; S. W. Tromp's monumental studies and compilations of biometeorology, for example, or H. Brezowsky who shows statistically among German populations the rise in emboli, haemorrhages, asthmatic attacks, migraine attacks, myocardial infarcts, colic, angina pectoris, osteoarthritic complaints and neuroma pain during the warm and humid conditions of a preparing weather change. This holds true for thrombo-phlebitis, acute encephalopathy and meningococci meningitis also. In fact, Brezowsky is compelled to divide weather phases into two unequal groups. Group I is biologically favourable, being at a maximum in the high-pressure areas of the subtropics and the Arctic, and at a minimum in the temperate zones where the winds are westerly. In Central Europe the ratio of the favourable to unfavourable weather conditions is 1:2. Group I is fine weather, cool to mild, with few and scattered clouds, and fairly calm. Group II includes the preparing weather changes, the storms, the ground inversions and the retarded weather changes, with extreme changes of temperature and humidity. During violent alterations in temperature and humidity 'infarct and stroke, as far as they are related to embolic and haemorrhagic diseases, are also increased, as are many symptoms of general diseases'; the evidence is that they flare up with the weather in 'biotrophic waves'.[69]

Wordsworth had often seen the thorn of his poem of that title in calm and still weather, but failed to notice it until a certain stormy day: 'Cannot I by some invention do as much to make this thorn permanently an impressive object as the storm has made it to my eyes at this moment?' The weather had enhanced more than his visual sense.

Reiter quotes a study in which changes in taste, smell, hearing and touch were examined in relation to the weather, and Tromp concurs. Thunderstorms are particularly potent in altering the senses. There was a famous hurricane on 21 September 1938. It happened that the freshman class at Massachusetts State College in Amherst were taking psychological tests when the hurricane descended on them. The wind rose to 80 mph, and the day grew so dark that the lights had to be switched on. It was expected that there would be poor results in the test, but, months later, when the 'hurricane papers' were examined, they were found to be exceptional. Ordinarily this college stood in the seventy-fifth percentile among other colleges; the papers done during the hurricane raised it to the ninety-fifth, exceeding any grade before or since. Weather conditions had apparently increased the intelligence of the students.

Ellsworth Huntington, who records this story in his seminal book on the influence of climate on mentality and social evolution, says he knew just how the students felt during the inspiration of that storm. Huntington happened at that time to be writing in New Haven in a room with thick stone walls, and with a window so high up that to anybody sitting down only a high tower and the sky were visible. He was aware that the wind was blowing hard, but he was so busy that he resisted looking out of the window. When he stopped writing and left the room, the rain had finished and the sky was clearing. He was astonished at the amount he had written, and amazed too to 'see great elms lying prone across the street . . . Something connected with that hurricane evidently acted as a powerful mental stimulant . . . which was not temperature, humidity, wind or lightning.' The effect of the hurricane was 'like that which makes people sing or whistle at the end of a storm or hurry to the library to get a book they have long purposed to read'. There is a remarkable statistical section in the book on the seasonal and weather changes in library fiction and non-fiction borrowing. Library figures have world-wide scope, and Huntington demonstrates that they reflect changes in mental acuity and disposition with the seasonal changes of weather. 'It was also like the easing of aches and pains experienced by sufferers from various diseases and the almost miraculous recovery of people who are at death's door, which occur at such times. Other related occurrences are a temporary drop in the general deathrate, high marks among students, and fast, accurate work among factory hands as diverse as cigar makers in Florida and brass workers in Connecticut.' Needless to say he supports all this with figures in what appears to be an unanswerable world-wide case.[70] Man's intelligence, at least partly, is his atmosphere.

The dismissal of the weather by the mainstream of Western thought, as Arden Reed points out, is quite a recent development. The shift occurred during the 'Enlightenment' of the eighteenth century. From Aristotle to the Renaissance, the weather was a major concern in Western philosophy and literature. The Enlightenment thinkers appeared to lose interest, and 'their changing attitude may be understood in the context of the development of modern science, which depended on exact, rigorous measurement of a wholly regulated environment, and this necessarily excluded the weather as a variable that could not be controlled. Hence physicists came to conduct their experiments in chambers free of atmospheric turbulence and, in short, science moved indoors.'[71] The Enlightenment, in fact, *repressed* the weather. This movement of thought and the science that went with it led to the extraordinary exploitation of nature and control of human populations in the artificial environments of the factories and the mega-cities, which we call the Industrial Revolution. It is no wonder that the repression of weather went with all the other conscious and unconscious repressions necessary to the accomplishment of this change. It is difficult to forgive our forefathers for the intellectual dishonesty of ignoring what it was not expedient to understand, while professing reason. Since weather was natural and could not be controlled, it was ignored. It has become another of the plagues of Thebes, and millions suffer because part of the causative picture of their illnesses has been repressed. Fred Hoyle has advanced the theory that flu epidemics have an extra-terrestrial origin since they mysteriously jump from place to place without evident cross-infection, and that the virus falls 'vertically from the atmosphere.'[72] This would be more interesting if the patterns of weather stress had been taken into consideration beforehand as an aetiology. Again, since weather causes changes in mentality, it can cause visions also which, it is arguable, can drive the over-sensitive mad. We have already cited evidence for olfactory sensitivity in what are called schizophrenics: there are now many studies which correlate mental disturbance with weather change.[73] Unfortunately so far nobody has investigated the content of the dreams, visions or hallucinations of the patients, and whether by symbols they portray weather passions and weather calms, as if the atmosphere (as it was to the Chinese and the Greeks) were full of irascible dragons or quarrelling parents. One weather-sensitive declares: 'I have never yet been known to be wrong in this matter and I can not only state with precision the time of the coming [weather] change but also the duration of the change and its relative intensity . . . The manner in which I am able to foretell the weather changes is simply this. I have learned that I invariably feel what is known as mental depression, slight or severe, and the reverse as the case may be, in advance of weather changes. The depression comes on rapidly, sometimes suddenly, and sometimes very gradually. It may last for only a few minutes, for hours, and sometimes for a day or a little more . . . I have no reason to believe that I am alone in this special weather sensitiveness . . . The periods of suicidal tendency will coincide with about three or four days in advance of atmospheric depressions coming on during finer weather conditions of the atmosphere.'[74] That weather-sensitive 30 per cent of the population has immediate cause to complain of that long-ago repression of weather by the Enlightenment.

Coleridge was one who could fine-tune his depression. His weather sensitivity was an essential element in his poetic sensibility, as he acknowledged. It would manifest itself *either in poetry or in rheumatism* after close contact with nature, as when he slept out in wet fields by the river after a quarrel with his brother, or when once he swam in his clothes, or with his move to the damp climate of the Lake District. When repressed, his dark or animal senses showed themselves as illness, and when the repression was overcome by working it through in poetry, illness was replaced by insight and the convalescent condition, which he regarded as a state of genius. After one attack he wrote, 'My new and tender health is all over me like a voluptuous feeling,' and thus illness when transcended by poetic work 'helped to reveal himself to himself; it sharpened his pleasures and pains in all areas of his life . . .' He wrote: 'I am harassed with the rheumatism in my head and shoulders, not without arm-and-thigh twitches – but when the pain intermits it leaves my sensitive frame *so* sensitive.'[75]

His dark senses were constantly in play, the frustration of them bringing illness. Weather and organic nature combined in a synaesthetic multi-media event, and this was the ground of all perception before it was divided up in daily living: the Primary Imagination giving way to the Secondary. Poetry was forever seeking a conscious return to this state, which existed all the time, whether he knew it or not. In 'The Aeolian Harp' he saw the stringed framework placed in the window for the breeze scented by the beanfield to play upon, a figure for this constant, inspired activity in nature: 'And what if all of animated nature / Be but organic harps diversely fram'd,' and the spirit everywhere played upon them 'with a light in sound, a sound-like power in light'. John Beer points out how very direct Coleridge's feeling for scented flowers was, 'as if he believed all flowers to retain some paradisal quality'.[76]

After a day of sickness, Coleridge records a vision of the dark senses in a repressed and negative aspect in weather-change conditions of a light overcast: 'O after what a day of distempered Sleeps, out of which I woke, all sense of Time & Circumstance utterly lost

. . . I get up / am calm, like one lownded – / as I lifted up the Sash, & looked out at the Sky, for the first minute I thought it all dark, a starless sky . . . / – but I looked again at the Sky – & there were many Stars, so dim & dingy that they might have put into Paracelsus's Fancy his whim of the Astra tenebricosa, that radiated cold and darkness . . . '[77] It is the dark light from the moon and stars which is doing this. So far as his gout and rheumatism were concerned, he knew that damp air was part of the cause yet, because it could affect him under several blankets in a warm room with a fire, he felt that a deficiency of 'electrical, or other imponderable fluid instrumental to vital action' was the essential factor.[78]

Sulman says that a certain type of weather-sensitive may exhibit 'dermographia' or writing on the skin.[79] Sometimes lovers delight in doing this with a fingernail, leaving red lines that turn into white lines, due to a local production of histamine and norepinephrine, and it is usually the woman's skin which has this sensitivity. The skin – that great organ, electrical as the brain and deriving, as the brain does, from embryonic ectoderm – is the seat of the sexual sense, touch, Blake's Fifth Window. It records and exhibits emotion, as we have seen in discussing thermography, and its I R rainbow is accompanied by electrical changes which can also be measured. An extra-sensual skin is one of the female secondary sexual characteristics, and a full relaxed skin open to its feelings is one of the blisses of the post-coital state: the 'skin orgasm'.

Coleridge evidently had a woman's skin, and could see also into the I R, although he thought, as his time would think, that it was a symptom of diseased nerves: 'I have myself once seen (i.e. appeared to see) my own body under the Bed cloaths flashing silver Light from whatever part I prest it – and the same proceed from the tips of my fingers. I have thus written, as it were, my name, Greek words, cyphers &c on my Thigh: and instantly seen them together with the Thigh in brilliant letters of silver Light.'[80] This note was interspersed with a discussion of animal magnetism, and Coleridge compared his Primary Consciousness to 'quicksilver': infinitely mobile, reflecting everything, like the 'dry water' of the alchemists and the charged cloud of the fleeting-floating pheromone maser. It is the skin that initially makes these pictures, and reflects the weather: 'The exquisite Affectability of my Skin, & the instant Sympathy of my Stomach and mesenteries with the Affections of the Skin . . . & in my miserable barometrical Dependence of my Stomach Sensations

on the *weather*, especially damp & wet-stormy weather . . . '
Wordsworth's 'hypochondria' was evidently also like this, but not to
such an extent. Coleridge considers the parallel action of a hot
climate: 'What if it brought out a deforming Eruption on my Face &
Body, leaving my inner Life sound and full of faculty?' but it is the
dank English climate that pursues him and leaves him eventually so
that *'my sole sensuality was not to be in pain'*. He nevertheless knows
the source of his dejection, and that the doctors are partly to blame,
and wonders: 'Whether Gout and Rheumatism – or, to speak more
guardedly, whether certain Diseases at least, which are now classed
under Gout and Rheumatism, are not mainly and primarily
cutaneous? And whether the Skin be not a Terra Incognita in
Medicine? And whether this Ignorance, if it exist, does not imply
broad fundamental Error in the Theory of Medicine . . . ' He knew
that the laudanum he took brought visions in place of the pain, and
discussed a hypothetical man in 'whom a *pernicious Drug* shall make
capable of conceiving & bringing forth thoughts, hidden in him
before, which shall call forth the deepest feelings of his best, greatest
and sanest Contemporaries . . . the dire poison for a delusive time
has made the body . . . a fitter instrument for the all-powerful
soul . . . '[81] that is, the soul in connection with nature. Humphrey
House notes Coleridge's awkward self-consciousness in much of his
published prose.[82] He 'muffs the tone' as if he were unsure of being
understood: that 'delusive' is a part of this, and the hypothetical
mask – yet he is sure of the importance of his perceptions. Nobody,
least of all the doctors or scientists of the time, could tell him whether
these experiences were delusions or no. It was the intellectual as
much as the physical climate which brought him and many others to
that last repression where his sole sensuality was absence of pain.

The weather-sensitive reader might try the effect of that plant-
growth hormone aspirin on twinges of rheumatism as the English
weather assumes its usual warm damp low-pressure state. If it is
taken at night, the sufferer will very likely obtain rest, and the pain
will be turned into vivid dreams. Is this why the willow (*Salix*),
from which salicylates come, was always considered a magical plant,
sacred to water and witches? If the reader now works at those
dreams, perhaps taking them further by 'active imagination' into
poetry, it may be that the balance between mind and body will shift,
and the weather may stimulate the imagination instead of bringing
pain. It is significant that the Romantics always associated imagin-

ation with a mist or cloud.[83] There is a wonderful and justly famous scene in Wordsworth's 'Prelude' in which the poet from the peak of Snowdon sees the moon brooding in clear sky over a radiant sea of cloud. There is a chasm in the cloud from which mounts 'the roar of waters, torrents, streams / Innumerable, roaring with one voice'. To Wordsworth it seems 'the perfect image of a mighty mind'.[84]

So it was with Coleridge; the moon rising, shedding its unitive visible light and its invisible and biologically active 'natural radiation' of I R, seemed to him like the creative word, the Logos, in continual utterance to his deepest levels, just out of hearing. His skin knew, no doubt, what his eyes scarcely told him. 'In looking at objects of Nature while I am thinking, as at yonder moon dim-glimmering thro' the dewy window-pane, I seem rather to be seeking, as it were *asking*, a symbolical language for something within me that already and forever exists, than observing anything new . . . I have always an obscure feeling as if that new phaenomenon were the dim Awaking of a forgotten or hidden Truth of my inner Nature . . . It is Logos, the Creator! and the Evolver!'[85]

Coleridge's 'Dejection: An Ode' must be the most famous analysis of pre-storm weather ever written. The poem begins with a new moon, which shows within its horns a slight albedo of the rest of the moon's disc. This ancient storm-sign – like a full and new moon in one – may be due to the moon's catching the reflected earth-light of storm-clouds in our atmosphere. 'For lo! the new-moon winter-bright! And overspread with phantom light . . . / I see the old moon in her lap, fortelling / The coming-on of rain and squally blast.'

He wishes that the storm were already raging – 'And the slant night-shower driving loud and fast!' – since that was the stimulus which 'sent my soul abroad' and the sounds of weather: 'Might now perhaps their wonted impulse give, / Might startle this dull pain, and make it move and live!'

The unpleasant atmosphere before a storm has caused a depression, maybe accompanied by an increase of the neurotransmitter serotonin in the brain; he is in the *neuralgic margin* of the storm. Depression is, however, also 'withheld knowledge', and the disciplined thought-processes of the act of poetic composition take him below the surface towards that knowledge.

The 'dull pain' is the depression, the 'katabasis' or 'going down'; it is the pressure of weather re-composing the human psyche. Nature is full of this pressure, and realisation delays, while the storm delays, in 'A stifled, drowsy, unimpassioned grief' which can find no outlet even in contemplating 'Yon crescent Moon, as fixed as if it grew / In its own cloudless, starless lake of blue . . .'

Although he sees natural objects as 'so excellently fair', still 'I see, not feel, how beautiful they are!' The feeling-senses beyond appearances are at that moment in abeyance. Coleridge blames himself: 'I may not hope from outward forms to win/The passion and the life, whose fountains are within'. He believes according to the doctrines of his time and with his surface mind (and contrary to what the poem itself will tell him): 'We receive but what we give, /And in our life alone does Nature live.' From the human soul, and not from nature, 'must issue forth / A light, a glory, a fair luminous cloud / Enveloping the earth –' for ' . . . in our life alone does Nature live: / Ours is her wedding garment, ours her shroud!'

It is as with Oedipus, the human being alone is the measure of things. The magic stuff – like the fleeting-floating charged 'cloud of glory' that accompanies the child in Wordsworth's 'Immortality Ode' – only comes from people, 'this fair luminous mist', 'cloud at once and shower' (resembling the 'clouds and rain' of the Chinese love-books in which the running of fluids and the condensations that can be felt occurring in the act of love reflect nature's atmospheric copulations). It is: 'Joy the luminous cloud . . . All melodies the echoes of that voice, / All colours a suffusion from that light,' but human joy only.

The dejection deepens, for Coleridge at that moment believes that this human joy is no longer potent against his afflictions; it used to be, but now 'each visitation / Suspends what nature gave me at my birth, / My shaping Spirit of Imagination.' Suddenly, as though he has spoken the correct magic word – not 'human Joy' but 'My shaping spirit of Imagination' – Coleridge finds that he can dismiss these 'viper thoughts'. The storm has broken and the wind howls; it 'long has raved unnoticed' as it did for Ellsworth Huntington, surprised by the amount he had written in his New England room.

Now the imagination rides on the wind over the world, as though it were the wind's perceptions, human and natural at once, simultaneously embodying themselves in superb poetry. Coleridge is free, he has come through and the agony and release of his psyche have left, in his poem, a piece of knowledge no longer withheld, by which we can study and ameliorate the same processes in ourselves.

In the blindness of non-feeling, 'A stifled, drowsy, unimpassioned grief', the riddle is posed: 'What is the nature of dejection?' and the answer given: 'It is withheld knowledge.' 'What is that knowledge?' 'The Shaping Spirit of Imagination.' 'What gives imagination?' 'Nature does.'

Scientists of the time were not immune to such visions. It was simply that they did not fit. The great Cornishman Humphry Davy left a beautiful account in an early notebook: 'Today, for the first time in my life, I have had a distinct sympathy with nature. I was lying on the top of a rock to leeward; the wind was high, and everything in motion . . . the whole sky was in motion . . . everything was alive, and myself part of the series of visual impressions; I should have felt pain in tearing a leaf from one of the trees.'

At the end of his life, after all his scientific work, Davy produced a visionary essay 'Consolations in Travel'. The narrator sits in the Colosseum and is given by a guide ('The Genius') a revelation of the universe. Again, it almost seems the moon is the guide through a reverie in which one sense enters the modalities of another: ' . . . My reverie became deeper, the ruins surrounding me appeared to vanish from my sight, the light of the moon became more intense, and the orb itself seemed to expand in a flood of splendour. At the same time that my visual organs appeared to be singularly affected, the most melodious sounds filled my ear; softer, yet at the same time deeper and fuller, than I had ever heard in the most harmonious and perfect concert.'[86]

4 Total Dowsing

Coleridge believed that the effect of temperature and humidity on his rheumatism was increased because of the lack of 'electrical, or other imponderable fluid instrumental to vital action', since he could feel the inclement weather even under blankets in a room with a roaring fire.[87] Weir Mitchell thought that the 'separate factors of storms, such as lessened pressure, rising temperature, greater humidity, winds,' did not account for the 'neuralgia' attendant on storms. He thought that it was either a combination of these, or 'some as yet unknown agency productive of evil. Such an agency may be either electricity or magnetism.' The aurora borealis was remarkably brilliant in 1867–8. Mitchell had a patient, who was an army captain with 'neuralgia of a leg stump', and who kept a detailed diary day by day of his stump's reaction to the weather. Whenever the aurora borealis shone (Darius calls it 'ether coursing in a maze of light') the stump hurt. Later statistical work on amputees, traffic and industrial accidents, reaction times and deathrates has shown that the measurement of 'sferics' (atmospheric electricity) is an excellent index of how biologically active any weather event may happen to be.[88]

There is now so much evidence that electricity and magnetism in all their various forms profoundly affect living organisms, including man, that it is difficult to know where to start.[89] It is not new ground, but it appears to be so because our society has shown a particular resistance to this idea. Like weather itself, the influence of electricity has been thrown out, and it is returning with a vengeance. We shall see that the motives for this ignorance were not disinterested, and belonged to a late phase in the Industrial Revolution: the electrification of the world. An understanding of the biological effects of electricity would not have permitted that development.

Weather sensitivity is the most obvious bioelectrical effect. Again, it is something nearly everybody knows about. It affects '30 per cent of the population in an overt reaction and the rest in an occult response'; that is, they react without knowing it. Urine analysis will demonstrate how changing weather by its electricity reaches right into our glands, well in advance of temperature or humidity alterations. Male and female sex hormones, thyroid, growth hormones, insulin and calcium metabolism hormones are all measurably affected.

The typical weather-sensitive, then, is reacting to atmospheric electricity. According to Sulman, 'Timing of the patients' complaints showed that most of their sufferings could be related to high air electricity, rather than to excessive heat or humidity. Sferics [atmospherics, such as you can hear on a radio] preceded weather change by one to two days and caused symptoms of the "serotonin irritation syndrome".'

This is the 'neuralgic margin' of the storm, and it seems that Weir Mitchell was right, and was seen to be right once the sferics monitor, the ion counter and the electrofield scanner had been invented, and the instrumental observations could be made.

Serotonin is a hormone produced in the brain and the intestines. Over-production occurs in response to atmospheric electricity and can result in insomnia, irritability, migraine, vomiting, palpitations, a feeling of electric currents on the skin and hair and many other symptoms, as Coleridge knew. Weather sensitivity of this kind resembles what happens to heavy smokers when they give up tobacco, and probably for related reasons; that is, effects on the chemical neuroregulators. Sferics correlate with death frequency, just as the storm fronts do in Huntington's account, and with muscular reaction-time – which obviously has important implications concerning efficiency at sport or work.[90]

'It is a pity that just the excellent personalities suffer most from the adverse effects of the atmosphere,' remarked Goethe. He himself was weather sensitive, and by all accounts earthquake sensitive also. Goethe was once discovered by his servant gazing at the sky. 'Listen,' he said, 'there is now an earthquake or one is just going to take place.' The weather was very cloudy, very still and sultry. A few weeks later the news reached Weimar that on that night (5 April 1783) Messina had been partly destroyed by an earthquake, which would have been accompanied by strong sferics.[91]

The list of notabilities who suffered from weather sensitivity is long and impressive. Women are more sensitive than men, due to their glandular make-up which 'produces less resistant stress hormones than men'. Some 80 per cent of the sensitives can actually predict the weather. Sulman's important aphorism is worth quoting again: 'We do great injustice to the electro-sensitive patients, who rightly complain of their serotonin sufferings, when we treat them as psychiatric patients. They have a sixth sense that makes them suffer and therefore deserve our help.'

Sulman, working out of Jerusalem, lists no fewer than twelve sources of environmental electricity which have strong and measurable effects on humans. These are ionisation, sferics, electrofields, aerosols, sun radiation, cosmic radiation, magnetic fields, radar, radioactive fallout, high-tension wires, waterhole radiation (water seeping through porous material and producing electromagnetic fields and air ionisation and emitting gamma rays) and 'technics' by which he means electrical appliances in factories and homes.[92]

It is worth noting under this last category that 'electro-sensitive people may react with the serotonin syndrome to passing electric street cars, telephones, radio receivers, television apparatuses, radar, infra-red heaters, U V generators and even to the extension wires crossing their living rooms. These reactions can be accentuated by the presence of good reflectors in a house, such as mirrors, marble plates, etc., which create undulations.'[93] This seems on the one hand madness; on the other good *feng shui* counsel: according to the ancient art of Chinese geomancy, reflectors like mirrors will contain, reflect and enhance the mysterious *ch'i* force which Western scientists responsive to and interested in nature appear to be re-discovering.[94] These scientists would surely include the members of the International Society of Biometeorology, which was founded in 1956, with headquarters in Leiden, under the secretariat of Dr Solco W. Tromp. In 1980 it consisted of more than 500 scientists from over fifty countries.

It is clear that biometeorology, which studies the nature and changes in every aspect of our environment, is also a direct study of that 'continuum' which has been a main subject of this book and was a chief concern of the Romantic nature-philosophers. It is the same subject under another name, and arguably one of the most important sciences of the present time.

It has 'manifold ramifications', which include rationales for the chemical as well as the electrical, magnetic and other physical features of that continuum which I have been discussing, and also for 'whole-body' effects not limited to the special sense organs, such as the nose or the eye. That is, *the body appears to respond as a whole, by a kind of diffused or comprehensive sense, to certain of these environmental influences, especially the electrical and magnetic ones.* This is as the Romantics believed.

It is as though we are understanding now what Blake intuited, that the senses were, in Eden, spread over the whole being. It might seem, then, that our bodies still live in Eden, but our minds refuse to know it. There is a magical tradition that women never left Eden; men may turn out to be unfortunate poison-victims of their sexual stress hormones, which minimise these weather effects.

The 'whole-body reaction' also takes us close to the idea of perception by synaesthesia, in which all the senses merge and combine. Weather is surely a whole-body experience; our eyes see the rain, but our whole bodies feel it is raining – it touches us, its music sounds on roads and buildings, and there are Zen gardens tuned by leaf and gutter to sound a special chord to the rain. Rain releases wonderful smells too, but we sense also a different electricity in the air, an ionisation. But there is more than this to it, much more.

Dr Tromp's meticulously accurate and scientific first book, pub-lished in 1949, takes us a good deal further towards a strong physically scientific grasp of these matters. It is really a most remarkable and thorough compilation. If there were no other source for my argument on the communion of humans and animals within a natural plenum, then this astonishing book would suffice. In point of fact, nearly every part of it I have found corroborated by more recent work. The book is scientifically accurate, and based not only upon 1,496 references to the experimental literature in several languages, but on the author's own published papers arising from his work in the laboratory and in the field as geologist and meteorologist. He speaks more than once in the book of that 'wonderful web of electromagnetic forces which seem to regulate all living processes on earth'. The dowsing or water-divining reflex – the twitch of the arm muscles that indicates a field-change – is only one of the human responses behind which lies this 'webwork of forces' of which animals and plants are, as it were, initiated and active presences. It is like a great collective mind, which we call Unconscious, for the reason that we are for the main part unconscious of it. We are capable of more, far more; which is why I have called this section 'Total Dowsing'.

It is not easy to summarise Tromp's 500-plus pages, packed as they are with information, but the difficulty is lessened by his systematic approach. He says that the stimuli registered by diviners are 'unconsciously perceptible by nearly everybody (not only a favoured few)' and that 'after being registered by our nervous systems they can be amplified and transformed into phenomena known in the ordinary perceptible world'. He also says that practically all parapsychological phenomena can be attributed to this sensitivity. In the core of the book he systematically lists the phenomena that have been shown to affect us, under the categories of (a) electric stimulation; (b) magnetic stimulation; (c) electromagnetic stimulation; (d) acoustic stimulation; and (e) stimulation by volatile components.[95]

Under 'electric stimulation' we have a truly wonderful array of electrical responses, comparable to what is well established in animal biology. We respond first to the atmospheric fields, which include the influence of ionic currents in the air. These directly stimulate the nerve endings in the skin, thus affecting *touch*. Ions are absorbed by the lungs – electricity in the very air we breathe – and this influences respiration and blood-pressure. Fluctuations in the patterns of ions are caused by variations in cosmic radiations, in the radioactivity of the soil, by fluctuations in the electrical gradients of the atmosphere and of the earth itself, by variations in the amounts of moisture, by temperature and atmospheric pressure, and the presence of metal; and therefore can theroretically carry subliminal or conscious information from all these sources by the 'dark' senses beyond sight, the feelings, and the dowsing reflex, mostly through the skin, and the whole surface of the lungs.

Moreover, the air carries electrical information by its gradient of charge, which has an average value of 120–150 volts per metre. This means that a person of average height carries a charge of about 200 volts' difference between the head and the feet. If the living body is earthed, this will have a direct effect on the nerves and on the flow of air-ions, and this will be a different electrical pattern from what obtains if the body is insulated: if you walk on moist earth it *feels* different from the way it feels in a building with plastic floors and ceilings.

For example, office buildings accumulate static charges, and most office work is done in effect within the plates of a high-tension capacitor. The room is a capacitor; it will discharge rhythmically, producing sub-thunder. Think of this next time you feel irritable in your high-street bank with its plastic ceilings and carpet of nylon. Measurements have shown that the normal use of such rooms gives rise to fluctuating potentials due to electrostatic charges on clothing, the moving about of people, and the use of electrical equipment. It is probable that those who succeed in business are the ones who are insensitive to the electrical environment of the office, which is not conducive to the optimum functioning of the body.

It is possible too that part of the feeling people get about their cars is due to the way the shaped metal body of the vehicle sheds variations in environmental fields, thus producing a protected space, a kind of 'Faraday cage', in which we can feel our own feelings, not think nature's thoughts for her. It may be such feelings that fill the roads with cars for the traditional family drive on Sundays, or that led D. H. Lawrence to write thus about a man driving a car with a woman to whom he is about to make love: 'He felt as if he were seated in immemorial potency, like the great carven statues of real Egypt, as real and fulfilled with subtle strength as these are, with a vague inscrutable smile on their lips. He knew what it was to have the strange and magical current of force in his back and loins, and down his legs, force so perfect that it stayed him immobile, and left his face subtly, mindlessly smiling. He knew what it was to be awake and potent in that other basic mind, the deepest physical control,

magical, mystical, a force in darkness, like electricity.'[96] Everybody
has seen a man driving his car like this, in perfect personal equilib-
rium. And families too, watching nature, like a cinema show,
through their untroubled windscreen.

These electrical gradients in the atmosphere are altered by, and
can therefore carry information about, the topography of the surroundings – houses, trees, fields, etc.; all will be sub-visible in the
electrical senses and potentially accessible to consciousness.

Weather, of course, alters the atmospheric fields – in clear air
there is a low gradient and in fog there is a high one; there is a low
gradient above the sea and high positive and negative gradients
fluctuating in snowfall and thunderstorms, which must account in
part for the depression and fascination caused by these kinds of
weather. The hypnoidal state that we go into when we are watching
the flakes flicker in a snowfall, the fascination and poetic feel of it,
then, is no pathetic fallacy, but an effect that reaches right into us by
means of the electricity which surrounds and penetrates us, right
down to the nerves and the drift of electrons in the protoplasmic
lattice.

Currents within the earth alter these atmospheric charges also.
For instance, if there is water circulating among iron and other ores,
a tremendous subterranean electrical battery is formed, with a
negative centre situated above the ore body and the weak acids
formed by the action of the water on the ore constituting the battery
electrolyte. Usually the current travels downwards through the ore,
and then upwards, spreading over the nearby landscape. As a living
being moves over these infinitely detailed underground sources of
electrical black 'light', the charge between head and feet changes, as
it does during the day, with the rising and setting of the sun and the
moon, and also day by day, the smallest changes occurring during
April to September and the largest ones from October to March.
There are yearly fluctuations too; and an eleven-year period linked
to sunspots.

Thus there are atmospheric and geophysical fields. Moreover, the
conductivity of the soil influences the rate at which your body-
electricity leaks, and interacts with the atmospheric gradient and the
battery earth-currents already mentioned, since these flow differently according to rock composition and changes in water content –
which is itself affected by rain, heat and atmospheric pressure.

Naturally, the travelling earth-currents, with which you interact, vary with local geology, the presence of conductors, faults, folds, subterranean caves, ore bodies, stratification, ground water level, distribution and shape of standing and running water, with the magnetic field and the electrical field in *its* complexity, the presence of rails, pipes, power circuits, foundations of houses and their shapes, and indeed anything that is there. The *feel* of everything changes moment by moment.

We also have our own electrical field. It has a polarity between head and feet, left and right sides of the body, and the polarity has its daily fluctuations. It alters also if you approach a conductor, or with your own nervous tone, with dust potentials, and all the effects already mentioned. You may feel it leak away near metal or water, and you can hear its pressure on a transistor radio when the sounds alter as you approach. Your field interacts with that of everybody else in a room, and with the environment around you, above your head and below your feet. Our body-field 'wobbles' with the earth-field like fruit in a jelly.

Your skin potentials, a part of this field, include diffusion potentials, membrane potentials, injury potentials, compression potentials, all of which are direct currents; your pulsing or alternating currents include your heart, diaphragm and brain electricity, the skin nerve endings and your muscular movement. These potentials alter with skin resistance and this fluctuates according to posture, temperature, humidity, the composition of your sweat, emotion, any drugs, fatigue; there is a daily rhythm (high resistance in the morning, decreasing after a midday meal, increasing again in the evening) and a yearly one; and there are effects from capacitance changes in the body due to alterations in its volume and the volume of its cavities, photochemical and photodynamic effects, the menstrual cycle, the interacting presence of animals and plants and fellow humans, besides interaction with everything already mentioned.

The patterns of charge and current on the skin also vary profoundly depending on the material of the clothes you are wearing, the way the fibres move over each other, creating a focus of charge in the space between crossing threads of the weave, an electrical coat of many colours.

'Rub synthetic fibres of different sorts against each other and even more electrons are ripped off . . . Every movement in a synthetic shirt starts some such electron stripping, and an electrostatic space-warp forms out from where it happened . . . ' Dust will be pulled into this field: 'Sometimes the particle doesn't even touch down on anything, but is just held quivering for hours in the gap between two fibers by the force-field beaming out of it.'

If the synthetic shirts are tightly cut, 'The electrostatic field wending out from the rubbing fibers will to some extent be counterbalanced by the identical, but oppositely charged, electrical field wending out from the continually friction-charged skin underneath . . .'[97] Thus, the cut of what we wear, and the way our clothes fasten and open, bears in upon us through sensory modalities other than the visualisations of fashion: we know how different the *feel* of clothes may be from their appearance, although the ideal seems to be comfortable clothes that look good.

Our feelings about clothes, like our feelings about cars, are profoundly altered by influences of which we are normally unaware. We adjust the micro-climate of a shirt or blouse by altering the dimensions of the convection flue or chimney at the throat, thereby altering temperature and humidity; but that alteration is accompanied by electrical changes too (to say nothing of the olfactory and I R influences already mentioned). Clothes, then, are a kind of switch-gear, with their buttons and flaps.

Certain clothes become intolerable or otherwise with changes in the electrical weather, as certain rooms do; temperature and humidity are important, but not solely so. Clothes, like a visible aura, seem appropriate or inappropriate, ceremonious or casual, comfortable or uncomfortable, according to circumstances and place; and, whatever we believe we know about dressing, the electrical environment will be having its say through atmospheric and geophysical fields, through geomagnetism and ionic currents in detailed figuration.

'At one time he had thought that there must have been more in such sights than he could merely see, perhaps not in them at all, behind them or beyond them but somehow connected with them, and plenty of poems had seemed to tell him the same story. But although he had stayed on the alert for quite a long while to catch a glimpse of what could not be seen, nothing answering remotely to any of his guesses or inklings had ever looked like turning up.'[98] This is the anti-romantic Amis hero, in a recent Booker prizewinner, gazing at the local scenery from a hilltop, 'who would like to believe but can't'. This apparently rational, sceptical attitude is far less reasonable than it looks; it ignores the data: not only the scientific data about what is really 'out there' that is given by authorities like Tromp, but the testimony of many ordinary people too. Clearly there is something 'out there' for migrating birds navigating by geomagnetism, far more than they can 'merely see'; and the nearest thing to this among humans is the 'sense of direction'.

Robin Baker of Manchester University thought that this human ability might also be geomagnetic, and in a now famous series of experiments tested the sense of direction of a busload of students by asking them to point the direction home after a tortuous blindfolded journey. The experiments showed that a statistically acceptable proportion of the students could do this accurately – but not when bar magnets were soldered to the helmets they wore, which probably therefore interfered with the natural magnetic sense. This 'sixth sense' is now well verified (although strangely enough the experiments do not work so well in America). Baker has written a book suggesting that it must have been important in evolution. One of his subjects could tell by a taste in her mouth and odd sensations in the fillings of her teeth whether her test helmet was magnetically activated or whether it merely bore one of the brass control rods; Baker suggests also that experiments on blind people who might have been obliged to develop their magnetic sense further than sighted humans would be interesting. It appears that women have a more consistent sense of direction than do men, and prefer to rely on this non-visual intuition.[99]

For Tromp, the magnetic effects include magneto-striction, which means that the tissues change in size with the magnetic field; the Faraday effect, which lines up liquid crystals in protoplasm; and magnetic influences on the ionic movements in cells and on their metabolism, and nerve induction currents. These are whole-body effects, although some recent work by Robin Baker and colleagues has discovered concentrations of iron in the human sinus bones which form the nasal cavity, and these may act as localised special sense organs for magnetism.[100]

The magnetic fields vary on land above igneous massifs, volcanic lava flows, above flows and faults in the sea-bed, and with geological compositiongenerally; also with the kinds of mineral present, especially iron ores, and with the presence of metal pipes, reinforced concrete, stoves or any magnetic components.

It is these influences that must have been integrated into a subliminal landscape by Robin Baker's female subjects (he says the males relied more on visual cues). There are also daily changes in the earth's magnetic field: thirteen-day changes, lunar variations, an eleven-year period and the likelihood of magnetic storms. In addition, vertical iron bars, rock flows and lava flows will become permanent magnets by induction (with the North Pole at the base), as will horizontal iron bars; and lightning where it strikes creates rock magnets.

There is now a more recent survey of what is known of geomagnetism and life in the work of the Russian A. P. Dubrov, for 'life came into being and has evolved in the presence of the geomagnetic field'. Dubrov shows how important the 'whole-body' effects must be. There is a high sensitivity of the water molecule to the geomagnetic field, and all biological reactions take place in the presence of water. The geomagnetic field also demonstrably affects the permeability of membrane in the nerves, the cell walls and the vascular system. This must work on the whole nervous system and its bioelectric activity 'whose basis is the membrane mechanism of asymmetry of sodium and potassium ions'.

There is also the magnetic field of each organism interacting with the geomagnetic field, and the former is probably based on the magnetic properties of the branching blood; both brain and heart are surrounded with a measurable pulsing magnetic field.[101] A person able to sense the magnetic field of the blood, like the person cured of blindness by Jesus's spittle, would see 'men like trees walking'. If, on the other hand, a person were able to sense the fleeting-floating pheromone maser surrounding the body, they might visualise it as Castaneda's Don Juan did, as a kind of glowing egg. Clearly, more than one kind of 'subtle body' exists, as is rumoured in the occult literature. Tromp agrees with Callahan that 'practically all living and non-living matter emanates volatile inorganic or organic compounds: in other words *every object in nature is surrounded by a kind of aura composed of volatile compounds*' and these interact together 'particularly due to the colloidal structure of the proteins of living matter'. Tromp also says that due to the 'great diffusion speed of these volatile compounds and their rather rectilinear diffusion this emanation behaves as a kind of radiation'.[102]

Tromp also speaks of how odour will add to the subliminal colouring of absolutely anywhere to those willing to open their senses: both volcanic and non-volcanic soils produce individual and detailed impressions of what they are made of, and the smell of the place varies with the weather.

He is also interesting on the subject of the electrical shadow that people can leave behind them, lying on a bed or sitting at a table. The trace disappears when the furniture is earthed, much in the same way as an electrocardiogram diagram remains 'restless' after a person gets up until the table is earthed. When the person leaves, a residual trace still remains. (This phenomenon is also seen in the infra-red 'heat photographs'.) The trace will have a very complicated relationship with the magnetic, ionic and electromagnetic surroundings. Someone with strong body-electricity is likely to create semi-permanent traces in surrounding objects, in their room and possessions. Some people have such strong body-electricity that a cardiogram cannot be taken. Even dressing and undressing creates quite large electrostatic potentials, and sparks can sometimes be seen. If the person undresses on an insulating surface, such as a nylon carpet, the charge is enough to start a neon tube glowing. Glowing phenomena can also be seen in a dark room during deep breathing with strong inhalation and expiration. Merely rising from a chair can create a potential of thousands of volts.

People who naturally generate very high electrical charges are sometimes called *hommes torpilles*, or human torpedoes: they are sometimes able to move a compass needle and create light-emission phenomena. The renowned medium Eusapia Palladino was one such person; she kept up a constant movement with her feet on the floor during manifestations, which would have increased the charge. Tromp notes that the experiments with this medium gave extraordinary results in Italy and in the South of France, but failed in England during rainy weather.[103]

I think the point about the continuum has been sufficiently well made. It is there, and we potentially have access to it in a number of ways: by intellectual means, by evidence and by instrumentation; we have as yet to see how it can be *lived*.

I have not dwelt much on the influence of the audio dimension, which flows in and out and interchanges with all the other multimedia. Charles Townes, the pioneer of the laser, has shown how acoustic waves can form a maser in a gas just as radiation does: a 'phonon maser'. There are now studies of how infra-sonics and supersonics affect the living organism. It is likely that our breathing rhythm, voice tone and lung capacity are among the interfaces here. The human chest is supposed to resonate at about 60 cycles per second; it has been found, however, that energy below 30 cycles per second produces 'clear-cut modulation effects on respiration and speech'.[104]

That particular frequency of 60 cycles (in Europe 50 cycles) turns out to be very important, as it is the rate at which the electricity supply alternates or 'vibrates'. It is also the continual background of our lives in the industrialised world, 'for it will be heard (together with its harmonics) in the operation of all electrical devices from lights and amplifiers to generators'. It will be heard, whether we know it or not. Try turning off your electricity at the mains. Almost immediately the house *feels* different: you notice the sound when it has gone.

Why does Sunday feel different from other days? Because the greater part of the current used in factories and shops is turned off, and so the sound of where you live has altered and, with the sound changing, so will all the vibrational effects which it causes and with which it intermeshes, from piezoelectricity in rocks to the alteration of the droplet size in water aerosols, mists, clouds and the like. Perhaps that is why 'it always rains on Sunday' and Bank Holidays.

R. Murray Schafer says that when the note C is tuned to 256 cycles, the resonant frequency of the background electrical supply is B natural. In ear-training exercises, students apparently find B natural 'much the easiest pitch to retain and recall spontaneously'. In Europe the resonant electrical frequency of 50 cycles is G sharp, and Schafer found his students uttering this note quite naturally as a core tone. He once plotted the 'soundscape' of a village in Sweden. The electrical equipment emitted resonant harmonics and, in the quiet of night, the street lighting, signs and generators produced a series of steady pitches: 'We were surprised to find that together they produced a G sharp major triad, which the F sharp whistles of passing trains turned into a dominant seventh chord.' Thus the town played them melodies.[105]

What Tromp adumbrated in the 1940s about the interactions of the EM continuum with living organisms has been fully studied in more recent years. One of the best summaries is by Becker and Marino who say, 'The earth has a natural electromagnetic background, produced by the earth itself and by cosmic sources, and the age-old question as to whether this background can be detected by living organisms has now been answered in the affirmative – the earth's electromagnetic background is an important environmental factor for all living things.'[106] They also tell the sad story of how 'animal electricity' was ignored in favour of a mechanistic approach to the electric current.

In 1791 the Italian physicist Luigi Galvani published his reports of experiments in which he touched the exposed crural nerve of dissected frogs' legs with a scalpel blade while an electrostatic machine was producing sparks in the same room; the result was that the legs twitched. Galvani supposed that it was the 'animal electricity' released from the leg by the application of metal that caused the reaction, although it was actually the current induced in the scalpel by the sparks. The twitch was even stronger when the leg was placed on a plate of one metal and the nerve touched with a rod of another, with no electric machine operating. Two years later Alessandro Volta published his experiments which *appeared* to show that Galvani was wrong to talk about 'animal electricity', since you could produce quantities of electricity without any frogs' legs at all, merely by constructing a battery of alternating metal plates separated by brine-soaked paper. The presence of a living thing was unnecessary for the production of an electric current – and this is true – but an unwarrantable and illogical further step was taken when it was concluded that there was, therefore, no true electricity in the living thing – that bimetallic electricity was the only true electricity.

The fact that Volta was right did not prove Galvani wrong – especially as the latter had demonstrated animal electricity without any metal in the circuit at all! An exposed spinal cord of a frog was brought in contact with a frog's leg, and the leg twitched, showing that current had flowed from the tissues. We know now that these are injury currents.

Quite powerful batteries were constructed entirely from animal tissue. The physicist Ritter – one of the company of German high Romantics – published his own counter-proofs to Volta's mechanistic experiments in his *Proof that the Process of Galvanism accompanies the Vital Process in the Animal Kingdom at all Times*. We know him now to be right; as we have seen from Tromp and others, Ritter's Romantic vision was of the continuum between all living things, but this did not suit the time, or the impulse of those in power. Ritter 'associated Galvanism with the very principles of life, envisaging the whole organic world as a network of galvanic circuits . . . "in Galvanism," he said, "the earth attains self-reflection"'.[107]

So little did Galvani's animal electricity suit the time that he lost his job, his home and his fortune. Volta offered his new science to Napoleon, and received honours and awards for it, although he made no other contribution to science. Becker points out that a treatise by von Humboldt, which came out just before Galvani's death, 'clearly established that both Galvani and Volta were simultaneously right and wrong. Bimetallic electricity existed and so did animal electricity . . . Nevertheless, all the advantages lay with Volta. His world of bimetallic electricity was both a quantum jump in technology and a simple, easily verifiable phenomenon. Galvani's world of living things, on the other hand, was incredibly complex and imperfectly understood as it remains even today.'[108] Technological society was once again advanced by a deliberate act of self-blinding in the presence of the living riddles of the Sphinx.

The conflict between vitalism and mechanism continued. The preferred hypothesis was that living things were mere machines, and could be taken apart and put together again like machines. Any idea of a vital 'field' was anathema. It became very dangerous to job and career to affirm that EM had any power in living things or role in their function. While all traces of vitalism were being expunged in science, in the real world of medical practice electricity was still used for a range of troubles, from stimulating the healing of recalcitrant fractures to the cure of mental disorders. In 1884 Bigelow wrote: '10,000 physicians within the borders of the United States use electricity as a therapeutic agent daily in their practice.' However, after the infamous Flexner Report in 1910, electrotherapy became scientifically unsupportable practice.

Had the scientists concluded, as the physicians understood, that EM had a profound effect on living tissue, then the way might not have been so open for Marconi to demonstrate the practicality of sending the first EM radio signals across the Atlantic from Cornwall, or for Edison to invent the electric lamp and the first generators for domestic and industrial use, without apparent harm to humans.

People were naturally nervous about the new electric fluid that was entering their homes, so Edison mounted demonstrations with dogs and human beings to show that they could stay in a strong magnetic field for a considerable time without any ill effect. Edison's subjects reported no sensation at all. One becomes suspicious that they were paid to say that, especially as other experiments carried out at the same time by d'Arsonval and Beer showed that changing magnetic fields applied to the human head gave rise to very definite sensations indeed: in fact people see lights, the 'magnetic phosphene', and this is confirmed in modern work.

The evidence continued to accumulate, unheeded by the scientific establishment. Leduc produced electro-narcosis with an alternating current in 1920, and this effect was used clinically in France and Russia. Cerletti in 1938 began using electroshock for the treatment of schizophrenia, and in 1929 Hans Berger recorded brain waves, using sensitive instruments attached to the skull. (Barbara Brown, among others, later showed that the brain waves were matched by corresponding emotional currents in the skin: 'skin talk'.)[109] In the 1930s Burr began measuring the steady-state or direct current (DC) potentials on the surface of many living organisms, including trees, and their changes in a variety of circumstances, including changes of weather. He formulated the notion of a bioelectric field that was 'generated by the sum total of electrical activity of all the cells of the organism'. Burr thought that by feedback this field controlled and directed growth, development and sleep.

Lund, Barth, Leao, Gerard and Libet expanded the subject. The last two concluded as a result of their experiments that the 'basic functions of the brain were controlled by these DC potentials'. This finding is in contrast to the more orthodox theory which holds that the nerve impulse is no current; rather it is ionic depolarisation travelling down the nerve membrane. This 'satisfactorily explained how the impulse could be observed electrically and yet not be electrical in nature . . .' but chemical. The observation of DC potentials has opened the way to a less mechanistic idea.

With the appearance too of the theory of semiconductors, the drifting of electrons within a crystal lattice, and the likelihood of these currents joining together in extended systems *independent of the nerve structure*, 'with common energy levels permitting semiconduction flows over long distances', the way has opened to the alternative view that bioelectricity can form complex total patterns in the organism, independent of visible anatomical structures, and over and above the merely mechanical concepts.[110]

Such ideas take account of natural form and flow and patterning, which permits intimate, even protoplasmic, interaction of the living organism with its environment. As Becker says, 'Discovery of the DC system showed how the interaction could work without [gross] energy transfer; it gave living things a way of "sensing" the fields directly.'[111] Thus, there is 'magic stuff' on this level too, a 'life-force like a wind or a subtle flame' which animates organisms like Aeolian harps that are sensitive to the movements of the 'all-pervading aethyr'. The basis is a 'whole body' feeling-together, or synaesthesia.

The protoplasm is not a mere chemical jelly, but a semi-fluid electrical crystal which, like its mineral counterparts in rocks, radio transistors and light meters, possesses properties which include semi-conductivity (which directs and rectifies currents), photo-conductivity (which generates and switches currents when light shines on the crystal) and piezoelectricity (which generates currents when pressure is applied, or causes a crystal to move when an electric current is applied).

In such crystals – of which we are made – there would be electron flow transmitting signals within the lattices, interaction between its electronic structure and variations in the external EM field, and an organised pattern of electric potentials, responding to the equally complex pattern of EM signals constantly altering around us. There is no 'onlooker consciousness' appropriate here.[112]

A vivid and simple way of visualising what probably happens on the molecular level when a living organism encounters an EM field was demonstrated by J. R. Bowman. He used an array of toy compasses, and described what happened when you passed a magnet near them. Depending on how you handle the magnet, an impulse can propagate along the compass needles, or, sometimes, the first one spins round and no impulse is passed. In some cases the compass needles assume a complex and unpredictable static pattern, and in others a slight movement of the first needle is amplified by resonance further along the train, as the magnets react with each other and the intrusive north or south pole. Bowman says, 'I challenge any IBM machine to compute what will happen. The interactions are now exceedingly complicated.' Becker and Marino see this as a model of how molecules acting like dipole magnets in neural tissue could respond with finer grain detail to EM fields.[113] Again, the natural analogy is with the Aeolian harp.

Another side to all this is very sinister. Humans have changed the electromagnetism of the earth to a greater degree than they have changed any other natural feature, with frequencies and magnitudes never before present. It is beginning to be plain what a health risk these stray frequencies constitute. It has been shown that depression and suicide follow the pattern of high-tension overland wiring; the Russians know more about this or follow a better practice than we do, as their official control of high-tension wiring near where people are living is much stricter than in the West.

Even in the first days of radar it was known that operators would react unfavourably, and such side-effects as annoying clicks in the ear and intense headaches were noted. It has been shown that the dimensions of the human body are such that its water-content forms a wave-guide or aerial to radar frequencies, which form small shock-waves in the body fluids. It is these which can be heard travelling in the cochlea.[114]

There is an amusing but accurate study which shows the degree of ionisation in the ordinary American bathroom; perhaps we bathe as much to alter our body-electricity as to clean off the grime.[115] Less amusing are the figures which show the alterations of ionisation and field consequent on the operation of citizens' radio. Even deaf people can hear microwaves pulsed at 300–3,000 megahertz as booming, hissing, clicking or buzzing. In 1973 Joseph C. Sharp heard and understood words beamed to him as a pulsed-microwave audio-gram – in other words he demonstrated that the human subject itself could be a radio receiver. There are many serious and direct hazards to health consequent on EM usage that are nowadays seen as comprehensible and inevitable.[116]

Some may wonder whether part of the harvest of this invisible pollution may be the comparative rarity of visionary experience in the modern world, and the predominance of a removed, over-analytical, repelling 'onlooker' intelligence in its place, resembling that of the Amis hero (who will not see because he cannot feel). If this is so, such an intelligence has produced conditions favouring its evolution and survival.

The entrance to the natural EM senses is now guarded by artificially monstrous EM waves carrying every kind of pattern irrelevant to nature, from TV sit-coms to defence radar broadcasts. It is as though we have covered the whole surface of the globe with a slum of slovenly, impalpable constructions during the past eighty years or so since Marconi. They are literally skyscrapers in as much as they touch the ionosphere and are reflected from it. They are tenements full of the disorderly displays of sit-coms and the sterile reflections of military radar.

It is claimed that both the Americans and Russians are broadcasting at each other microwaves near to the brain's natural resonance, from aerial arrays like the antennae of giant moths. This is a development of the scandal caused when the Russians were found to be broadcasting deleterious microwaves at the American Embassy in Moscow, which were supposed to be for surveillance purposes but turned out to have harmful physiological effects.[117] Cole and Graf envisage the conditions on primordial earth: 'The atmospheric electrical currents were very large and, coupled with the conducting core of the earth, resonated at about 10 Hz [cycles per second].' This suggests that organic structures formed at that time might resonate to that frequency or in other ways be sensitive to it. It just so happens that in the brain waves of humans and all animals that demonstrate brain-wave or EEG patterns 'the dominant frequency from the point of total energy is 10 Hz'. Rutger Wever has constructed rooms that were entirely shielded from EM influence. In these rooms the normal daily rhythmic variations in body temperature, sleep and activity cycles, and urinary secretion of sodium, potassium and calcium, simply went to pieces. When, however, he introduced a 10 Hz electric field into those rooms without the subject's knowledge, the internal rhythms began to synchronise again.[118]

It is possible that it is this basic frequency that the Russian-American broadcasts are attempting to subvert; if it were successful, it would have the effect of blinding us to our birthright, the basic tone of the earth, and brainwashing away our ability to *feel* our world. This would be a terrible mutilation that might well lead to a world despair 'of unknown origin', and many 'Theban plagues'. We would forget our roots, our love of the earth and of each other, 'earthe upon earthe'.

In the continuum, the *form* and the interaction of forms is of more importance than the magnitudes of energy (which may be very small). The orthodox explanation of nerve function as a leakage of chemicals across membranes can only apply to the 10 per cent of the brain which is composed of cells that are likely to operate in this way. It is probable that it is 'these extra cellular electrical currents that exert the primary controlling action on the neurones', and not only in the brain either, but through the whole body. Here we have a rationale for the skin-feelings of healers, who describe such currents as being perceived within their own 'aura' or electrical field. Most magical systems rely on the perception and cultivation of auras by subjective exercises. (We shall see later that the 'charged cloud' both within and around the skin is as important to the practising magician as it was to the Romantic poets and still is to the meteorologist.)

Becker thinks of two complementary brain-systems. It is the neurones in the brain which operate like a digital yes-no switching system, sophisticated but limited; but it is the DC fields which are the more primitive analogue system, working by form and pattern as a kind of internal 'charged cloud'.[119]

Two modes of mental action which correspond with this were distinguished by the German Romantic philosopher A. W. Schlegel: the non-poetic and the poetic views. 'The non-poetic view is the one which considers that once the senses have perceived things and intellect has determined what they are, everything is settled once and for all . . . ' On the other hand, 'The poetic view is the one which continues to interpret them and never assigns any limit to their plentitude . . . '[120] for, as we have seen, the world of the unconscious senses is so resourceful that we in the defensive isolation of our conscious minds can only approach it by our *feelings*, and those *sensations* which seem full to us, and, as we say, satisfying. Such sensations seem 'romantic and ghostly' (which was G. W. Pabst's definition of what real life was like) and have that tinge of otherness which is a riddle to our conscious minds, and draws them to further comprehension.

Thus, it is not the yes-no world of pragmatic reductionism which is the common human 'magic stuff', but rather that visionary mode which appears to everybody in dreams and intuitions. It appears, too, like a vision held within language as it is used by children like Sean Thomas, lovers and poets. It is the metaphorical mode, the analogue or simulating mode, the infinitely malleable, transforming 'magic stuff'. Everybody knows how language can be used both in the digital yes-no mode, and in the resonating play-mode that makes discoveries by posing riddles and making the ordinary world strange: 'Be playful and know I am God.' The Sphinx's mode is analogue; Oedipus' mode is the 'no' of the yes-no digital: the turn-off.

Call it carnal knowledge, because, as science has also found, the body itself is the most sensitive and accurate instrument we have. Its read-out is our feelings and our sense of reality; and what it perceives thus by the unconscious senses is no mere subjective fantasy.

The late-Romantic symbolists called this way of understanding *le rêve*: that 'special organisation of consciousness where *volupté* and *connaissance* are fused', including in this term waking dreams and hypnoidal states.[121] Carnal knowledge is the biblical term, meaning 'knowledge obtained through the body', and is carried over in its beneficent connotations from a pre-patriarchal, pre-biblical age. Barbara Walker uses the word *horasis* for the knowledge obtained by sexual communion with an enlightened woman – in Hebrew *zona*, meaning both prostitute and prophetess. She says *horasis* is the word 'misleadingly translated "visions"' used in the description of the arrival of the Holy Spirit at Pentecost like a 'mighty rushing wind' (Acts 2: 17), terms which recall both the charged human atmosphere and the enlightening effect of storms.[122]

The Hebrew word for 'carnal knowledge' is *Daath*, which to the magical cabbalist signifies that apple which was plucked from the Tree of Life. The centre of *Daath* is said to be at the throat, the organ which resonates language in both its digital and analogue modes, and is therefore the bridge between the conscious and the unconscious minds, the place where the breath balances. In Hindu yoga, the throat is the dreaming centre.

Becker and Marino point out that not all information gathered by the usual senses is 'processed at the conscious level, and there is no physiological principle that would preclude the subliminal detection of EMFs [electromagnetic fields] by the nervous system'.[123] In fact, unconscious scanning goes on all the time. It seems more than ever likely that what we know as the visionary or poetic mode is our response via the unconscious senses to what is really there in the environment. We are not trying to 'explain it away': it is rather that *we symbolise this kind of awareness*.

How we symbolise it depends on the mythology we are provided with. Human beings will see the same forces in different ways, which will partly depend on the capacity of their culture to respond: the images provided. Thus it is possible in the modern world that flying saucer visions are the way in which the powerful whirling EM fields produced by earth tremors or the shearing of rock in piezoelectric geological structures are symbolised. To say this is not to depreciate the vision. It must have been like this with the Delphic oracle, in which a priestess prophesied on her tripod over a cleft in the earth from which subterranean vapours arose: those physiologically active vapours carried data, recorded in human language by the priestess. Our ability to sustain such perceptions and make use of them depends on the strength and relevance of our mythology. No Greek in ancient times would take any step, political, religious or otherwise, without first consulting the Delphic pythoness. She brought Oedipus to his crossroads. Pythoness? Earth energy has at all times and in all places been symbolised by a serpent, sphinx or dragon. For Ezra Pound it was the energy which both attends love-making and pervades the earth itself: 'fluid CHTHONOS' he calls it, 'ICHOR of CHTHONIOS', 'Kore, the shining of the dark', 'the shining of the dark whore Persephone'.[124]

Our approach to reality, our sense of reality, cannot assume that the text of nature, the book of life, is a cryptogram concealing just a single meaning. Rather, it is an expanding riddle of a multiplicity of resonating images.

'There is no single thing . . . that is so cut and dried that one cannot attend to its secret whisper which says "I am more than just my appearance".' Mandelstam says, 'The earth moans with metaphors.' In Roger Cardinal's words, 'If each object quivers with readiness to imply something other than itself, if each perception is a word in a poem dense with connotations, then the poet's selection of any given subject of speculation will become . . . a means of attuning himself to the rhythms and harmonies of reality at large.' A magic symbol approaching us from the real world either by magic practice or by dreaming, a Romantic poem, will be part of the tuning of our sense of reality into a world more marvellous than we have ever allowed ourselves to believe. Roger Cardinal is correct when he says, 'The notion of a network of correspondence is *not* an outmoded Romantic illusion: it represents a crucial intuition . . .'[125] The ancient figure was of a net of jewels, in which each jewel reflects every other, and the whole. The bedewed web resonating light: it stands too for the living body and the resonance of the earth which created it.

5   Vision at Land's End

Why, on a fitfully sunlit day in winter at Land's End in Cornwall, do the long wings of this little fly standing on the weed create a strobe effect in the sunlight, so that the wings show motionless within the blur of their motion? This sight cheers me after a morning's hard and difficult work using a terminology of science that is harsh and mechanical. The wings seem to me like a tuning-fork resonating to some quality in the light that I am beginning to feel as the ragged coast-scene takes hold. Is it in some manner vibrating to the genius of the place? The clouds blow hard across the sky, and the waves pound hard on the cliff, so that I can feel the deep note of the rock under my feet. It is an exciting sound, this slow drum-beat in the cliff, and it is as if the air itself were charged by this sound. Drum-cliff.

Having just written this chapter, the information I have mingles with the poetry in the scene. I must try, as best I may, to follow the great example of Coleridge, whose train of thought proceeded from perceptions, which in turn gave him feelings, which transformed into intuitions, which he then thought about, and returned those ideas to the scene, thus opening his senses to more perceptions. It is a dangerous business, this thinking, as he acknowledged, for unless he took great care, it would 'steal from him all the Natural Man'. In the 'Dejection Ode' it led, as he warned, to dejection. I must therefore be resolute and, instead of writing poetry now, return my thoughts to the scene via my present work, this book, for if they are true, these things have been too long unsaid.

I and my companion could rest solely in the drum-beat of the cliff, or in the motion-in-rest of the long dress of the little fly on its umbellifer: two vibrations strangely linked by the feeling of the place. I know that that feeling, and the more precisely-picturing intuition, which has shown me the wing-beat of the fly in the music of the rock, is the medium by which many marvels which are actually there may be revealed. The actual insect, the actual sound, is the vehicle or symbol of these further marvels, for it is thus that they show themselves to our thoughts, on this side as it were, and participate in a further reality out there.

The feeling-in-the-air, which draws me again and again to this place as though it connected me to the whole world, I will call a perception and not a subjective illusion; perhaps by study I may see more because I feel more. I know, as we two walk the cliff-path underneath, that the clouds are charged with that life-force we call electricity and, as they scud over, their fields press on our own, which press back. I see them beginning to build into a thunder-anvil, and I feel something in the sight which is more than an appreciation of their manifest forms; I begin to feel them vibrate with a faint seen-echo-thunder that leaves with a prickling of hairs as the high white castle blows out to sea harmlessly.

The sun has come out, but there are still clouds in the sky. The sun beams down upon them, and its power charges up the water-vapour and ice-crystals of which they are composed, and in which are dissolved the essences of living things, drawn up from the land: the distillations of trees, flowers, animals and people which begin to re-radiate and add the tone of their lives to the light which excites these molecules: nature's memory, or one of nature's memories.

This must be why I see so many shapes in the clouds! There, that one is shaped exactly like a map of this part of the coast; that one like a floating version of the woodland on the hill over there; that one like a crowd of faces. I know the clouds are the crests of the water-vapour that pours up from the land, and so, as the crests of the sea-waves echo off the rocks of the coastline in a visible shaped margin, their forms cannot be independent of their source. I know that just as every cloud has a light-shadow, it has an electrical shadow too, which I feel by my sense of touch, by my whole skin, for the ionisation of the ground alters as each cloud passes over, and my lungs breathe this charged air. But within the clouds too, those complex organic molecules and assemblages of water are charged also by the sunlight beating upon them. It is said that their electrons move up to a higher-energy shell, and then the merest touch of the correct frequency will cause them to drop a shell. As they do so they emit in-phase EM frequencies, which may bounce around inside the cloud until their energy bursts them free, emitting infra-visible flashes like a laser, producing invisible collision-rainbows or interference patterns as they intermesh with their source in the sunshine.

I know that inside the clouds the audio pulses of the wind echo too, like vast resonant chambers which are floating electrostatic machines and transducers of radiant energy also, masers tuned by the whole balance of things to emit as that balance will. Now I feel awe at the concept, 'masers tuned by the whole balance of things' as though they were a choir uttering universal music.

What can I experience from all this? There is a glamour in the scene, which deepens. The tone of the sunlight alters like a varying taste. There are shadows and tones in my thought which alter as the clouds alter, but which seem to be sustained also by the drum-beat under my feet. I look at my companion, and she alters too in this glamour, and I realise too that I see more and feel it as a direct consequence of her being present. She also glows a little. At least I think she does this, but it is difficult to separate this perception (even if I wanted to) from the knowledge that we have a short time ago been making love. I know that this has sensitised us, and we have been re-tuned by orgasm to all that we see and feel now; our skins have an altered pattern of heat and electricity and are differently alive, and our dark senses are alert to the world and to each other, reacting to one another's reactions, like the amplifications inside that resonant laser-chamber of the cloud, not just on the verbal level or by caress. Such things alter the pattern in the living crystals we are (a prettier terminology than some) and in the DC energies flowing through us, which, like the charged clouds floating above, hold in them a form or analogue of all we experience.

To our fancy that rock-formation round which the sea-spray bursts seems like some Gothic library full of piezoelectrical light in which people are turning over pages. As the rock reads in its crystals all the pressures that surround it, so we read the scene from the impulses induced in the electrical lattice of our whole body, with its piezoelectrical hair and skeleton; the pressure of the light on those dish-aerials called eyes seeming almost the least of these effects.

Thus we react to each other's reactions and in them, somewhere, are all the resources of our unconscious senses, our dowsing reflexes, re-broadcasting to one another among the world's broadcasts, throughout a continually changing, continuously held field of resonance, like a choir of visibles and invisibles.

The wave-guides which are our skins are holding on them standing waves, intertwining with our body electricity, like rainbow snakes. The reception of these energies depends on all the factors we have mentioned and very many we have not, including our bodily posture, the clothes we are wearing, the beat of the sea-wave pattern as the tide changes; and, as the piezoelectricity changes with that pounding of the sea in the geological formations, they are themselves twisted into fresh broadcasts because of their rock-tide, pulled by moon and sun.

And, as the wind beats on the waves and the sea-bed alters its broadcasts, so the field and feeling of that immense liquid crystal – the sea – changes its nature, and is modulated by all the wave-patterns of the world, and all the resonances that the world encounters in its sea of outer space.

It is a complexity of an order even greater than that of the human body, so how can we deny that feeling in it of a strong presence or soul, only a portion of which is visible, and whom we may still feel with our eyes closed, both within our bodies and in the drum-beat of the cliff? Thought and explanation will steal from me 'all the natural man' unless I know this presence so far as I can, on the natural level, on the pagan level, as a presence, an enigmatic one, with many features which are more than human and other than human too, as in the vision of the Sphinx.

And it is at this level, the level of personality, that my questions may be answered, for if I put them as if to a machine I am likely to receive mechanical answers. I drop my eyes once more to the long-winged fly, tiny initiate of this world, with the drum-beat of the rock firmly gripped in the soles of my feet. I think of the moment in *Oedipus at Colonus* when, surrounded by his children, he declares in horror: 'Look at us all: I am brother to my daughters, and they are sisters to their father . . . ' 'Look at us,' he says, 'we are all from the same womb,' and that is true of everything alive, and horrifies only Oedipus the patriarch.

THREE
MARY LUCIFER

'... *Nature speaks upwards to the known senses of man, downwards to unknown senses of his ... every process in nature, rightly observed, wakens in us a new organ of cognition ... creating in the wake of an ever-creative nature ...*'[1]

'*Who has divined the high meaning of the earthly body?*'[2]

'*She who ate, and tempted her consort to eat, and was herself the apple ...*'[3]

1 The Colour of the Holy Spirit

Joachim of Floris (d.1202) believed that history was to be divided into three ages. There was first the Old Testament age of the Father and then, with the birth of Jesus, the age of the Son. The last age was to be that of the Holy Spirit, when the hierarchy of Rome would be dissolved, and the whole world would become a Church with its members in direct communion with God. However, if we follow the evidence of Massey, Graves, Bachofen and others, we must believe that the age of the Mother was first of all. We have seen how one of the great symbols which ushered in the age of masculinist Father–Son conflict was that of Laius–Oedipus. Now it seems that the great 'cultural symbol' presiding over the transitions of our age into whatever type of society may be coming is that of the Black Goddess.

It may appear that the Holy Spirit and the Black Goddess are identical. We have met her image already in this book as the Black Wisdom of Solomon's ecstatic hymn, and she speaks in her own voice in Ecclesiasticus: 'It was I who covered the earth like a mist ... Alone I made a circuit of the sky and traversed the depths of the abyss ... I grew like a cedar of Lebanon, like a cypress on the slopes of Hermon, like a date-palm at Engedi, like roses at Jericho ... like a fair olive tree in the vale or like a plane-tree planted beside the water ... I was redolent of spices; I spread my fragrance like choice myrrh ... like a terebinth I spread out my branches, laden with honour and grace. I put forth lovely shoots like the vine ... Whoever feeds on me will be hungry for more, and whoever drinks from me will thirst for more ...'[4]

We have also met her as the Sphinx rejected by Oedipus, as the

Dark Girl of the Eastern Love-Books,[5] the Queen of Sheba, the 'black but comely' Shulamite and the Fallen Daughter or Animal Soul. There is often in her manifestations the image of a tree, and of living perfume, and I ask the reader to recall the information on previous pages as to the nature and extent of our unconscious olfactory communion with the continuum of nature. As Havelock Ellis has remarked, 'During religious excitement a real and pleasant odour is present in the atmosphere.'[6] There is a meticulous biblical instruction direct from the Lord to Moses concerning the Wisdom-perfumes appropriate to the atmosphere of the Tabernacle: myrrh, cinnamon, calamus, galbanum, frankincense and others in Exodus 30: 23ff. It is remarkable how often in both Whitman and Words-worth the experience of poetic inspiration is connected with the experience of lying under trees, and with respiration.[7] The tree is a tremendous electrical machine connecting earth and sky, and in its presence the normal potential difference in humans between head and foot is reduced; it is also an energetic chemical laboratory of psychoactive pheromones. To say this is not to reduce the value of poetic inspiration, but to point to its reality and certainty in the body.

The Holy Spirit is traditionally feminine.[8] Her emblem, the dove, is a yoni-image with a long history both in India (*paravata*, the symbol of lust) and as the love-goddess's totem. As *Ruach* in the Bible she hovers or broods over the waters as a creative mist. She is seen sometimes as the weather and the wind, as a storm or a whirlwind. We have seen in discussing Coleridge's 'Dejection: An Ode' the depth of religious and imaginative insight that may attend a change of weather: indeed, he uses the ancient image of a creative mist. The word *Ruach* combines the meanings of 'breath, mind, spirit', as does the Greek *pneuma*. There are instances in which *Ruach* is also identified as 'air, gas from the womb'.

Jung saw the Holy Spirit as Sophia enabled by the opening of Job's soul in his dialogue with the frenzied Hebrew male God to enter human history once again.[9] The Holy Spirit was present in the electrical flames of Pentecost, the anniversary of which, celebrated at Whitsun, is at present of so comparatively small an importance in the main Christian sects. It is good Christian as well as Jungian practice to look to the inferior, the despised and the neglected for the fresh revelation, to the discarded builder's rubble for the corner-stone, or the dung-heap for the *prima materia* of the alchemist's stone.

Indeed, it is among the outcasts and outsiders that the Black Goddess has lingered through recorded history. To the respectable and the self-regarding she is dangerous Lilith, she-demon of the night and the storm, and flies long-haired through 'Sumerian, Babylonian, Assyrian, Canaanite, Persian, Hebrew, Arabic and Teutonic mythology'.[10] She was particularly shunned in Mesopotamian Semitic mythology by those who anathematised all erotic experience except that which led to the conception of children.

Thus she became the night-demoness, the succubus-incubus, the left-hand wife-husband who consorts with those who sleep alone and who blesses or curses them with nocturnal orgasms and erotic dreams (glorified as Madame St Urzulie in voodoo, which calls her to heal people by means of these same nocturnal experiences). She was the child-killing witch of the menstrual period, when the womb fills with blood instead of offspring: the Lamashtu of Syria.

In this latter form she was the winged Lilith, the strangleress, which is the meaning of the Greek word Sphinx, and this turns out to be a calumny. The original Sphinx was Anuket, the clasper or container, who, with Satet, contained and channelled the Nile at what is now Aswan.[11] At the time of the inundation the whole fertility of Egypt would pour in red mud-laden waters through her granite cliffs inscribed with votive carvings: ' . . . the waters, which had been running of a dull green hue, are suddenly troubled and turn crimson. The red oxide of iron mixes with the liquid and gives it a gory gleam in the sunlight, making it run like a river of blood.'[12] In modern times the Russian-funded Aswan Dam has raised the watertable, causing floods, destroying the local fishing industry, and promoting schistosomiasis on an epidemic scale. Moreover, the fertility sediment is deposited in Lake Nasser, where it is unavailable. The Egyptian fields therefore have to be artificially fertilised. Gigantic chemical fertiliser plants have been built, and the dam operates at capacity merely to supply the electricity for these. It is another case of the clever moron creating 'Theban' plagues.[13]

The 'baby-killer' Lilith was known throughout the world as 'Dame Donkey Legs, Vixen Bogy, Blood Sucker, Woman of Harlotry, Alien Woman, Impure Female, End of All Flesh, End of Day, *bruha*, *strega*, witch, hag, snatcher and enchantress'. She was cursed as 'serpent, dog, donkey and owl, screeching night jar or strix' yet she was also *'the soul of every living creature that creepeth'*;[14] that is to say, of everything that had not risen on its Freudian two legs.

Thus she is also the animal soul of the world, the *All-Tier*, like the fantasy Altaira of the *Forbidden Planet*, that without which we 'may not perceive or feel the Joys of the Universe', the Fallen Daughter.

Lilith was Adam's first wife, who was refused equality by God, and therefore fled to the Red Sea and became a storm-demon and bred storm-demons and nightmares. She was also the dam of Leviathan, whose submission to God is such a feature of the book of Job, and the bride of 'Samael the Devil and King Ashmodai'. Yet again she is simultaneously the Queen of Sheba and 'is even the consort of God himself while the Shekhina is in exile'.[15] Barbara Black Koltuv says that the attempts to suppress and deny the Black Goddess date from the 6th century BC, but that 'she returns ever more', and 'will continue to do so until the Messiah comes and drives the unclean spirits from the land'. Yet there is a persistent rumour that she herself is the Messiah, come to redeem the divided souls of women, and to unite the known senses with the unknown, higher with lower, by virtue of her ability to circuit the sky and traverse the depths of the abyss.[16]

How telling it is therefore that the archetype of the Black Goddess reaches not only into the future, but right back to the beginning of our time. Genetic research by scientists at the University of California suggests 'that everybody on the planet is descended from the same woman. She . . . lived in Africa about 300,000 years ago, and descendants of the group she belonged to eventually migrated out of Africa, giving rise to all the people living today.'[17]

My readers will have understood how the figure of this personage presides over the meditations of this book. I have given reasons to consider how science, in studying human communication within the species, with the environment and with the living things sharing and creating the environment, should take account of all those neglected yet verifiable channels of knowledge which I have called the 'unconscious' or 'subliminal' senses, which have to do with the invisible, are beyond vision, yet which control it. 'Science offers a surer path to God than religion . . .' says Paul Davies.[18] After all, science itself poses the question: 'Only 1 per cent of the amount of matter predicted by the latest cosmological theories can be seen in bright stars and galaxies. What form does the invisible 99 per cent of the universe take?'[19] and ' . . . there may exist matter like the stuff we know, having the same kinds of particles and forces, which to our senses is almost undetectable . . . The two forms of matter could co-exist in the universe, almost blind to one another's existence . . . this phenomenon of almost hidden matter . . . '[20] Evidently, the Queen of Night has the largest kingdom.

There was recently established what is humorously called 'Arthur's Seat' – the Arthur Koestler Chair of Parapsychology at Edinburgh. It is the first such professorship in the British Isles. The terms of this post are of considerable interest, for there must be a growing public for a real 'science of the invisibles', what G. H. Schubert called the 'Night-Side of the Natural Sciences'.

In a recent radio talk,[21] Robert Morris, the present incumbent, made three particularly significant remarks. He spoke of a rich area of research in ESP in which the *body* rather than the mind appears to be implicated in unknown modes of communication. There is no content or image of a visual kind to such ESP experiences: it is a matter of *non-visual bodily feelings*.

Professor Morris also declared his interest in those subtle means of passing messages which are often exploited by showmen. The interviewer mentioned that Professor Morris kept books of mentalism and stage magic in his university room. Morris spoke of the remarkable abilities of 'muscle-readers'. We have seen some instances of this when discussing Helen Keller.

Lastly he spoke of colleagues whose beliefs could shift from agnosticism to a belief 'that there is an extraordinary miraculous substance about us'.

This seemed in context a casual figure of speech, yet we have seen that 'magic stuff' exists and acts around us without ceasing. The magician J. H. Brennan describes the Lodge Room of a Magical Order: 'The effect of that room was staggering. If you have ever walked any distance on a frosty winter's day before pushing open a door into a centrally-heated building, you will know what I mean by a wall of air. There was a wall of air at the doorway of the Lodge Room. But its essence was not heat but something else, something that could be sensed perfectly (and, it seemed, at a physical level) by the nerve endings beneath the skin of the face . . . '[22]

Everybody has experienced this feeling – consider the physical enhancement of atmosphere in a church at the height of a ceremony, at the theatre or concert hall, at a football match, in a room where people have been making love, or during the mutations of a storm. I have demonstrated that such feelings refer to actual and veridical happenings. If the model of the pheromone maser I have proposed operates in such atmospheres, then it, or something like it, should be verifiable by instrumentation, and be of interest to professors of parapsychology.

This is because, in creating a ritual atmosphere, we are also creating a charged gas that is sensitive not only to ourselves, but to outside atmospheric and cosmic influences: a kind of radio set or radiation detector; we have shown the case for this in the last chapter, and we shall see too that it fits the procedures of magic.

It is, again, the spirit of the Black Goddess who presides over the strongest currents in modern magic, 'black magic' as it is fearfully called by those who, like Oedipus, fear the Sphinx. 'Black' here means 'invisible' and is no more to do with evil than 'black theatre' is. Black theatre is when the curtain goes up on a stage where the footlights are glaring into the audience's eyes, and so all beyond them seems deepest darkness. A stand with sheet music floats in as if by magic, and a white chair appears from nowhere and sits in front of it. Then a violin enters, carried by a pair of white gloves, which begin to play.

The animation, disappearance and appearance of visible objects out of black nothing seems miraculous. Yet we know that actors dressed from head to foot in black are doing it, invisible against the black background. It is an image, surely, of the creative mind in its waking dream, guiding us through the mysteries of an intelligible yet invisible underlying reality. This reality *grips us*, and, while there are experiences for which there are no images, if we see, then we see with a synaesthetic eye, and call such images 'symbols'. Sensation is then visualised – in the visionary mode, not the optic one.

What we call 'black magic', and shudder at, is black only in the sense that it is a science of the invisibles.

The same magician, J. H. Brennan, evokes in his ritual the Lady Wisdom of Darkness, *Aimah Elohim Shekinah*. He asks her to ligature his outer senses so that his inner ones will awake, to clothe him in her black cloud of unknowing, 'to place a veil between me and all things belonging to the outer and material world'[23] so that he may pass through the Gate of the Invisible by the magic of the Divine Light, which needs more than eyes to see it. It is like the 'black light' of Divine Ipseity in Islamic mysticism: ' . . . the light of lights (*nur al-an war*), that by which all visible lights are made visible, is both light and darkness, that is, visible because it *brings* about vision, but [is] in itself invisible.' Its appearance heralds 'superconsciousness'.[24]

It is to be recalled that the central object of worship in Islam is a black stone, the Ka'aba, the male servitors of which are called 'the Sons of the Old Woman', meaning the moon.[25]

Kenneth Grant quotes a saying of the Great Goddess Nuit, declaring herself now, as in the past of the ancient Apocrypha: 'My colour [kala] is black to the blind, but the blue and gold are seen of the seeing.'[26] Of the Tarot Moon-Quest it is said: 'The Knight upon this quest has to rely on the three lower senses: touch, taste and smell.'[27] It is as though the moon threw down a black body upon earth visible only to the subliminal senses, which thereby became illuminated. The stars do this also. Nuit is the goddess of the night sky full of stars and full of radiance we cannot see. In the film *2001: A Space Odyssey* one recalls the black obelisk like a doorway which, once entered, is full of stars and which sends off pulses of evolutionary energy. Less well known is Paul Valéry's poem 'The Young Fate', of which Albert Cook says 'Yet the repressed returns in force, and Valéry's most famous long poem presents the ruminations of a giant female Fate spread out upon the stars of the night sky.' The Young Fate 'has just cried beneath the bite of the serpent' and the conflict in this great modern poem is: 'The body perceived under the sign of contemplation . . . contrasted to the body under the sign of experience, or fertility.'[28]

The cloud of blackness or invisibility, the creative mist within which a magician could work, has a long and notable history, from Merlin's magic weather-mists that could decide the outcome of important battles, to the French Rosicrucian clouds. Of these Thomas Vaughan says that 'the fraternity of R.C. can move in this *white mist*'. Golden Dawn initiates were alleged to have the power of surrounding themselves with a 'Shroud of Darkness and Mystery' which looked like 'a cloud or veil'. Steve Richards, who has written a short book on this theme, equates this mist or charged cloud with the ectoplasm of the spiritualists and with some aspects of the human aura. He gives exercises for extending the sight into the ultraviolet and tells us if we do them we may experience 'chromatic onomatopoeia', when colours will sound and sounds will colour, as in Baudelaire's '*Correspondences*'. (One remembers that Baudelaire's black mistress, Jeanne Duval, was '*Noire et pourtant lumineuse*' – 'Black and shining with it'.)[29]

The cloud of invisibility itself is collected by scooping it out of the air with the hands, having sharpened the sight with the exercises already given. The advanced student will realise that the cloud is the same with which a God surrounds himself: 'God, the vast and shrouded One'. To perform magical invisibility and exercise the power that comes with it one should proceed by 'rites of assumption' to enter in imagination the being of minerals, plants, animals and then other humans, before entering that of the God-form. 'If you are successful, and I mean successful in an advanced sense, you will be able to see through the eyes and hear with the ears of Harpocrates, just as with less advanced forms of assumption you learn to see with the eyes and hear with the ears of some other mortal.'[30] Since Harpocrates 'looks out upon heavenly scenes and listens to celestial music', this is an assumption to Heaven, or a state, literally, of enthusiasm, *enthousiazein*: one has entered the God. Yeats, who had done these exercises, knew this condition: 'While on the shop and street I gazed / My body of a sudden blazed; / And twenty minutes more or less / It seemed, so great my happiness, / That I was blessèd and could bless.' This coherent 'black' or 'invisible' cloud, mediating non-ordinary experiences, is clearly the 'magic stuff' already discussed.

The 'chromatic onomatopoeia' of magic is the synaesthesia of the poets. George Whalley, writing on Coleridge, says: ' . . . the appeal is not to any one sense but to *an interinanimation of all the senses* [my italics] combined into a tactual impression of great power – a condition that psychologists call synaesthesia. This may well be a prime characteristic of all poetic perception, of the poetic sense of language, and perhaps of all our refined and developed sensory experience.'[31] Rimbaud refers to this experience when he says: '*Il s'agit d'arriver à l'inconnu par le dérèglement de* tous les sens' ('The point is to arrive at the unknown by the disordering of *all the senses*'). That 'disordering' is contentious; the word is better translated 'de-schooling'.[32] (Please see also the Appendix on the synaesthesia of the born-blind.) Whalley says Rimbaud's statement is the essence of poetic: ' . . . metaphor disorients the individual senses so that they excite and fertilise each other . . . In this way Poetic establishes a novel interpretation of thought and feeling . . . In Poetic, sight can be converted into sound and texture and even scent; single words can assume physical shape, contour, fibre; groups of words may take on meanings not implied by their grammatical relations; savour, aroma, cachet may be conveyed in texture and rhythm.'[33] Bertocci summarises the characteristics of the privileged or visionary moment when he says: 'It is characterised by synaesthesia in the vertical sense, i.e. in which colours speak and perfumes tell of thoughts, as well as in the horizontal sense, i.e. where "perfumes, colours and sounds answer each other's call".'[34] But first the visionary, poet or magician must pass through the Cloud of Unknowing, the blackness, the depression where all the senses seem closed, until the unconscious senses flower with the conscious ones, upwards to the known senses, downwards to the unknown ones. The magician will be assisted in his synaesthesia by established vertical and horizontal correspondences, in his temple, resonances between colours, sounds, materials, incenses, planets and god-forms with their attributes and stories which he will learn until they are second nature. Exactly the same applies to any religious or sporting procedure, from a church service to the team-spirit rituals and fetishes of a public school.

In other words, this type of exercise, which also includes methods so apparently widely separated as Goethe's 'exact sensorial fantasy', Jung's 'active imagination' and the Silva Mind-Control Method, involves attending to the imagination in order to experience a state of unknowing which is actually charged with knowledge, to partake of which requires a profound shift of consciousness. This unknowing, in my terms, is the synaesthetic plenum of the unconscious or subliminal senses, responding to a continuum of such complexity and grandeur in nature that it can only be approached by means of ignorance and emptying, with symbolic and imaginative guides, and under rules which comprehend the imagination in the Romantic sense: as a device for exploring the fringes of our knowledge, and of tuning in to hitherto unapprehended realities. Thus Goethe believed: '. . . every process in nature, rightly observed, wakens in us a new organ or cognition . . . creating in the wake of an ever-creative nature . . .'[35]

Sometimes this imagination is understood, as by Jung, as a Somatic unconscious; or, as by Mindell, as a Dream Body; or traditionally as a synaesthetic Magic Body or Subtle Body. Some of the magical methods and exercises are designed to increase the sensitivity of the space surrounding the skin, by imagining it filled, as it is, with electromagnetism in various invisible colours, and subject to the four elements, which means in effect fluctuating environmental influences like those described by Tromp.[36]

Traditionally, the invisible 'radiant body' (*augoeides*) or 'star-like body' (*astroeides*) was understood to be the chief organ of spiritual knowledge, in preparation for the formation of the 'resurrection Body'. Origen's words echo Blake's on touch: 'In that spiritual body the whole of us will see, the whole hear, the whole serve as hands, the whole as feet.' Synesius says that God must be approached by synaesthetic imagination, the common sense: 'For this is the one sense of all senses, seeing that the spirit (*pneuma*), whereby the imagination is brought into play, is the most general sensory and the first body of the soul . . . Now hearing and sight are not senses, but organs of sense, servants of the common sense, as it were door-keepers, who notify their mistress of the sense-objects outside . . . Whereas she in all portions of her is simple sense. For she hears with the whole of the spirit [the common sensory], and sees with the whole of it; and so she does for the rest of the senses . . . and they each proceed from the animal [i.e. the spirit] . . .'[37]

I ask the reader to note here that ancient use again of the word for 'breath' – *pneuma* or *Ruach* – as an equivalent for the spirit that arouses the imagination, and to consider once more the power and complexity of the communications by breath and air that I have outlined in the last chapter; and, again, the connection in this passage of 'spirit' with 'animal': ' . . . by its means things divine are joined with lowest things . . . Indeed it goes down even as low as irrational creatures, so as the better to extend itself.'

2 The Great Whore

There are extremely beautiful accounts, both traditional and modern, of an opening of the senses (which are the imagination) leading to a participation in the continuum – the hither side of which is understood as a subtle body, or a state in which one reaches out beyond the skin with a something which is both within and all around, which may be intense feeling, or a kind of crackling electricity, like the 'dry water' of the alchemists, and all the senses have become that 'common sense'.

In a sexual context, this is as though the energy of an orgasm involves the whole skin, the skin of one's partner, and the immediate surroundings as well. A modern Taoist master calls this the 'Valley Orgasm': 'continual rolling expansion of the orgasm throughout the whole body'. He attributes it to the flow of bioelectricity intensified and made aware, the same current that flows through all living things.[38] We have seen how this is now conceptually possible to the Western mind with the development of semiconductor theory; it is to be hoped that now Westerners know it is there, they will at last be able to feel it. The bioelectricity, according to the Taoist, is that same *ch'i* we met when discussing *feng shui*, and corresponds exactly to the continuum and the mesmeric fluid.

Another modern Taoist master recommends the raising of these energies by individual practice rather than in sexual pairs. He distinguishes various varieties and echoes of the *ch'i*: that which is born from the body is called *ching*, a word which means 'sperm'. It is said to be the body's primary energy, that which forms both sperm and ova. It is to be remembered that the traditional view of the energies of menstruation is that the whole power of the ovum, which is capable of forming a person, a child, is released upon its break-up at the period for the use of its owner. *Ching* is to be transmuted into *ch'i*, which is an aspect of will, and then into *shen*, which is true consciousness. 'Not to know the intercourse of male and female and yet to have an erection is the arising of *ching*' and 'when a growing baby boy is asleep, he has absolutely no consciousness of sexual desires but he may have an erection' and this is *ching*; yet during all dreaming both men and women show the reactions of sexual excitement.

The feeling of 'happiness orgasm' comes from *ching*. With its further transmutation, there is 'lightness' and 'the top of the head feels fresh and cool as if cream were being gently poured over it. The Buddhists and Taoists call this "internal baptism" . . . the body will feel warm and harmonious and as if one is experiencing a strong internal orgasm.' The feelings are 'difficult to describe', but the Chinese say that one is 'internally touched by wonderful pleasures'.[39]

It is interesting to compare this with Middle-Eastern sexual-religious practices, and the images of them which we have inherited. Mari-Ishtar, the Great Whore, anointed her consort Tammuz (with whom Jesus was identified) and thereby made him a Christ. This was in preparation for his descent into the underworld, from which he would return at her bidding. She, or her priestess, was called the Great Whore because this was a sexual rite of *horasis*, of whole-body orgasm that would take the consort into the visionary knowledgeable continuum. It was a rite of crossing, from which he would return transformed. In the same way Jesus said that Mary Magdalene anointed him for his burial. Only women could perform these rites in the goddess's name, and this is why no men attended his tomb, only Mary Magdalene and her women. A chief symbol of the Magdalene in Christian art was the cruse of holy oil – the external sign of the inner baptism experienced by the Taoist. We shall see more of the Magdalene as sexual initiator later.[40]

The knowledge the man initiated by women would return with would be *samadhi*, which was said to be shared originally by all living creatures. Instead of an Oedipus, such a man would be a re-born magician, a prophet, like Tiresias. In her article on prostitution Barbara Walker describes *samadhi* as 'the unique combination of beauty and kindness called *charis* (in Latin *caritas*) . . . like Hindu *karuna*, a combination of mother-love, tenderness, comfort, mystical enlightenment, and sex' that was dispensed by the *devadasis* of Hindu temples and the prostitute-priestesses in Middle-Eastern temples. 'Hesiod said the sensual magic of the sacred whores or Horae "mellowed the behaviour of men" . . . Communing in this way with a holy whore, man could realise the spiritual enlightenment called *horasis*. This word appears in the New Testament (Acts 2:17) misleadingly translated "visions".'[41] The chapter in Acts refers to the coming of the Holy Spirit at Pentecost: 'and suddenly there came a sound from Heaven as of a rushing mighty wind . . . And there appeared unto them cloven tongues like as of fire, and it sat upon each of them . . .'

We have seen how an enhanced response to the movements of air-masses and to the electrical transactions all around us, in which our bodies partake, is part of the relaxation of the unconscious senses into the natural continuum. As the modern Taoist master Nan says: 'The heart, mind and chest will feel joyful and open.' Barbara Walker's concept of the *horasis* closes the gap between sexual and religious experience (or, since the word 'religion' has been so soiled, 'revelatory' experience). But the revelation of the *horasis* takes us into the 'marvels of the commonplace', as Gerald Massey says all revelation should be; that is, of the infinite natural wonders: ' . . . the joy and pleasure is like that experienced by a person who drinks good vintage wine . . . '[42]

Blake sometimes speaks like a Taoist, as indeed all the Romantics do, but he more often than the others in a sexual context: 'Embraces are Comminglings from the Head even to the Feet, / And not a pompous High Priest entering by a secret place.' John Trinick in a remarkable book equates the dry water, the 'homogeneous metallic water' or 'Mercury of the Philosophers', the 'water-which-wets-not-the-hand-and-is-itself-a-fire', with the magnetic fluid of animal magnetism. His study sets out as the investigation of a symbol, the *mysterium conjunctionis* of Jung, but is drawn inevitably towards acknowledging the fusion of the imaginative with the physical.[43] A footnote, added after the main text was completed, refers to some modern case-histories in which the sexual electricity was seen. The description recalls Coleridge's experience with the silvery light over his thighs.

One couple lay for an hour together on a couch, without having sex: 'Then we separated from each other and stood up; thereupon my wife became visible. She was outlined with a nimbus of greenish-blue mystic light which radiated from her. It was like a halo, except for the fact that it encircled not only her head but her whole body . . . ' The couple could produce painful sparks from each other, but the alarming electrical effects did not occur if they had intercourse lasting not less than half an hour. The woman's sparks were stronger during her menstrual period.

Another couple experienced a like flow through the skin where it naturally touched; the impression was that a 'million sources of delight merged into one and streamed to the skin', but this delight was reduced if they had not taken a bath beforehand. If it faded away a shower or a rub-down with a wet towel would restore the conductivity of their skins so that 'they could go back to bed and re-enter their state of superhuman bliss without difficulty', yet ordinary genital intercourse was avoided.

They felt that this was 'a prevision of the after-life' and the author comments that he was convinced that 'Platonic love is, more probably, something of this kind [rather] than a purely spiritual relationship.' The author, Rudolf von Urban, specifically relates these experiences to observations on human bioelectricity such as those we discussed in the last chapter.[44] Morton Smith, the New Testament scholar, adduces evidence that it was in this way that Jesus initiated his disciples.[45]

Abilities of this kind would be part of the holy whore's *karuna* or *charis*, and are found today in witchcraft circles which practise touch-magic: the touch of the high priestess within the circle will immediately produce a waking-dream in the skin, an entry into the 'astral' by whole-body *horasis*.

Charis was the name of the female Christ of the Gnostics, whose natural blood of menstruation was held to redeem mankind. Massey says: 'The blood of Charis preceded the blood of Christ, and but for the purification by the blood of Charis, there would have been no doctrine of the purification of souls by the blood of Christ. The Eucharist was a celebration of Charis before it was assigned to the Christ.' These experiences are clearly continuous with the Pentecostal inspiration; thus the Gnostic Marcus says 'Behold, Charis has descended upon thee; open thy mouth and prophesy; open thy mouth and thou shalt prophesy.'[46] The reader will have noted the Christ-like imagery of the fruit and the vine in the passage above where Wisdom is declaring herself, and the reversal of the New Testament image of the living water that quenches all thirst (which must be the water of death), in that he who partakes of Wisdom desires more.

It is clear now why Wisdom is also a Tree. 'The same Tree of Knowledge that supplied the fruit which damned the primal pair in the Genesis is the Tree of Wisdom in the Apocrypha.'[47] It is only in the Judeo-Christian mythology that the snake is evil and the Tree dangerous: Greek and Sumerian Edens are paradises of trees haunted by oracular serpents. Eden in these and Renaissance mythologies stands for the 'littoral' or in-between zone joining this world and *that* one: the interface of the continuum.[48]

All this seems fable if the 'how' is missing. But we now know more of the 'how'; science subverting its orthodoxy has shown us how we may believe in wonders that everybody experiences, but which, as with the Romantic movement, are not developed because there are no 'explanations' of how, and so one becomes incredulous. With Trinick, we can see how his symbol of the *mysterium conjunctionis* passes into living reality because the 'how' is there: there *is* bioelectricity, and the progress of a storm out of the desert *can* so affect people's minds that in one state they are ill, or in another, more harmonious state, they may prophesy, as in the magic circle or at Pentecost. We can see how St Gregory of Nyssa could experience the unconsuming fire of his own *ch'i*: he said that one may become 'related to that which is without weight, light and aerial . . . He, then, who . . . has made his soul dry like the spider, has put on this aerial tunic. It extends from the head to the extremity of the feet . . .'[49]

Once a friend of mine had made love to his wife at a very relaxed time, but in the bedroom where their nine-year-old daughter was also sleeping. Love-making was of necessity quiet and slow, otherwise the child would have woken.

He tells how he slept, and then woke a short time afterwards with a beautiful feeling in his skin from the love-making, as though it were open and enlarged and no longer a barrier, and through it he could also feel his wife's self sleeping by him and interpenetrating his skin, as though their bodies had intermingled in the warm space between them. After a short time of simply lying there and enjoying this 'afterglow', he opened his eyes and found that the room was full of a golden-coloured gossamer arranged in a webwork that emanated from fluffy centres of gold, and this webwork extended as if in care to the small bed of their daughter.

He thought this was a mere dream reflecting his relaxed state, until he saw the passage I have just quoted from St Gregory, the one from Synesius above, and the following from Plutarch: 'Others . . . take away from this passion its furious character . . . so that there remains in the soul a clean light together with warmth. This warmth . . . brings to pass a marvellous and fruitful opening out, as though of a flowering or fruiting plant; it is like that of pores, which open to give forth persuasion and affection; but little time is needed to pass beyond the body of the loved one to pass inwards to the roots of the being, and to attach oneself to the soul, now perceptible to the cleansed vision.' He was also impressed by the Arabic poet, who spoke of how 'The hand of love has woven about us all night a tunic of kisses . . .'[50]

Later on he made a cento or patchwork of quotations from a particular book on the Middle-English mystics, to illustrate the sheer physicality of such 'mystical' experiences. ' . . . *thi gostly eyes . . . a blinde beholdyng unto the naked being . . . Odor Divino as the senses open . . . the Holy Rauch and the Divine Schmack . . . the fragrance of God often solidifies to become a cloud overshadowing the soul and we endlessly be alle hyd in God . . . Hym delectably smelling . . . Christi Bonus Odor . . . A sweet smel of oonheed, or unyoun which the Devil cannot smell . . . A good mirknes and a rich noughte . . . a gostli felyng in the soul . . . taast of goostly felyng in God . . . He is oure clothing that for loue wrappeth us . . .*'[51]

He introduced me to this same book, by Riehle, and its message was strong. It seems that the closest connection between the Middle-English Christian mystics and visionary movements on the continent, such as the Brothers and Sisters of the Free Spirit and the Friends of God (Hieronymus Bosch was said to be a member of the former), was in the area of female mysticism, as with Julian of Norwich and Margery Kempe.

Riehle from his documents distinguishes a variety of important ideas, such as the *inner eye* of the soul; in Eckhart there is an outer eye for the ordinary world and an inner eye for knowing eternal being. One must in a sense become blind to know God. Synaesthesia is frequent: Richard Rolle (who shows a clear affinity with female mysticism) links images of music and fire with other sense experiences. Hilton speaks of the 'harps of the souls'; it seems that in John Chrysostom 'the man who subordinates the body to the soul is called a harp'. 'Allegories of the sense of smell are also an essential ingredient in all accounts of the mystical union of man with God': this is the '*Odor Divino*', the holy '*Rauch*' and the '*Divine Schmack*'. Touch, too, for these mystics is part of the 'vision'. Mary Magdalene as the woman with the issue of blood, who touched the hem of Jesus's garment, is seen as a figure of the soul.

The word '*feling*' is used to mean the ability to experience God through the powers of the soul, and the concept *nous* is rendered in the Vulgate as *sensus*; *nous* in ancient Greek is another of those words which move between 'spirit', 'breath' and 'heart'. As already mentioned, there is a wish for the soul to *touch* God. The realm of the transcendental is a *savour which can be felt*. The Song of Songs with its Black Shulamite (the word may mean 'solomoness' or 'peaceful') is a central text, almost an instruction manual.

God lives in a divine dark which 'is invisible because of its overbright brightness'. One must enter the dark theatre of the soul by the annihilation of the self, but the first stage of contemplation is an increased feeling of the body, a '*nakid thought & a blynde feling of thin owne beyng*', according to Riehle.

Ese is necessary to the mystic, and Riehle says this is the same term that is used to describe the state of bliss which the lovers in *Troylus and Cryseyde* achieve in the physical act of love-making, the 'lightness' of the Taoist, the deep relaxation of the 'relaxation response'. The mystic is like the bride made drunk by the lover, and this is taken from the Song of Songs, and resembles the Taoist's account of his 'happiness orgasm', like being drunk on 'good vintage wine'. The mutual caresses of the lovers in the Song of Songs also lead to the theme of love-play between God and the soul, the 'Game of Love' or of Hide and Seek, like the Queen of Sheba's riddles. The soul is the bed of God, and there is a mystical kiss of God and the soul which is also found in the Isis cult.[52]

I mentioned the painter Hieronymus Bosch (d.1516). The argument that his wonderful visions came from an association with a late Gnostic order and their techniques is to me strong. The Adamites (another name for the Brethren and Sisters) accorded women sacramental equality, in contrast with the Church. They practised a 'sexual secret' which was said to have been used by Adam in Paradise, and it is said that Bosch's altar-piece *The Millennium* gave 'immortal expression to this Adamite eroticism'. Wilhelm Fränger quotes Novalis on this 'alchemy of love': 'Soul and body touch each other in the act: chemically, galvanically or electrically or fierily . . . the mystical organs . . . the mere thought of which, the silent movement of which, is in itself sensual pleasure.'[53]

Books such as von Urban's and Trinick's have updated or rediscovered these experiences. After all, elaborate ritual or preparation is not required – only a way of 'seeing'. Thus both William and Catherine Blake 'used to sit staring into the fire in which they saw images . . . sex . . . it is actually a way into Eternity . . . So I believe that Blake, in the dreamy post-coitional state, found an unusual effervescence of ideas, and this was what he meant by passing into the World of the Poetic Imagination by the Fifth Window.'[54]

The message in my terms is that the imagination is capable of super-sensory perception (ESSP) but needs training or purifying. It must also work with the less familiar senses, with which it can test the darkness. 'Before, however, the imagination can receive God, the incomings [of the accustomed senses must] flee away out of it.' It must expect the unexpected, in the 'gostli senses', the black theatre. By imagination, therefore, is meant not the streams of conversations and images that rush through the mind in its usual state. These are in fact part of our accustomed *discontinuity* of consciousness. It is rather in the first instance that blackness which to the full ego is depression, but which to one who can wait or transform, as the Sphinx teaches, is that satisfactory emptiness that is achieved in relaxation and meditation, the '*ese*', the 'post-coitional state', the 'valley' or 'happiness orgasm', when 'the heart, mind and chest will feel open and free', the 'lightness', the 'relaxation response'. Such a state allows the 'common sense' of all senses together – synaesthesia – to operate and proceed to intuition. It is pure black theatre: the mind empties and the vivacious images enter and the invisible musician begins to play, and be heard. And one may ask questions, and the answers appear.

In the literature on the Romantics poetic experiences are sometimes called 'privileged moments', and the phrase is a bad one. It must have been invented by people interested in maintaining privilege against common birthright. The privilege here is of access, and it is open to everybody, most particularly in the sexual embrace. Almost every human being comes closest to poetry and what is meant by 'the Kingdom of Heaven on Earth' at some time in their lives by this means. Relaxation, vision, an enhancement of body and mind is known by direct experience, yet because of its wholeness and power it is the chief subject of taboo and imposed disgust. I am talking about sex for the mutual illumination of the partners, which in nearly every major religion is expressly forbidden: sex is supposed by most religions to be for procreation solely.

In the modern world, copulation for its own sake has seemed the natural reaction to puritan one-sidedness, but in its wake many fresh 'Theban plagues' have arisen: herpes, non-specific urethritis, AIDS. This last is a disease of the immune system, which we have seen is a chief communicator between body and mind. The new science of psychoimmunology shows how the immune system responds to events and can actually learn from them, but it is a late-comer on the scene, and sexuality has inherited a world-view in which little relationship between sexual soma and psyche seems possible. Lovers struggle, with consequent damage and disease to both psyche and soma, in an adverse milieu in which neither science nor established religion can see any purpose to sex other than procreation. The ancient view of non-procreative love was the reverse of this, and arose from exclusively human characteristics, which may yet paradoxically repair the broken bridge to the community of nature. In it body and mind are one: the flesh thinks, the mind feels; the animal unity is achieved – and something more. The Sphinx is answered.

The reason why I say 'exclusively human' is that there is an erotic peak among a majority of humans *when no child can be conceived*. This is a human (and higher primate) characteristic not shared by other animals. It occurs at menstruation. Among animals, mating behaviour, the oestrus, is coupled with the ripening of the egg. Humans have this peak too, but they have another, around or during menstruation, when the possibility of a child is almost nil. Both male and female experience these peaks, the man in response to the woman's cycle.[55]

The erotic peak at ovulation has been the only one acknowledged by Church and Darwinian science alike, because it advances the species, and breeds children. The other kind of sex, the 'sterile' kind, sex without physical conception, 'whore's sex', has been repressed and outlawed for centuries, and attributed to the influence of demons, such as that aspect of the Black Goddess called Lilith. Yet, as the *horasis* and the gift of the initiatrix Magdalene, Mari-Ishtar, it is the chief means of conscious individual evolution, exceeding the knowledge of schools and universities. It is the knowledge of the Black Goddess of the dark vision beyond sight, whose emblem is the Magdalene's issue of blood, and the redeeming blood of Charis.

It seems that in the black theatre of the mind of the great theologian Paul Tillich the words 'Nature, also, Mourns for a Lost Good' had an unexpected and further significance than the one I discussed in Chapter One. It was, literally, a pornographic significance (*porne*: a whore).

Hannah Tillich describes entering her husband's room during his private showing of a porn film: 'There was the familiar cross shooting up the wall . . . A naked girl hung on it . . . More and more crosses appeared, all with women tied and exposed . . . ' Mary Daly says: 'I suggest that theologians have always fantasised a female hanging on the cross . . . Indeed, these sadomasochistic fantasies were the juice/sap of his impressive theologising.'[56] They were the torment of exiled Charis calling to the Christian theologian unable to connect his sexuality to his faith – they were his riddling Sphinx. Women know one cross as the choice between the potentials of motherhood and those of a different individuality, and it hurts and bleeds and calls out with all the resources of the body. Moreover, a sexually developed woman will know as one of these alternatives the sexual Crossing-and-Return of Mari-Ishtar. Perhaps Tillich was also calling out for the Magdalene initiatrix it is said his master found.[57] I saw a student come into realisation of his own talent by doodling a cross on successive pages of his notebook – as the pages advanced the shaft sank into a reflective puddle and the crucifix reflection of the male figure above came into view. Down below was the suffering body of a woman.

3 The Black Goddess

'The Black Goddess is so far hardly more than a word of hope whispered among the few who have served their apprenticeship to the White Goddess. She promises a new pacific bond between men and women, corresponding to a final reality of love . . . She will lead man back to that sure instinct of love which he long ago forfeited by intellectual pride.'[58]

That great Doctor of the Church, Thomas Aquinas, was in his late years converted to the worship of the Black Goddess. ' . . . The long-repressed anima appeared to Thomas, in that vision, shortly before his death, in the guise of Wisdom and the bride.' She appears as a Muse, a 'feminine *pneuma* who enkindles and inspires' his work; 'the black earth is itself Wisdom', or Wisdom is its soul which also, like Ishtar, descends to the centre of earth; and she who is 'the playmate of Yaweh' 'suddenly appeared to him in personal form' with the effect of a thunderclap when 'he had taken her merely as an abstract idea'. The bride is a 'sweet-smelling *pneuma* and is thus identified with the Holy Spirit'.[59]

Even in his earlier writings, as the architect of Church orthodoxy, Thomas Aquinas advocated a science of the invisibles. He maintained that the presence of an angel could induce the *physiological* movement of humours and spirits in a way that would simultaneously present a person with a supersensible vision and enhance their intellect so that they were capable of interpreting it.

There was a passing also of invisible spirits through the medium of visible light when a man fell in love, and, when these spirits passed from the eyes of the lady and entered into the man's nature, a process could be set in motion that led to the creation of the *intelletto d'amore*: 'The process would seem to involve a transformation of sexual energy, through which the love of the lady's exterior form would dissolve into love of the miraculous revelation of her soul . . .'[60] The invisible thus became sensible, by the operation of spirits dependent on the physiological workings of the body.

This was the belief of the *fedeli d'amore* of thirteenth-century Italy – the 'faithful followers of love' – among whose number was Dante, and whose antecedents were said to include the Templars.[61]

What is certain is that Dante's art 'has its most direct origins in the discoveries of the troubadours writing in Southern France from the beginning of the twelfth century', and that for these singers of the cult of love it was no mere matter of simple sexual attraction but that 'the experience of being in love totally altered their perceptions of the world . . . as they were driven to explore the essence of their sexual beings, so they experienced ever higher levels of consciousness in instantaneous but ever memorable moments of illumination . . .'[62]

It is possible to trace a whole tradition of *maithuna* (Tantric visionary sexuality) in the literature of Romance.[63] Some of it is indeed grossly erotic.[64] Guilhem Montanhagol wrote: 'A lover should on no account desire what would dishonour his lady-love.' Barbara Walker comments crisply: ' . . . probably meaning an unwelcome pregnancy'.[65] Thus this kind of love is not on the ovulation side.

The love was both sensual and divine, as we have seen with the Middle-English mystics. Thus, to Guinizzelli, 'The girl he sees wearing a hat of grey squirrel fur so proudly that she leaves him trembling like a snake's chopped-off head is also the lady with the semblance of an angel.' For these Italian poets their goddess was again the Wisdom (Sapientia) of the Solomonic books: the eternally pre-existing companion of Christ – 'I was daily his delight, rejoicing always before him' – and the playmate of Yaweh. The Song of Solomon was their text through the sermons of St Bernard. They paid particular attention to their visions and dreams and, as in Dante's *Divine Comedy*, the actual initiatory power of the woman was acknowledged. 'It may be that what these poets had in common was a method of contemplation that expanded consciousness in them so that they were made open to the illumination of Sapientia . . .'[66] and this opened to them the world of imagination as perception. This method of contemplation was probably language charged with sexual illumination ' . . . expressing in words not simply the ineffable experience of mystical illumination but that illumination experienced through woman, in whom divine and earthly love were united as one'.[67]

Call her Mary Lucifer – 'Mary the Light-Giver' – as the Magdalene was known. She was the companion of Jesus and 'there was no grace that He refused her, nor any mark of affection that He withheld from her'.[68]

In the *Pistis Sophia*, a third-century Gnostic scripture, Mary Magdalene became the questioner of Jesus, much in the manner of the riddling of the Queen of Sheba or of the catechism of the oriental love-books between Parvati and Shiva, or between the Dark Girl and the Yellow Emperor. Again and again the Magdalene, and what Ean Begg calls the 'whore wisdom', was associated with the establishment of cults of the Black Virgin, particularly in Southern France, the Cult of Love, and the Gnostic sects. Begg says that one of the directions the Black Virgin cult points towards is *the alternative Church of Mary Magdalene*, James, Zacchaeus, Gnosticism, Cathars, Templars and alchemists'.[69]

It is as though Mary Lucifer beckons from the invisible, from the blackness, to those who can enter and return, their lives-in-the-body enhanced and nourishing the soul. For the German poet Rilke, the world must pass into its invisibility before it can be *felt*: 'Earth, do you not wish this: to arise invisibly within us? Is this not your dream, to be invisible also one day? Earth! Invisible!'[70] He also speaks of the 'vision-in-the-dark-angel'.

When discussing Rilke the literary critic Hartman echoes the parapsychologist Morris concerning the E S S P of 'Nature's untranslatable concreteness' in that it is a matter of 'non-visual bodily feelings'. If it is seen, it is 'seen with the edge of the eyes . . . There is in the mind an instant of radiation . . . no singular percept . . .' Then the mind returns to its sleep. But 'What is the meaning of this sleep that must precede and follow such apperception?' It is black theatre, for it 'is a readiness of the body and a suspense of the will enabling total reception from the senses'. It is a girl observed, 'the beloved announced by all creation,' and at the 'crossroad of the senses' she may then return, 'made of invisible images and inaudible sounds'.[71]

Let me say why I think this presiding image of the world's hope-in-love is represented as black, and why she is feminine also. I suggest again that she is black because she is the symbol and gateway to everything we could know in the apparent blackness beyond visible sight; because she represents all those forces that surround us which are not perceived in the eyes, but which extend from the visible spectrum into unexplored modes of being, to which animals seem closer than we are, at the 'crossroad of the senses'.

Guinizzelli's experience with the lady in the grey squirrel hat shows how the initiatory lady can be, must be, a fusion of angel and animal, the Sphinx.

She is black because she is also, as Isis was with her temples of dream incubation, the goddess of the vision of the night, the dream, and goddess too of all those marvels we see by inner light when our eyes are closed. Thus the Black Virgin is sometimes referred to as Notre-Dame de Lumière: Black Light.[72]

She is black also because she is the goddess of clairvoyance, clear-seeing and the second sight – and in truth of first sight as well – the lover's light of touch in bed, and the dark light of touch in the womb. She is the Goddess of Intimacy, of being 'in touch' and of that fifth window, the skin, which is black and blind until those other kinds of light come into it.

She is the Black Goddess also because she lives in the darkness men have created by their blindness. She is sometimes represented as blind or blindfolded, as Justice is, or as the blind Shekhina who has wept her eyes out in the exile to which men have consigned her. She is also blind Salome, haunting Jung's autobiography.

Jung used to imagine a deep descent. Once, he found there an old man with a white beard, and a beautiful young girl, who was blind, and called Salome. The old man explained that he was Elijah, and they 'had a black serpent living with them which displayed an unmistakable fondness' for Jung. His comment was that Salome 'is blind because she does not see the meaning of things'.[73]

This astonishing statement in my opinion protects Jung from some of the uncomfortable scientific facts that I have attempted to uncover. Much in the same way as Tillich took the 'juice/sap' of his theologising from his fantasies of the crucified Charis, so the blind woman with the black snake (as we shall see) is an impressive vision of the oracular woman with second sight (that not depending on the eyes) at her catamenic time of prophecy. I suspect Jung knew that Elijah, the prophet, was dependent on his 'trance-maiden', as Jung himself depended for the 'juice/sap' of his psychology on the visions of women, as we shall see the 'black magicians' do.[74]

The Black Goddess: what symbol of transformation could be more appropriate than the rich darkness, the black earth of Isis the alchemist, in our world where, whatever the degree of poverty, no one is ever far away in any country from the television set with its brightly trivial patter, potent optical illusions or screen chattering with venal calculations? And, in a patriarchal culture, what other figure than the female mediator, the personal anima in continuum with *anima mundi*? Chipping away at Oedipal complacency, how moody she makes him with her weather changes rooted in the unconscious senses, and what a wonderful richness of connection with the real world these imply. And in a culture that has outlawed sex-without-procreation, what more transformative actuality than the initiatrix who lies with a man through the night and changes him utterly?

Modern depth psychology started with Freud's Oedipus, and stuck with him for a long time. It was thought that the Oedipus complex was the mainspring of human evolution, when it is more probably the image of disaster. Later workers in depth psychology have as an alternative pointed to the truly evolutionary figure of the Black Goddess. Ean Begg is one of this important group.

Begg confirms that Jung himself distinguished two poles in the feminine archetype: the Virgin and the Whore. In Christian mythology the Virgin is assumed bodily and crowned by the Sun. Thus 'the Eva cycle is fulfilled'. But 'the Magdalene is still the lost sheep and still, as the Black Virgin, the secret, dark wisdom of the serpent, sells herself to all who desire her'. Thus the ovulation, 'Eva', is differentiated from the 'black sheep' or black serpent of the menstrual pole of the cycle.[75]

For Begg, the Black Virgin 'plays the leading role in the mysteries of death, rebirth and the underworld'. In well over 200 famous Western European shrines of the Virgin, her image is black. She is the 'shadow aspect of the Madonna' relating to heretical knowledge. Blindness and its cure are a province of Sicilian Persephone, a pagan Black Virgin. Candlemas (2 February) is important to the Black Madonna (as it is to the witches). At Ephesus she may have been a black stone, like the Ka'aba, and a famous statue of Cybele had a black stone for a head.[76] He says: 'Black is the colour of the unknown, the unconscious, and it is there that we must seek whatever it was that was repressed and lost . . . '

Lilith is described with her Sphinx-like, part-animal nature, called Lamia in the Vulgate, as the 'image of the fallen, expelled feminine principle that turns negative and wreaks revenge on mothers and their children' (because non-ovulatory). Yet she 'is a ladder on which one can ascend to the rungs of prophecy', just as 'the Sphinx is well known for her perilous riddles . . . yet is hymned as the wise virgin . . . '[77] Only in India has her cult persisted unbroken through the centuries of Kali-Lalita, the *dark flame*.[78] However, in the nineteenth century Michel Vintras, under the Black Virgin's auspices at Sion-Vaudemont, preached again Joachim's prophecy of the advent of the age of the Holy Spirit and a redemption brought about by the Virgin mediatrix and her priestesses, in which the sexual act would be the high sacrament, restoring the original androgyny.[79] Could this be the wonderfully perfumed feminine *pneuma* or Muse known to Aquinas 'who kindles and inspires' and makes a one body out of the separate beings of her worshippers? Certainly the wonderful Gnostic hymn of the Black Goddess speaking as Prunikos (the 'lewd') quoted by Begg begins to suggest this, and the experience of coming closer to the invisible and actual creatrix:

> For I am the first and the last.
> I am the honoured one and the scorned one.
> I am the whore and the holy one . . .
> I am the one whom they call Life
> and you have called Death.
> I am the knowledge of my enquiry,
> and the finding of those who seek after me . . .
> I am the substance and the one who has no substance.
> What is inside you is what is outside of you
> and the one who fashions you on the outside
> is the one who shaped the inside of you.
> And what you see outside of you, you see inside of you;
> It is visible and it is your garment.[80]

4 Love-Streams

Begg gives some credence to the Order of the Prieuré Notre-Dame de Sion, now known to millions of modern readers through the international best-seller *The Holy Blood and the Holy Grail*.[81] This is a magnificent conception, if true, that 'Mary Magdalene sailed to Provence after the Crucifixion, bringing with her the wisdom of the feminine principle that was to blossom anew in Catharism and in the cult of the Black Virgin in Southern France,'[82] and that the Prieuré was later established to protect this wisdom with a succession of alleged grand masters.

These included the alchemist Nicolas Flamel; Botticelli; Leonardo da Vinci; Robert Fludd, also an alchemist; as was Johann Valentin Andreae, the founder of the Rosicrucians; Robert Boyle, the 'Sceptical Chymist'; Isaac Newton (whose alchemical papers greatly exceed in number his mathematical ones, and who only published the *Principia* because Halley the astronomer insisted and paid for the publication himself); Victor Hugo; Claude Debussy and Jean Cocteau.

Moreover, the Magdalene was supposed to have carried the child of Jesus with her to establish the holy blood-line of the Merovingian dynasty, and the Prieuré exists partly to restore this to its throne. This might be confusing the mental children or the supersensible vision of the gnosis with the physical lineage; but, though it is not easy to believe quite all the authors of *The Holy Blood and the Holy Grail* say, the phenomenal success of the book shows how thirsty the world is for the Magdalene's survival.

There have been some fascinating spin-offs too, which take us closer to 'black magic' and the actual cultivation of supersensible experience. One of these is *Genisis* by David Wood, which has the imprimatur not only of Henry Lincoln, one of the authors of *The Holy Blood and the Holy Grail*, but also of the grand master of what I take to be a neo-Gnostic order, the MAAT Lodge (Egyptian).

Recalling the scientific tale told above, that all races alike are descended from one African woman, this book argues from further investigations at Rennes-le-Château, where the secrets of the Prieuré first declared themselves, that the true secrets were indeed those of Isis, but that she was an extra-terrestrial visitor responsible for the mutations of the pre-human primates that led to the human race.

One of the secrets this visitor left with us is supposed to be a way of controlling our own evolution by simultaneously presenting a person 'with a supersensible vision and enhancing their intellect so that they were capable of interpreting it', in the words I used in discussing the Florentine poets. The method of Isis was kept as a secret by the Gnostic sects, and was a part of the love-feast among those who believed that true communion with each other and with other worlds was gained by the imbibition of each other's sexual fluids. The theology of this was that the god-substances, scattered through the universe, were only truly brought together in humans, and the collected essences could be shared, hence re-creating the undivided god or goddess: 'I am dispersed in all things, and in gathering me you gather yourself.'

Something like this remains among the sex-magic practices of present times. *Genisis* puts it thus: 'Heavily veiled in the allegories of the alchemists and the Brotherhood of the Rose Cross was the unbelievable suggestion that in some way a minute trace of a very potent liquid seeped from the brain of a woman and collected in the womb or vaginal cavity . . . It would further appear that this secretion was cyclic on a monthly basis. Alternatively, a certain amount may remain *in situ* and be expelled during the menstrual cycle.'

This, David Wood thinks, may be one of the Wedding Song secrets in the Song of Solomon, and ' . . . the meaning behind the age-old mystery of the Rose and the Lily of the Valley . . . Was the Elixir being continuously generated in every female body and expelled twice a month? . . . It is suggested that to imbibe this fluid elevates the mind; this is liquid intelligence; the bridge between the conscious and super-mind.'[83]

Given now our contemporary data on pheromones and semiochemicals and how the action of these may re-adjust the whole emotional and therefore the endocrine system of a human being and its nervous response, it seems quite credible that with the secretion of potent substances, which certainly does occur, at the two culminations of the menstrual cycle (at ovulation and menstruation), a re-adjustment of the masculine intelligence could be effected. If both partners consumed the mingled elements, as in the Marcian communions, where they were thought to be the actual bodies of god and goddess, then presumably both would benefit.

Israel Regardie was one of the first to come out in the open about this, but he spoke in guarded alchemical terms concerning what is called 'The Mass of the Holy Ghost'. Louis Culling later on was more explicit.[84]

I have had the benefit of some conversation with two neo-Gnostic initiates, who represent the English branch of a magical society based in the United States. The society was founded by a woman, an analytical psychologist, and its present American head is also an initiate of a branch of OTO (of which more later).

As with all sex-alchemical orders, its aim is the Great Work, which is the transformation of human consciousness and its re-adjustment to a more fruitful and feminist path of evolution. Another of its aims is to preserve and study the works of Gerald Massey. In the English branch, at least, its central object of contemplation is the Black Goddess, seen as the Virgin of the World, *anima mundi*, Star Maiden and the gateway to other worlds.

My interlocutors prefer to be known as Frater S.C. and Soror S.M. I asked them why they took the titles of 'brother' and 'sister', upon which S.C. quoted Solomon's hymn to me: 'Say unto Wisdom,

Thou art my Sister.' He then said, 'We are all siblings if we have the same Sister.' This seemed to me a good answer to Oedipus the patriarch, with whose horror the last chapter closed.

I asked my friends what they thought of *Genisis* and they agreed that it was less important whether it was factually correct in detail than that it associated the figure of the Black Goddess with such high, solemn and evolutionary thoughts. Solemnity was not much in evidence when S.C. then quoted Walker Percy: 'Being geniuses of the orgasm is far more demanding than Calvinism.'

I was surprised that they were prepared to discuss some of the secret sexual methods of alchemy and Gnostic communion, but they explained that, although these would always have a very definite effect on the people who practised them, the full benefit could only be obtained by those whose minds were prepared by some system of belief in the goddess's actuality.

This need not be metaphysical, and probably in the present age was better not so. I quoted Paul Davies on science being the best way to God, and they replied that the litany of the goddess was being newly invented every second. There was danger in existing forms of worship in so far as they resembled that of the angry Father-God. It was less that their goddess desired *worship* than that she rejoiced in *being imagined*.

I asked what other systems of belief were appropriate. They said they preferred the word 'experience' to 'belief'.

We had Begg's *The Cult of the Black Virgin* there, and they said it was excellent. However, S.M. pointed to a passage which reads 'To the Gnostic, the importance of objective phenomena lies in their underlying symbolic significance . . . ' She said, 'We believe the converse as well; that the importance of symbols lies in their underlying objective significance – in their ability to take us further into the world as well as into ourselves. Gnosis implies direct objective experience.'

A genuine experience of depth psychology would do, and was sometimes equivalent to or better than the first stages of formal magical initiation.[85] They hoped that the book I was writing (this one) would help, and this was why they wanted to talk to me.

One alternative to a 'belief system' was the gift of language, like a magic mirror. Experience in punning and metaphor such as the poet's would catch synaesthetic intimations of the supersensible 'at the crossroads of the senses'. They said that poetry and prophetic speech were a continuum with each other and with sexual experience. The orgasm, if prolonged, was like nothing so much as the poetry, say, of Neruda or St-John Perse.

They explained to me that men and women together did indeed produce an elixir, and it could be tasted. Sometimes it was like honey, sometimes metallic.[86] Sometimes it fizzed on the tongue, like champagne. It could be made at the various culminations of the menstrual cycle, usually signalled by the female partner's sexual 'high'. The male and female fluids mingled electrically in the alchemical vessel or 'curcubite' of the vagina and were potentiated by the succussion[87] there of the partners' movements, and irradiated by the activated metabolism of the whole body. This irradiation could always be felt, and sometimes seen, playing about the skin like wildfire.

Both partners should have as many orgasms as they felt right . . . here I queried how many and what kinds of orgasms did they expect a man to have! The answer given to me was that orgasm was no more equivalent to ejaculation or climax in the man than in the woman, and that men could delay or multiply the climax in the interest of the orgasm by appropriate training and a gift of nature.[88]

Ideally both partners should have their final climaxes simultaneously, the male then providing his fluid to mingle with the female's.[89] In this basic practice this could then remain *in situ* and be absorbed by the genital skin if the partners used some posture – the 'scissors' was an easy one – in which they could remain for a long time in genital contact. During this process they would experience their own and each other's 'afterglow' and 'streaming' which would merge into dream and hypnogogic states, and back again. (I said that bioenergetic therapists like Lowen had described as much[90] and S.C. replied, 'Precisely – science is a way to God.') Sometimes the barrier of the skin where it touched seemed to disappear, and a one body made of the two was felt; sometimes this formed around them for a considerable distance, and its presence in the room could be felt for hours after. Others could enter and share this '*pneuma*' and, although S.C. and S.M. were silent about their temple methods, I gathered that this 'mutual angel' could be contributed to by other adepts, and that it either was, or communicated with, their goddess. Even with only the two partners, requests could be made and questions put at this time, and they could 'call each other down' to deeper states.[91]

These half-waking dreams would also contain images of the supersensible; and on rising the skin would be so enhanced that it would supply all the senses with fresh energy and further-than-usual responses. This was by the same token the time to do creative work of any kind, since a dedication to what we call 'creative work' is an essential in catching the new apprehensions of the greater world ('*unus mundus*' was the alchemical term S.C. used).

S.M. pointed out that plenty of people did these things anyway, but the magic intention came when one established beforehand a *purpose*, which one could then re-introduce into one's enhanced state during and after the congress; though one could also use the method for pure contemplation, and that was best.

Cuddling with intromission but without climax – sometimes called Dianism – was also important to master. 'Qodosh' – a goddess-name meaning 'rainbow' and 'holy' – was a practice attended by consumption of the elixir, which must however remain in the shared vessel or 'curcubite' for at least five minutes. Since the air must not get to it, it must be transferred by mouth and a 'kiss of peace' to the woman. This amounted to a circulation of the energies of the bodies, such as the Taoists do internally in Chinese sexual alchemy.[92] S.M. laughed as she recalled the cinema image of Dracula bent over his prey, blood running from the corners of his mouth: this was how S.C. looked at that point in Qodosh during her period! Soixante-neuf could also be used.

I asked them what they thought of the modern theories of semiochemicals and pheromones and the electrical charging of the body. They laughed again and said it was well known to them and to other societies like theirs: the invisible colours given off by the excited bodies were called '*kalas*' and the seven alchemical 'metals' were the different secretions given off by seven particularly excitable parts of the body, also known as '*chakras*'.

Of these in the present age, the throat *chakra*, Viśuddha or Daath, was vitally important, as it was the bridge between body and mind, and the gateway of repressed and neglected knowledge, the way to Wisdom's 'other tree' which could be recovered through its particular function of prophetic language. The word 'secretion' itself responded to the troubadour 'green language' of punning and metaphor: it meant the 'secret-ions' of the body's currents and charged perfumes.

I looked a bit doubtful at that, so S.M. asked me why I thought

S.C. wore a pentacle ring on his middle finger. He showed me the silver star with a red stone set at its centre. I said I knew it represented symbolically the womanly star, the star at the core of the apple, showing 'as above so below', for under the night sky full of stars the apple orchard of the earth is packed with earthly penta-grams – just slice an apple and see – and that with the red stone at its centre it meant the womanly star of the five days of her period.

S.M. laughed and said, 'Very nicely put . . .' and S.C. grinned and said to me, 'Symbols, symbols . . . Peter, this is my fucking-finger, and if I stroke her clitoris with it she diffuses beneficent metals which soon begin to transform the room and our familiar bodies. We believe these are the perfumes which are also the magnetic sounds that the sun and moon and the planets make as they trace out the dark body of our goddess earth in her serpent-winding journey through space . . .' Then they gave me the information about Callahan and his moths which I put in Chapter One, for the dusk-haunting Privet Hawk moth, *Sphinx ligustri*, is apparently the animal patron – the Sphinx – of their English Lodge.[93]

5 The Black Snake

Later I found pictures of the geomagnetic field which is traced out by the dark magnetic core of the earth in balance and exchange with the magnetic fields of the sun, the moon and the planets. The electro-magnetic influences of these bodies appear traced on our atmosphere as on a cathode ray screen, both visibly as the aurora and invisibly too.[94]

The pictures of the field resembled a great hooded, winged angel. It is in this field, the invisible body and robes of the visible earth, as it were, that the cosmic influences work, and communicate such influence as they may have to all the living creatures of earth, as our section on geomagnetism in Chapter Two has already suggested. It is as though Gaia wears a robe of magnetism embroidered with the sun, planets and stars: 'I saw a woman clothed with the sky' (witches perform 'skyclad' – naked). I remembered the accounts of Orphic initiates ascending as on wings to a vision of the earth as the great coiling *krater* or cauldron of the goddess, and I wondered whether my friends had not truly seen by the flesh and blood instrumentation of sexually enhanced bodies the true black body of Gaia, observed also by the scientists in their terms, through their differently electronic instruments.

What Frater S.C. and Soror S.M. were able to tell me about their sexual practices, leading to sensory enhancement and an entry into the natural continuum, is fully borne out by such published accounts as exist. These experiences, as the couple suggested to me, are hard to handle in our culture which is practised in avoiding them. It has probably distorted their nature even in those who are capable of them.

I note that neither of the two most popular, detailed, accurate and, in their own terms, helpful modern sex books (Alex Comfort's *The Joy of Sex* and *More Joy of Sex*) gives more than a hint of anything but purely physical sensation as the accompaniment of sex.

Perhaps this is the reason why sexuality has begun to be plagued by new diseases which represent the repression of the mental spiritual experiences that can otherwise come, and are the refusal of enhanced understanding, as it was in Thebes.

Massey's books throughout are full of the Wisdom that finds marvels in nature, which in itself is the true magic. John Mumford discusses the basic principles of sex-yoga in a way that few would find objectionable or difficult. Firstly he says that sex properly done produces hyperacuity of the senses, including the normally unconscious ones. He calls this ESP, and he means, like myself, 'Extra-Sensual Perception'; that is, 'converting the whole skin into one extensive, massive genital organ'.

His second principle is Sex for Positive Thinking: ' . . . a sexually aroused human is hypersuggestible. Correct use and knowledge of this (sometimes called "sex magic") allows an individual consciously to inculcate his unconscious with life-affirming – rather than life-negating – attitudes.' In other words, it is the most powerful opportunity for self-training by hypnosis or (in its green language or punning sense) transformation by 'trance-formation'.

This leads him to the Art of Mental Creation. The conscious mind at any peak of arousal can ejaculate its seed or germinal idea into the deep unconscious for incubation. 'Gestation continues in the unconscious womb until the sudden birth of the idea as a "flash" or "inspiration" which emerges – fully formed – into consciousness.'[95]

Kenneth Grant's profound, remarkable and far-ranging books are probably the fullest contemporary statement of a practical on-going neo-Gnostic view that we possess. Much is luminously plain, and much that is difficult in these books acts as 'magical formulae' which unfold in the passing of time, and in this sense they are books that 'do things' as well as say them, as Massey's are.

Grant is the current head of the famous OTO (Ordo Templi Orientis – the initials of which Mumford says stand also for 'Order to Ov'. '"To Ov" is a Greek term meaning an emanation of liquid or astral fire' or, as S.C. and S.M. would call it, wildfire, 'dry water' or 'living metal'). Much of Kenneth Grant's writing is concerned with recovering knowledge of the repressed or demonic forces represented by such figures as Lilith. The typhonian and stellar forms have to do with repressed feminine power: the old dragon. Again, there is secret access via Daath to the 'shadow tree' of dark Wisdom. It is as though this access is the place of the missing Apple.

The basic practices correspond to those we have already described, for 'the mental exaltation generated by a magically controlled orgasm forms a lucent lens-like window past which streams the vivid astral imagery of the subconscious mind'. The black theatre throngs with its imagery. The inner senses are awakened, and can be focused or incarnated by dwelling on a particular image, as they 'are dynamic links with the deeper centres of consciousness'.

The purpose is to obtain a spiritual or magical child rather than a physical one, so the so-called 'sterile' methods of intercourse such as oral sex, menstrual sex, karezza and masturbation are used. Lilith, the 'child-stealer', is connected with the 'lunar current of periodicity'. There is a dream body, or body of light: 'The stellar or astral body is also called the Desire Body because it is the vehicle of sentience in the human organism,' and '"the Sphinx is . . . an apt Hieroglyph of the Great Work"'.[96]

The female partner is the source of wisdom in the heterosexual practices; she is the *suvasini*, or sweet-smelling one, who emits the *kalas*, rays or emanations, which 'equate with the psychologically modified somatic secretions of the erogenous zones that have not yet been investigated by physical science'. That was in 1972; as we have seen, scientific information is now available which justifies these traditional insights. The operations of the endocrine glands are adjusted by the 'secret-ions' of the *kalas*. 'The exudation and imbibition of magical *kalas* inherent in human fluids' is the main study of the ancient science called *Sri Vidya*, and '"The Alchemist's metals were *living* substances"'.[97]

The woman imparts magical visions by the light of her womb; she becomes the Uterus or Utterer of information when she becomes inspired or possessed. Eyes tight-closed in trance, she is Jung's Salome, with her magical black snake, as below.

The sacramental supper is the Mass of the Holy Ghost, where the male and female essences are mingled and consumed. The yoni, like the eye, is the source of images. The body, particularly the woman's body, is the field of the interplay of bioelectrical or odic energies. 'The secretions of women are made in the laboratory of the Deity, the Temple of the Mother . . .' and are transmitted from the skies and discharged into the bloodstream via the endocrine glands. The essences are emitted particularly at the two culminations of the fertility cycle, ovulation and menstruation. Of the latter, Grant remarks: ' . . . the five-day eclipse was the seal of woman's nobility, the nobility that wears the scarlet mantle of nature herself . . .'[98]

Animals are seen as the first forms of primal consciousness, 'the primal forms of cosmic energies or "gods",'[99] and the magician's assumption of these forms, as in Chapter One above, was a way of contacting this consciousness. 'The Psalmist said that we are all mortal like animals . . . It would be truer to say, however, that *unlike* animals we are mortal.'[100] If a beast conjoins with a woman, as in the image of the Sphinx, the result is a god.

Grant tells us that the reason why the Left Hand Path is vilified is because its magic originates from woman: 'Woman, actual or imagined, as the prime instigator of orgasm . . . the *doubling* agent through which the mind reproduces and materialises its imagery.' The priestess sees 'clairvoyantly with her womb . . . this she does at the time of catamenia, when the astral forces are able to assume almost tangible form from the effluvia emanating from her vaginal vibrations'.

These are the 'perfumes or *kalas* of creative breath' and the black light of the goddess bathes the priest 'in a sweet-smelling perfume of sweat'. The subtle body or Tree of Life, Wisdom's Tree, is seen as a 'scintillant web of brilliance that courses through the denser masses of its shadowy physical counterpart'.[101]

One may believe that the 'fire serpent', or *kundalini*, the basic bioelectrical form, the black snake of invisible fire, flexes among the branches of this tree like a natural aerial of the body, as the standing wave of a television broadcast twines on its sigil-like aerial.

Grant brings Western magic close to its origins in the ancient stellar and lunar possession cults of Africa and in voodoo. Africa is the cradle of humanity and the origin of 'black' magic of the luminous night-time.

Among the Yoruba, Dahomey, Benin and neighbouring kingdoms Oduda is the chief goddess. Her name means 'the Black One' and she is a personification of the serpent current, as snake-tailed Lilith is. She presided over sacred prostitution in the city of Ado, where tradition asserts that the earth menstruates. The cult is *Obeah*. Gerald Massey is quoted by Grant: 'Dr Hahn derives the word Aub from a Hottentot root, Au, meaning to flow, or bleed. The motion of the serpent made it a type of that which flows – water flows, blood flows – and the serpent flows along the ground . . .' My suggestion, as above, is that during arousal of the body this black snake of invisible fire striking in its tree may actually be 'seen' by the subliminal senses as well as felt, caught on the electrical structure of the body, the subtle body or Tree of Life, acting as a shaped aerial or waveguide to environmental energies.

This then would be the origin of such images as the serpent-woman, and of the oracular or temptation serpent in Eden's tree; a figure repeated by the serpent on the cross of the modern spiritualists, which some would argue is a possession cult. This latter figure derives from the brazen serpent nailed to a cross that Moses constructed for the Israelites to counter a plague of 'fiery serpents' (Numbers 21). If powerful telluric energies were abroad, as with earthquakes, the snakes would awake in the *feng shui* wildfire of flesh and blood. Moses's device would then mean 'Catch the serpent energies in your Tree of Knowledge, and prophesy'.

Massey continues: 'The MQNR IMIM, or fountain of blood for the feminine pudenda Lev. 12: 7, which is likewise the Tepht (hole) of the Snake . . . The witch of Endor was described as a woman with knowledge of Aub (Ob) because the witch, whether African, Assyrian, Egyptian or European, is a pythoness, a serpent-woman possessed of the knowledge and wisdom of the Obeah or Ophite cult.'[102]

It was some such intuition in Keats (whose poetry is full of the magnetic sleep preceding or containing visions)[103] which made him love and hate the serpent-woman Lamia. In the poem of that name the hero Lycius was all but married to this great Lilith-figure until she was destroyed at the wedding-feast by the rationalist philosopher, Apollonius, Keats's figure for the onlooker-consciousness: 'Do not all charms fly/At the mere touch of cold philosophy?'

Grant says that 'the original sacrifice of sperm, followed by the magnetic sleep or trance, was misinterpreted by later cults as the sacrifice of blood and the death of the body,' as in the Christian cult. He confirms that the original cross or crossing was the feminine source, where spirit was fixed in matter as a living baby or alternatively as a magically potent vaginal emanation.

The ordeal of the cross therefore involves passing over into that other spirit-world of enhanced senses and returning via the 'little death' *in full consciousness*. This is the origin of the cross as the symbol of the Mysteries of Death which were – from the first – of a psychosexual nature.' Grant says that the Greeks hid and replaced the initiated techniques for doing this by empty doctrines with no factual basis. It was the Greeks, 'with their myths unrelated and unrelatable to the genuine gnosis',[104] who were responsible, and we have seen this borne out in the myth of Oedipus.

The mysterious *prima materia* or starting-point for alchemy is said to be certain products of the body which in the initiate are returned and transformed by the irradiation of the 'fire-snake', just as S.C. and S.M. said. These products include semen and menstrual fluid, which are reputed to be hormonally very potent, and urine. Grant says the last can be a rejuvenation fluid and a bi-sexualising agent which, 'if ingested at certain times of the month, creates a condition wherein the initiate becomes androgynous and without fear'.[105] This again would be to participate like the animals in the thriving world of chemical communication. To Massey customs and language show that *female influence on the sexual sense was the earliest human power acknowledged by the male*', and maintains that he did not *worship* her any more than he did the animals, but rather recognised in her the 'embodiment of a superior potency' which was none the less a power he could turn to his own uses.

'She was the teacher of time in relation to the sexual instinct,' and his inflamer and inspirer: 'It is this radiance in women . . . that urges men to every sort of heroism, be it martial or poetic,' says Coomaraswamy, and recalls that where Radha stood this radiance made the ground shine 'bright as gold'.[106] S.C. stated that he had seen S.M.'s 'aura' shine around her in this colour.

Thus Sekhet, the lioness, is not only solar heat figured to the Egyptians as a goddess but 'she is also the divinity of sexual pleasure and strong drink; the fierce inspirer of the masculine potency'. Thus Shiva had his *sakti*, or 'energy'; in the same way, the

Lord was accompanied by his 'Wisdom' before the beginning of things.

The image of Sekhet's force is her hind parts, the source of her invisible fire, and the fire-feeling; the goddess is the *energiser* of the god. 'It was because the female was the *inspirer* of the breath of life, the quickener, that the spirit was considered to be of a feminine nature. Even the Hebrew *Ruach* or spirit of pubescence that descended on the male at puberty is feminine in gender, as if it were the *sakti* or feminine inspirer of the male!' [107]

It is the outward senses that are to be retroverted, turned inwards or backwards to stimulate the inner ones. *Apanga* means the eyes turning upwards at the moment of orgasm, and in this moment they see nothing, are blind outwardly. The five arrows of the senses having been turned inward like this 'stimulate a flow of nectar through the whole system . . . the fragrance of which is instrumental in awakening the Fire Snake . . . *Apanga* occurs only when the goddess is suffused with the flow of amrit, the nectar emitted from the flowers of the inturned sensualities, the fragrance and glow of the elixir of life itself.' [108]

There is, apparently, no necessity in this situation for physical connection of the worshipper or worshippers with their goddess: the power of the orgasm and the magic stuff that comes with it will suffuse the room or temple and 'the worshipper is inflamed with bliss'. In voodoo the possession may be indistinguishable from a sexual possession, and the slow orgasm or *status orgasmus* resulting *is* the presence of the *loa* or spirit.

The meditator's Guru may do as much: his presence is enough; and so may the star at the pop concert, or even the sound of him at the disco. Anyone who goes to the disco where the invisible charged atmosphere is beat upon or succussed by the music and the strobes, where EM turns to audio and back again, may expect to lose their mind for a while and have it returned renewed and oddly illuminated. So may a grandfather also become renewed by the atmosphere of delight emanated by his grandchildren at Christmas-time.

These things are also operations of 'the Elixir of Life or the perfumes of regeneration'. 'Today there are signs, at long last, that Kaula praxix [Kali tantrism] may be seen for what it really is – a scientific experiment with the psychosexual chemistry of the human body.' [109] This recalls Alex Comfort's hopes for a medicine based on pheromonal aroma therapy. Kali is the Black Goddess.

For Grant 'the keynote is blackness'. This blackness symbolises the Gate of Knowledge of the Black Goddess Nuit of 'Infinite Space and the Infinite Stars thereof': ISIS. It is also the abyss Daath which is so dangerous for the male magician, since through it come all the teratomas and demonic powers which are the repressed feminine Wisdom. If the *kalas* do come from the sky and the earth, these demons may be the utterance of indignities inflicted on the planet in industrial science's name. It is the Lost Daughter, Persephone, 'the Hé final' of the Tetragrammaton, Daath herself, who is returning.[110]

To the women, as our next section will show, this abyss may be found familiar and a friend. Grant[111] quotes Castaneda: 'Women . . . have their own abyss. Women menstruate . . . that was the door for them. During their period they become something else.' One of the female apprentices states that 'during our menstrual period *dreaming* becomes power . . . a crack opens in front of us during those days . . . two days before her period a woman can open that crack and step through into another world . . .'

One correspondent of Grant's comments that his magical sexual partner would lose 15 to 20 pounds in a night, because the serpent-fire used the water in her body. This suggests that the rite is performed during a premenstrual phase, when the woman would be likely to accumulate water. It can also be a time of energised disturbance that can only be satisfied 'so that the nectars flow' by profound sex. 'The end product of water is fire' – the ritual sex might very well bring on the period.

Grant describes a contemporary Gnostic cult deriving from voodoo and led by Michael Bertiaux. The Mystère Lycanthropique is performed, which is the assumption of the form of a wolf or other predatory animal on the dream plane by a process of 'dreaming true' or hypnotic dream control. Magical art is the art of 'visualising sensation'; that is, the art of synaesthesia and black theatre. There is a need, according to this cult, 'of regaining periodically the contents of the subconscious lost or repressed during man's transition from the animal kingdom to the world of humans'.[112] Union with these 'atavisms' is said to dissolve the ego-complex temporarily so that the animal's powers can be assimilated. We found other examples of this in shamanism in Chapter One, and in the experience of Laing's patient. It is Freud's human being getting down on all fours again, and we may see the process fabled in modern commercial cinema, showing how currently interested the public is, in *Wolfen*, *The Howling* and *Cat People*, the last with the image of the mother of the were-panthers sitting in her African tree like black Wisdom.

One of the characters in the novel of *The Wolfen* ruminates on 'the idea of canine senses and a primate brain'. Because a wolf's nose is '200 million times more sensitive' than the human's, 'the sheer quantity of information pouring in must literally be millions of times greater than that reaching a man through his eyes. The mind that gave meaning to all that information must be a miracle indeed. Maybe even greater than the mind of man.' One of the werewolves watches a human 'moving through the dense body-heat and smell of himself and, in the marvellous blindness of humans, not even noticing'. It thinks to itself: 'These poor creatures were blind in all except the visual sense. Nose-blind, ear-blind, touch-blind. They were the best prey in the world.' In the hunting pack the scent of the Wolfen follows them 'like a blaring noise'.[113]

Grant tells us: 'The Adepts of Ancient Egypt used this formula, of which the most ancient and enduring ornament is the Sphinx which combines the Woman and the Beast in a single form.' Bertiaux speaks of a new yoga of 'skin-to-skin immediate presence' and of the sexual organ 'shining like a magic mirror at the time of orgasm'.[114] This is like Coleridge's silver-lettered thighs, or the marital experiences of Von Urban's patients, or the Eskimo shamans who, according to Knud Rasmussen, spoke 'of a mysterious light which the shaman suddenly feels in his body, inside his head, within the brain, an inexplicable searchlight, a luminous fire, which enables him to see in the dark, both literally and metaphorically, for he can now, even with closed eyes, see through darkness . . .'[115]

6 Mere Deviltry

Lest this be thought mere deviltry, let me recall again how the preoccupation of the analytical psychologists, engaged in the practical work of healing modern humans by integrating the forces discovered by depth psychology, converge in this area.

M. T. Colonna writing in the *Journal of Analytical Psychology* equates the Black Moon with Lilith as the redemptive anima and the estranged part, which is nevertheless 'the inexhaustible source of creativity' for creative men who have found their inspiration here in 'the disruptive and magical feminine'.

It is 'the active confrontation with the Black Goddess that assumes significance for the creative act, because "down there" inspiration finds energy and participates in a process of magical awakening'. Because the Black Goddess challenges men with the severe task of restoration she brings anguish and 'confronts man with the necessity of reuniting the earthly and celestial woman in the divided anima'.

This goddess calls for a restoration of the Romantic vision, which Colonna terms '*Dionysian globality*', created out of both Eros and sex'. 'Only in welcoming the demonical can we avoid being possessed' and 'For ages we have separated sex from Eros in order to deny the latter.'[116]

James Hillman, who was once head of the C. G. Jung Institute at Zurich, echoes the same consistent theme, and notes the importance of the subliminal and invisible senses in the quest for wholeness. He quotes Heraclitus: 'Invisible connection is stronger than visible,' for 'to arrive at the basic structure of things we must go into their darkness'. 'Nature loves to hide' – the riddle of the Sphinx – and Hillman evokes a dark 'God of the Invisibles and his bride Persephone'. Hades – whose name was rarely used but who was referred to as the 'unseen one' and as Pluto 'the hidden wealth or the riches of the invisible' – 'is not an absence, but a hidden presence – even an invisible fullness'.

To relate to Hades, says Hillman, is to relate by asking of an experience what it has to do with death, the crossing. Thus everything can 'become deeper, moving from the visible connections to the invisible ones'. Eros itself was part of the brood of night and the brother of death (orgasm is 'the little brother of death'). If this were understood 'there would then be a closer bond between what goes on in dreams and love that fulfils itself in darkness'.

Hillman speaks also of this underworld being inhabited by spirits and ghosts which are 'invisible by nature, and not merely invisible because they have been forgotten or repressed'. To find the dark world is . . . 'to notice the fantasy in the moment, to witness the psyche's shadow play in our unconscious daily living . . . watching not just the physical reality in front of the eyeballs and by means of them, but seeing into the flickering patterns within that physical reality, and within the eyes themselves'; thus there is 'space enough to take in the same physical world but in another way'. He speaks of the soul as ' . . . a vaporous substance . . . a flowing participation . . .'

According to this analyst, the important dreams have access to the less used senses. If you can smell in a dream, then the dream-event is something 'essential, pneumatic, aesthetic, even etherial', for to Hillman 'smell is the undersense'. He quotes Heraclitus again: 'In Hades souls perceive by smelling.' He says: 'Perhaps psychic depths that are not revealed to the more visible, tangible senses require a perceptual mode, such as that of smell, that discriminates amidst what is hidden, a perception of intangibles by intangible means. Psychological work could call for a keen nostril, an ability to perceive subtle bodies, or the body subtly . . . it is the nostrils which discern the spirits.'

In this darkness animals are the soul-bearers; they help us to see in the dark. One goes into this dream darkness, as into the Cloud of Unknowing, without hope, then, 'as the mind's eye dilates in the dark, with increasing surprise and joy', there is a 'darkening of consciousness' which is 'less visual'. In practice, 'The place of one's sensitivity may move from eye to ear and then through the senses of touch, taste, and scent, so that we begin to perceive more and more in particulars, less and less in overviews. We become more and more aware of an animal discrimination going on below our reflections and guiding them.'[117]

Patricia Berry, another Jungian analyst, echoes all this and speaks in terms of goddesses. 'But there came to be a split between the upperworld aspect of Gaia's earth and its underworld aspect . . . The upperworld became a Demeter realm of concrete, daily life, devoid of the spiritual values, the sense of essence and the dark (and beneath the dark) carried by her underworld daughter, Persephone. For reunion with this underworld daughter, Demeter suffers inconsolably. And we without a religious sense that includes and connects us with the earth's depths and essential insubstantiality suffer as well.' Thus Persephone, who is a Black Goddess, is also the Lost Daughter. Apprenticeship to the White Goddess of the full moon, ovulation, physical fertility, is served in the upper world, with Demeter. Jung calls this 'paying the debt to nature' before the work of individuation starts.

In the underworld one is among the essences, the invisible aspects of the upperworld. 'Hades' means the 'invisible' or 'invisibility-giving' in contrast with 'Helios' (the sun) which means 'the visible and visible-making'.

But it is necessary to be at home with underworld essences in order to perceive surface-world differences: the non-visual guides and fulfils the visual because the magical art is the art of 'visualising sensation'.

'In this way, to notice upperworld differences is at the same time to perceive by means of an underworld consciousness of *in*visibles. Thus what we have called perception is not so in the ordinary sense of the word, but a deepening of concrete objects by perceiving them as germinations of the realm of Hades.'

Thus, 'the concrete natural world, unlike the mystical denial of it, is the very way and expression of soul. Demeter/Persephone sees so deeply into objects that she sees through them.'[118] Hekate, the third person of the feminine trinity, is the one that sees all from her cave. She is Mary Lucifer, and is called also *phosphorus*, the light-bringer. This suggests the *lumen naturae*, the light of nature, which we have met equally in the light that fills the shaman's body and the phosphorescence of desolate Coleridge's thigh.

Nathan Schwartz-Salant, an analytical psychologist practising in New York, emphasises that a valued but mysterious experience that occurs during the course of analysis is *not* sex-magic. It is certainly alchemy, and he uses the images of alchemy as described by Jung to characterise what he calls this *conjunctio* experience. It is like the conjunction of the immaterial bodies of analyst and client, and thus recalls the experiences of Frater S.C. and Soror S.M., the 'magic stuff' of Grant's priestess, and also the Oliphants' sympneuma mentioned in Chapter Two.

Schwartz-Salant differs from Jung, in that he considers the *conjunctio* (that condition sought after by the alchemists in their preparation of the stone that would heal all) not merely an 'unconscious ordering factor' that is discovered retrospectively in analysing dreams. He finds that it is 'an imaginal experience *between two people in the here and now*' (my italics; 'imaginal' means 'imagination' in the sense of a perceptive faculty, as I have discussed above).

The *conjunctio* produces kinship between the two persons, in an I-Thou relationship, which is an intense form of the 'transference' so essential to successful analytical work. This is the kinship that Frater S.C. and Soror S.M. referred to when they said that those who share the same sister are all kin. The relationship 'brings a sense of mutual respect, equality and concern on a very deep level, as if blood had been exchanged'.

Another term is *communitas*, implying 'not only the structure of communion or community but also a kind of "substance", as though it could be transmitted'. This substance is a 'paradoxical' combination of physical and psychic realities. We have seen how this could occur in actuality.

The *conjunctio* is also 'liminal', a term which in rites of passage denotes that state of separation from the 'surface-world' before one's reincorporation in a new status which results from the sojourn in the activated other world. Thus it is identical with the 'crossing'. 'It is in liminality that *communitas* emerges,' as, when in the liminality of sexual intercourse, the visionary no-time state of the magical orgasm, the partners become 'one flesh'. Thus 'the experience of the *conjunctio* is often one in which one feels neither male nor female, and the "self that hovers / in between" can be hermaphroditic' like the initiate blind Tiresias.

Schwartz-Salant describes such an experience, in the analytical hour, with no physical contact, as follows: ' . . . I experienced an erotic energy field between us. She also experienced it. As we both felt this energy, which seemed like something between us, my consciousness lowered a bit and, just as in active imagination, I saw a shimmering image, which partook of both of us, move upwards from where it was, near the ground . . . She said she knew that if she descended into her body, it would be too intense, that she was afraid. She stated that she now felt I was her friend, that it felt like an I-Thou relationship, and that she had never had such an experience before with anyone . . . A feeling of timelessness pervaded; I didn't know if one minute or twenty had passed . . . '

The analyst describes the *conjunctio* as 'gnosis-yielding', and he found that after it there was 'a transformation of inner sadistic anima or animus figures' and that he had seen this result many times; which is to say that the demons gave up their energy for use and awareness.[119] In another case-history Schwartz-Salant describes how a woman dreamed of a little black girl, called Kore (Persephone's other name), who expressed and understood her rage by turning into a wolf-child. He refers to the split-off 'Persephone-like souls' of his patients.[120]

For the analyst, the temenos of his room and the enclosure of his hour; for the Wiccan, the traditional magic circle; both are places in which experiences such as this *conjunctio* may equally occur by following the symbols wherever they may lead, especially the dark image of Mary Light-bearer, and creating objects that possess 'neither a purely physical nor a purely psychic reality but a paradoxical combination of them both'. These are the traditional magical tools of the witch, which by making and handling live in both worlds. The *conjunctio* is a rebirth, and all who undergo it emerge as kin. These are the relationships that so horrified the aged Oedipus at Colonus, but as if he had conceived children from his daughter-sisters as well as from his mother. Yet these were the ancient kinships figured between humans and nature-deities. As Goethe said, in nature everything exists in a state of radical inter-penetration and variously reveals the perduring archetypes.[121]

Schwartz-Salant says that 'in a sense, incest is committed on the level of the subtle body'. This is because it takes place in that temenos or activated space – called virtual space by aestheticians describing the magical effect of paintings – which is the womb of the dark goddess. Schwartz-Salant describes the process well, in terms which any magical initiator might be proud of, and which also suit our age. 'The energy of incest, which is a Dionysian-like effect that was never properly received in childhood, is now experienced with a "brother" or "sister" to the higher goal of creating kinship . . . Incestuous energy, perhaps better called Dionysian energy, gains a proper container in the analytic "*conjunctio*" '[122] – which, as Frater S.C. tolerantly admits, is an appropriate system of experience.

In other words, no person can assimilate the wonder and power of their own creation in the dark furnace of their mother's womb, when they recapitulate 9 billion years of evolution on planet Gaia, plant, animal, primate, in a mere nine months. Yet the personal mother's womb is only a knot or *ankh*, as it were, of the Great Mother's womb, which is all around us, full of the forces which made us, and which can remake us. We may obtain rebirth from it, as it were from Demeter's womb as our children, grandchildren and great-grandchildren; or from black daughter Persephone's womb as our own selves with more than mundane potentialities in play – it may be with evolutionary possibilities that are not suitable for discussion in Demeter's family circle where the children must be reared. It matters little whether we do this latter thing in the secular analyst's hour or in the magical space of the poet's page or painter's canvas or in the temple, Wiccan circle, or lover's bed – in all these places we can re-encounter the invisible powers that made us in whatever guise they come, and release a little more of their energies each time for our use and awareness.

7 Lucid Frenzy

And of course the women, the womb-bearers, have always known this. The Black Goddess may be to male artists, as she was to Robert Graves, 'so far hardly more than a word of hope whispered among the few who have served their apprenticeship to the White Goddess . . .' but many women artists have long proclaimed and practised her ways, which have been ignored by the male establishment until recent changes of consciousness, brought about largely by the women's movement.

The surrealist movement bears all the hallmarks of the Romantic-Gnostic, the temenos or sacred space being the canvas or the page of painter and poet. To quote Kenneth Grant again, 'The mental exaltation generated by a magically controlled orgasm forms a lucent lens-like window past which streams the vivid astral imagery of the subconscious mind.' This fact was well known to the surrealists: the word 'surrealism' should be understood to mean 'heightened reality' or 'beyond ordinary reality'.

André Breton, 'a figure of endless complexity and endless fascination,'[123] with his Surrealist manifesto nominally the founder of this movement, practised the magical art of 'visualising sensation'. He celebrates the parts of a woman's body as plants, fruits, trees, as though she were an odorous and electrical map of the universe, as in magical tradition she is, and among Surrealist poets the sexual organs of women were constantly compared to flowers.

'Flowers' is also a euphemism or metaphor for the period in a kind of punning green language which acknowledges that the woman is now a flow-er and the flow is perfumed, as with the *kalas*.

Breton remarked: *'C'est la terre qui, en quelque sorte, ordonne à travers la femme'* ('It is the earth, which, as it were, dictates/ordains through woman.')[124]

Nerval has a wonderful dream which shows the same spirit as Breton: 'The lady I followed, moving her lively body forward with a motion that caused the folds of her dress in changing taffeta to glitter, graciously placed her bare arm around a long stem of hollyhock, then started to grow under a clear ray of light in such a manner that the garden slowly took her form, trees and flower-beds becoming the roses and ornaments of her garment; while her figure and her arms printed their contours on the sky's purple clouds.'[125]

Jules Michelet's study of witchcraft, *La Sorcière*, influenced Breton profoundly. It altered his attitude to women, and was therefore a powerful force in the Surrealist movement, which was strongly supportive of women in many ways unique at the time.

Michelet was a nature-philosopher and historian who believed in the natural continuum, and in nature's artistic creativity; according to Edward K. Kaplan he 'has just begun to take his rightful place beside Victor Hugo and Honoré de Balzac as a luminary of French Romanticism'. He believed that 'women were necessary to humanise men' and argued this view in his first educational book *Priest, Woman and Family* (1845). He believed in the Earth as 'an animal, a mother' who possesses '"an expanding and burning soul", a molten mineral core endowed with a will to become living,' a Gaia suffused with electricities.

His beliefs were a product of direct experience, of gnosis from an unexpected quarter. 'His gradual conversion to a natural religion was completed during his therapeutic mud bathing at Acqui, Italy.' The ailing historian believed that his physical rejuvenation came from direct contact with the powers of Mother Earth, as with Pound's fluid CHTHONOS.

The earth was a vital source, and his immersion in that source and subsequent cure proved to him that this was more than a symbol. 'His immersion in the hot mud leads to an impressive intuition *by physical participation* of nature's spiritual substratum . . . "In my magnificent coffin of white marble, I underwent the first application of the black mud."'

He uses the French word *limon* in preference to the more common *boue*, as the former denotes the clay from which God formed Adam in the French Bible. Kaplan tells how reverie lulled Michelet's mind and then annulled the barrier between himself and the earth. 'Ideas disappeared in my profound absorption. The only idea which remained was that of *Terra mater*. I felt her plainly, caressing and pitying and warming her wounded child. From without? Internally also. For she interpenetrated my frame with her vivifying spirits, entered into and blended with me, insinuated into my being her very soul . . . So strong was the marriage, and more than a marriage, between me and the Earth! One might more fitly have called it *an exchange of nature*.'

There seemed to be an actual elixir, fluid CHTHONOS remaining on the skin: 'I was renewed. When I emerged, an indescribable unctuous gleam shone upon my body. A certain organic element, wholly distinct from minerals, and whose nature we are ignorant of, gives the effect of a living contact, of having communicated with the invisible soul . . . ' *La Sorcière* was published in 1862 long after this experience.[126]

From it Breton adopted Michelet's conclusions that the woman was endowed with two special creative gifts: *the inspiration of lucid frenzy* and the power of parthenogenesis or 'unaided conception'. Thus Breton and Aragon celebrated the fiftieth anniversary of hysteria by publishing photographs from the Salpêtrié hospital archives, and provided a redefinition of hysteria, or prophetic speech, from a mental disorder to a poetic precept. They wrote: 'Hysteria *is not a pathological* phenomenon and can in every way be considered as *a supreme means of expression*.'[127] This recalls the manner in which C. G. Jung elaborated his psychotherapeutic system on the basis of female ecstatic experience, in the Miller 'fantasies' and the Visions Seminars.

Whitney Chadwick remarks in her study that 'in recognising her intuitive connection with the magic realm of experience that governed creation, Surrealism offered the woman artist a self-image that united her roles as woman and creator in a way that neither the concept of the *femme-infant* nor that of the erotic muse could,' but this was rather the late fruit of Surrealism. The figures of the child-woman and her inspired automatisms and the collective Gradiva Muse (*G*isèle, *R*osine, *A*lice, *D*ora, *I*nès, *V*iolette) dominated its early years. One letter moved would alter the word to 'gravid': from trance-maiden to mother.

The prime artistic and magical need had seemed to be to effect a synthesis between male and female principles, between what was unconscious in the man – the world of women; and what was unconscious in the woman – the world of men. In this work, 'As a glorification of spiritual fecundity, the myth of the androgyne becomes a celebration of spiritual procreation.'[128] The fusion of man and woman had its obvious counterpart in the sexual act, but this could take place on more than the physical level, as in the *conjunctio* experience. But there were other priorities. The women artists found that other regions of the psyche not visible to men became a chief concern – their 'split-off, Persephone-like souls'.

The images formed by the male artists were not in themselves the gnosis for the women. It was essential for the latter to find the *feminine* gnosis, long cursed by men as sorcery and witchcraft, for themselves. If the old magical saying was true – that only man was cast forth from the garden of Eden, while woman remained behind – then that fact had been carefully concealed from the latter. The masculine images were the riddles presented; the answer was the gnosis itself but, before the great work could be accomplished, the riddles had to be solved, and not in the manner of Oedipus. Thus the women uncovered their own new-knowledge, restoring the Black Goddess for themselves to begin with, but now perhaps for the evolution of the world.

Whitney Chadwick says that all the Surrealist visions of women converge in the figure of the serpent-tailed Melusine, a fairy-woman avatar of Lilith. Breton's wife Elisa had the 'rosiness of flowers' and was to him a reincarnation of this being. 'Melusine concentrates the telluric forces of nature in herself . . . her transformation into a serpent that must remain hidden relates her to female Earth . . . Endowed with supernatural powers, Melusine holds the key to mysteries forbidden to men . . .'[129]

Melusine was also a fertility goddess, but the Demeter aspect of her power interested the Surrealists less than the art generated from interior sources. Chadwick says that the mere images of fecundity were soon discarded for an immediate here and now identification of the woman with the very core of nature. It was an assumption into the goddess herself. 'The blood trickles through the grass, is mingling with the dew, it evaporates and is replaced by the wind,' says Eluard when comparing Valentine Penrose's use of language to the natural transformations of nature itself, as though it and she were a magic mirror to those forces. She 'would return naturally to her underlying temperament of the benign witch'. Ithell Colquhoun commented years later: 'Breton's vision of the "free and adored woman" didn't always prove a practical help for women, especially painters.'[130]

Meret Oppenheim was among the first to identify the woman artist with forces mediated by the female magician or witch, the 'child of nature'. She worked with Max Ernst, whose forest paintings and *frottages* evoke a totemic world; Oppenheim's work reveals 'her belief in nature as the dwelling place of the female creative spirit'. She was also one of the few in Surrealist Paris of the 1930s to prefer Jung's view to that of the phallocentric Freud, and she found her intuitions confirmed by undergoing Jungian analysis: 'One could imagine that the first state was matriarchal . . . Eve has been damned, and the snake with her – by men.'[131]

Again, Leonora Carrington had drawn her imagery from hermetic sources long before she read *The White Goddess* in 1948, but said that reading it 'was the greatest revelation of my life'. Her painting and writing drew absolutely on the magical tradition. In one painting, *The Godmother* (1970), 'The central being with the invisible face, according to the artist, shows no differentiation between the five senses, and it also contains the sixth and seventh psychic senses.' Awakened being has a 'black monkey face' in this picture, and this is the Black Sun 'through which alchemical illumination and enlightenment are achieved. It represents the vision of the inner eye . . .'

Her novel *The Hearing Trumpet* is a female grail quest. The horn through which the heroine Marian hears stories of her various incarnations, the trumpet itself, is an 'organ of interior perception', a womb cornucopia: as Marian is ninety-two years old it is no longer fecund, except of insight. A painting on the walls of the community to which she is banished by her family leads her to acquire occult powers. It is the portrait of a former abbess who 'had wanted to obtain a precious liquid from the tomb of Mary Magdalene', an elixir of life. Such discoveries belonged particularly to the woman. Again in the painting *Lepidopteros*, the black swans refer to 'a secret matriarchal song . . . "I am the Black Swan, Queen of Them All."' *The Garden of Paracelsus* (1957) refers to the great fifteenth-century physician whose work was the foundation of modern medical science, but which also foreshadowed the magnetic theory of Mesmer. He believed 'that the universal spirit or astral body of man could be created by combining the quintessence of each animal, mineral and plant . . . that astral bodies communicate with each other . . .' and the painting suggests a direct experience of this world. Carrington's animals in her short story 'The House of Fear' (1937) replace male Surrealists' 'reliance on the image of woman as the mediating link' between the human and the marvels of natural life. The hyena is the fertile night; the horse an image of rebirth.[132]

Thus 'Surrealism followed a path that led inexorably towards the domain of Faust's Mothers,' those mysterious Chthonic deities. The associations between the powers of women and the telluric depths, the night and the moon, proved to be sources of strength and self-definition. It does seem rather one-sided that, as for Breton, erotic love was the way man's creative powers could be brought once again into close contact with the transforming energies that were the basis of the universe, and 'love was the means by which man moved into the circle of woman's magic powers . . . ' Graves's idea of the function of the poet is that he recognises the Muse's glory, of which *as a woman in this age she may be unconscious*. In return for reflecting it, she lends him her magical powers. This idea was movingly dramatised in the film *Diva*, for the great black singer had never heard her own voice, until the boy-hero recorded it surreptitiously at a concert and played it to her. Nobody, on the other hand, pointed to Bernard Shaw's *The Black Girl in Search of God* and cried out, 'It's you!' so she settled down to a life of child-bearing with a red-haired Irishman instead.

Notwithstanding the Surrealist insistence on the liberation of woman from the bondage of hearth and home, Chadwick says that theoretically she existed to complement the male creative cycle. However, men and women in the movement formed interacting but fairly independent groups. The women artists from the beginning showed needs and acted in ways which did not fit into any male myth. They set out to find their firm ground by affirming the fundamental forces that differentiated the feminine experience from the masculine. Ithell Colquhoun sent Penelope Shuttle, as elder to younger, a copy of her famous *Osmazone* (a word which seems to mean both 'smelling-place' and 'perfume of the whore'). This happened after Shuttle had sent a copy of *The Wise Wound* to the distinguished painter. Colquhoun's standpoint is as plain as any of the sources cited in the Shuttle–Redgrove book:

'One day in the translucent water I felt strange and found that my body was exuding a dark glue, not quite a blood. I knew what had happened: the revelation of the Plain years before had told me what to expect . . . Certain wise savages still put their women in a hut of reeds, away from the village . . . the tribe thus gives each woman a few days each month of rest and solitude, for contact with the night-side of her own nature. Will no one listen? This is what must be done, though it makes civilisation turn over. It is harmful to attempt a normal appearance – business, housework, the catching of trains – when normality is absent, and its place taken by intensified sensibility to hidden springs . . . Through retirement I became reconciled to the moon.'[133]

Chadwick says that it was indeed Ithell Colquhoun who

transformed what is usually a masculine identification of woman's creative powers with those of generative nature 'into an intuitive alchemy of natural forms'. Colquhoun uses 'natural forms as a starting-point for divinatory explorations'. She recalls how she visited the Bretons in Paris in the summer of 1939, when they were surrounded by a new group of young painters discussing a technique they called psychomorphology, which was 'an effort to tap that level of consciousness sometimes perceptible between sleeping and waking which consists of coloured organic (non-geometric) forms in a state of flux'.

Colquhoun published her *The Mantic Stain* in 1949. Her starting-point is the technique recommended by da Vinci, Blake and Ernst of allowing an apparently random stain on a wall to suggest every manner of fantastic and magical form. It is a reverie, a concentration and a relaxation, and a way of stimulating the inner senses to awake to their contents. Of course, no stain is random as its shape is dictated by all the forces around it. Colquhoun in this visual alchemy of transformation is pursuing the 'mantic or divinatory characteristics of the stained surface' and concludes that such techniques used in Surrealism are close to the ink splashes, sand, tea leaves and crystal globe of the clairvoyant. She identifies the so-called 'automatic techniques' of *sfumage, écremage, decalcomania* and powdering with the four elements of earth, air, fire and water as alchemical techniques, referring to alchemists such as Eirenaeus Philalethes. She has also written distinguished books on modern magic. For her it is these improvisatory or aleatory techniques that can catch the mutations and transformations of the other world competently; and the same is true with similar language techniques. She concludes that such methods 'all have an august ancestry in that they are traceably allied to the "great work" of alchemy'.[134]

It transpires that it is not the images of physical fecundity that have been of most use to contemporary women artists, not the Demeter surface-world; but rather the underground vision of the Black Goddess Persephone: the night – or supersensible – vision. In 1951 Alice Rahon wrote how 'in earliest times painting was magical . . . It was a key to the invisible.' She said the value of it was its power as a conjunction: 'Like the shaman, the sybil and the wizard, the painter had to make himself humble, so that he could share in the manifestation of spirits and forms.' There was a Persephone-like transformation of the Demeter world; for instance, Carrington found 'that mixing egg tempera seemed to mimic culinary procedure' and she and Varo evolved a vision of 'the woman creator whose creative and magical powers were a higher development of traditional domestic activities like cooking'.[135]

So close was the link between some women artists and the animal forms that the Sphinx image seemed inevitable. In Carrington it replaced, with the Animal Muses, the female Muse of the men Surrealists. Léonor Fini's *Chthonian Divinity Watching Over the Sleep of a Young Man* (1947) shows a black Sphinx presiding over the sleep of an androgynous youth. In this painter's work, 'The hybrid Sphinx mediates between the human and the bestial . . . a symbolic reunification of a human and civilised world that she views as lacking passion and animality, and an animal world in which the magical powers of animals may help humans to understand their own loss of connection to a more primordial nature.'

And, for Léonor Fini, woman is priestess and sorceress: 'By assuming the form of the Sphinx she exercises all the powers that have been lost to contemporary women.' She says, 'The man in my painting sleeps because he refuses the animus role of the social and constructed . . .'

Other Sphinxes of Fini, as in *Sphinx Philagria* (1945) and *Sphinx Regina* (1946), were described by her friend Jean Genet as existing in a world of 'swampy odours' and 'cruel kindness'. *Petite Sphinx Ermite* (1948) portrays a child-Sphinx dressed in black who seems exiled from this world that men refuse to help build, but the sexual power is biding its time in the form of a 'fleshy pink flower' hanging from the lintel of a doorway.[136] Her *Le Bout du Monde* (1949) shows a golden-haired, golden-skinned woman emerging from a reflecting watery surface which mirrors the same woman black-skinned and black-haired. Fini's picture is a perfect representation of the golden madonna of ovulation and motherhood with her counterpart, the exiled Black Goddess of supersensible eroticism of the other culmination of the fertility rhythm: the spiritually fertile menstrual period, in which disturbing underworld power is exercised.

Fini herself should have the last word in this: 'I have never been attracted by fecundity. It is the refusal of utility: participation in the continuity of the species is an abdication. In order to have children a humility nearly inconceivable in the modern world is necessary, a brutalised passivity or a mad pretension . . . Myself, I know that I belong with the idea of Lilith, the anti-Eve, and that my universe is of the spirit. Physical maternity instinctively repulses me.'[137] The Demeter role is not the only one.

How important this figure of Lilith-Melusine and its exile, as the demonic powers of wind, storm and water,[138] has been in world history, and how essential it is to women and all others that she returns is again clearly put in Barbara Black Koltuv's *The Book of Lilith*.[139] It appears that the whole of Judeo-Christianity was built on the repression of this figure, the putting down to the lowest depths of exile this wonderful magical part of women.

Jung calls Lilith the 'shamanistic anima'. Koltuv is another neo-Jungian analyst, actively midwifing this rebirth of the Black Goddess into modern society. She quotes a case-history of a woman in which the Shekhina (heavenly) and Lilith (earthly) aspects of the dreamer 'had come together and been transformed into a powerful image of the feminine self' which would now guide the patient.

Koltuv says: 'Lilith is that part of the Great Goddess that has been rejected and cast out in post-biblical times. She represents the qualities of the feminine self that the Shekhina alone does not carry.' These words recall strongly Fini's painting of the golden woman, conjoined with the black woman beneath the surface of the pool.

Koltuv enumerates these qualities. The first is 'lunar consciousness', for 'a woman experiences the Eve and Lilith sides of her nature in the ebb and flow of her menstrual cycle. In the first half of the cycle, Eve is ascendant; anticipating ovulation and perhaps conception she feels receptive, open and related. When conception does not occur, Lilith holds sway. Hope gives way to despair and the raging premenstrual witch carries her off to the desolate wilderness and bitterness of the menstrual hut.' However, as all I have quoted have shown, from 'black' magicians to modern women artists, that rage of non-conception in the physical sense is the gateway to magic and extra-sensual perception, for Lilith is also 'the rungs of the ladder of prophecy'. This Lilith magic refused, according to the Talmud, is the origin of the 'plagues of mankind'.

The second rejected quality of the goddess that Lilith represents 'is the body – instinctuality, and sexuality': the body alive with all its potentialities of the subliminal senses as it is with the animals.

Thirdly, Lilith represents 'prophetic inner logic . . . directly felt and experienced within oneself, unmediated by word of law'. Geoffrey Hartman in his seminal book on certain Romantic poets calls this the 'unmediated vision', the 'direct sensuous intuition of reality'. In particular, Koltuv says, 'Lilith is a younger aspect of the Goddess and does not have to wrest the power of the word from the father Gods. She already knows it.'

The fourth quality carried by Lilith, according to Koltuv, is to match up to the male God, father and creator, by adding to the Godhead the qualities of God the Mother and Creatrix. This seems weighted a little too much on the ovulation side, so I would add a fifth quality: that of initiatrix of the male magician out of his self-assumed regal authority in a world in which he has become with his science a mere onlooker or tourist (and with his royal simper not sure where he is, but believing he is king of it), through blindness and humility to rebirth. Such a reborn one would be sensitive to the woman's dark body of data and rhythm through his black senses, and closely associated with her wise blood.

8 Blackness Visible

In this process, it might seem that what the male magician desires most is to become both female, and black. We have suggested how the feminine can and might impart initiatory gifts, but what of blackness in its literal sense, of *négritude*? In studying African ways of knowledge it seems the 'black' magicians are trying to find a *négritude* in themselves. Is there any quality in this core blackness which carries such supremely desirable qualities? Certain writers would affirm that there is.

We have seen how Massey's insistence that Africa was the cradle of humanity has been vindicated by modern research, and will, I suspect, be further vindicated on the cultural level, by following his pointers.

Massey conjures up the African progenetrix, from whom we all may have sprung, in his figure of the ancient Egyptian child's doll of the 'black negroid Isis with her veil or net thrown back'. This was the veil that the inscription in the Isiac temples declared 'had been lifted by no man'. But a woman, or the goddess herself, may lift it.

Massey says of Egypt and the colours of skin there: 'All the four colours, black, red, yellow, and white, meet upon the monuments, and they all blend in Egyptian types. The red men and the yellow are there as Egyptians, with the background of black out of which the modifications emerge'; that is, black was the human beginning. 'The problem of origin cannot be worked back again from white, yellow, or red to black, as it can forwards from black . . . ' He speaks of the 'black blood-royal'. It seems certain to him 'that the black race is the most ancient, and that Africa is the primordial home . . . The genetrix represented as the Dea Multimammae, the Diana of Ephesus, is found as a black figure, nor is the hue mystical only, for the features are as negroid as were those of the black Isis in Egypt.' It is even suggested that the origin of white skin may have been from the sickness of leprosy.[140]

We should expect to find in at least some modern writers on *négritude* those qualities and that world-view which I have described in this book as Romantic–Gnostic.

This proves to be so. Léopold Sédar Senghor, for instance, in his essay 'The African Apprehension of Reality'[141] considers how the European will face an object only as an objective intelligence, a warrior, a man of will, a bird of prey; how he separates it from himself, distinguishes it, fixes it, kills it; and in a pitiless Cartesian analysis, dissects it, then makes use of it. Senghor quotes an old African sage he had talked to: 'White men are cannibals. They have no respect for life . . . It is life which makes human, not death. I am afraid it may all turn out very badly. The whites by their madness to destroy will in the end bring troubles upon us.'

Senghor says that an African's black skin is like a primordial night. Like night which unites all in feeling, he does not start out by distinguishing himself from stone, tree, man animal or social event. 'Once he has come under its influence, he takes it like a blind man, still living, into his hands. He does not fix it or kill it. He turns it over and over in his supple hands, he fingers it, he *feels* it.' The black man is in touch, discovering like a 'pure sensory field' *subjectively*, as an insect discovers with its feelers. Whereas the European like a bird of prey with greedy centripetal movement devours the object, the black man 'is *moved* to his bowels, going out in a centrifugal movement from the subject to the object on the waves sent out from the Other'. There is material energy, and there is psychic energy: 'Perhaps in the electric waves which set off nerve cells, the subject perceives both kinds.'

There is also a directly perceived continuum, which is rhythmi- cal, as in African music and dancing: ' . . . the movements of the brain and of the world: the beating of the heart, breathing, the rhythm of walking and making love, ebb and flow, succession of days and seasons and in general all the rhythms of the cosmos . . . It is this cosmic rhythm, with its variations and harmonies, which the object gives out . . . also at the height of the emotion the rhythms of the heart and breath fall into agreement with it . . . '

Senghor tells us how one of his African friends confesses that all beauty, of whatever kind, 'strikes him at the root of the belly and gives rise to a sexual feeling'. This is not only dancing or music or an African mask, but also the High Mass of Catholicism. But it is ESSP as well – for ' . . . the African's spirituality is rooted in his sensuality: in his physiology'.

Thus the African 'does not kill the other life, he strengthens his own life through it . . . [it is] an intimacy of mingled bodies, the acts of love from which the fruit of knowledge is born.'

It is a process of the dark senses, not the distancing eye. How does the Senegalese voter know that his deputy knows *him*? 'I want you to smell me,' he cries. 'To greet', in Wolof, has the same etymology as 'to breathe'. 'I smell, I dance the *Other*.' It is the 'reason-by-embrace'.

Also, there is no distinction between natural and supernatural needs; all events have *significance* to which the human being responds with *emotion*. This is by no means a failure of consciousness but 'on the contrary, the accession to a higher state of consciousness', complete consciousness because 'the subject moved and the moving object are united in an indissoluble synthesis'. Senghor asserts that 'it is this gift of emotion which explains *négritude*'. Elizabeth Sewell has called it 'post-logical thought'.[142]

Janheinz Jahn is concerned systematically to define neo-African culture. He discusses voodoo, and says that the possessed person maintains contact and understanding of where he is at all times, but that in the ecstatic condition mental conflicts are removed or smoothed out in the presence of the greater pattern of the possessing being, the *Ioa*. 'The heightening of the physical and mental powers . . . seems to us the true aim of all voodoo ceremonies; here lies the meaning, the social function and the value of voodoo . . . all serve only to increase the physical and mental powers . . . '

Thus arrives Legba, the opener of the highway of the gods, which streams upwards from the earth, through the main roof-post of the voodoo temple. Damballah comes along it and rides his mount, the human, who writhes in the dust like a serpent, the 'maker of invisible life apparent', or climbs up to the roof and hangs from the rafters:

the great fertility snake with his wife the rainbow-serpent Ayida-Oeddo. Then the beautiful and compassionate Erzulie-Freda-Dahomey strolls into the peristyle on *her* human mount, male or female, throwing kisses and seductive glances at all the men. It is she who will marry the discontented spouse of a difficult marriage, and appear in sexual dreams on Mondays, Wednesdays and Fridays, to impart sexual fulfilment and instruction as the 'other wife'. Or, indeed, like the calumny which was the medieval succubus-incubus of the witches (an avatar of Lilith), she will appear as the 'other husband' to satisfy the discontented wife; and thus repair the sick marriage.

In African thought as defined by this author, there are no separate things, there is only the force and the continuum. Everything is force and energy, so there is no real barrier, except that in men's minds, between the sacred and the profane. The dance is the human participation in this energy, and the 'possession' an assimilation or assumption to its greater patterns, the conscious acquiescence to them, the spiritual patterns which formulate life at its best and most intense.

Everybody knows the dance called the rumba, but how many whites know that, whenever or wherever it is danced all over the world, it is the Black Daughter of the Sea-Goddess who is dancing: '*Carida, caritas, love*'? Jahn has studied in his book the presentations of the basic philosophy of five different peoples who evidently have the Romantic vision immemorially established in their culture: Baluba, Rwandese, Dogon, Bambara and Haitians. Massey sees it in all original African culture.

Jahn says the artist, in particular the poet, is properly a magician, who by his or her transformations and feeling for everything releases for human use the powers of the universe through the power of the word, called *Nommo*. *Nommo* is also water and heat and the life-force itself. Language issues from the mouth in a hot water-vapour 'which is both water and word'. We have seen how the ancient Greeks believed this, with the inspiration of the *thymos* in the *phrenes* of their poets and heroes. The person who has power over the word directs the life-force.

For this person, 'The world is flesh and son of the flesh; on the sea and in the sky, on the dunes, on the rocks, in the wind, the Negro finds again the velvet of the human skin; in the belly of the sand, in the thighs of heaven, it is himself he is caressing; he is flesh of the flesh of the world . . . ' or, as the great Middle-English poem has it, he is 'Erthe Upon Erthe'.

Like Rilke he or she is 'porous to every breeze' and the Aeolian harp plays in his or her skin. He or she is alternately female and male, like Tiresias, for they merge one with the other in the sexual act, which is to them the celebration of the mystery of being. There is a compatability between all disciplines; the poet is doctor and theologian also, for a medical theory which contradicted a theological proposition which was not poetry would be an absurdity.

What we call the spirit world interpenetrates with our own, as in Senghor's poetry: 'Then I returned from Fa'oye, after drinking from the solemn tomb. And it was the hour when the spirits are visible, when the light is transparent . . . With my head on your breast . . . I would breathe the scent of our dead, that I might receive their life-giving voices and learn to live.'[143]

Such statements recall the parallel European vision, also struggling for its life, so marvellously compiled by Roger Cardinal: ' . . . such a magical state of receptivity to sense-impressions that colours, sounds and scents seem to merge into one . . . ' for 'love gives another stimulus to a deep reading of nature's text; the loved one emits a paradisal light in which all things are seen to connect in a paradisal light,' because of '"the fusion of the five senses that is imagination"' maybe in an encounter 'with a girl who transmits her sensuality through the heady mimosa scent that radiates from her body', for 'the source of the energy which illuminates all aspects of the analogical universe is erotic energy'.[144]

Sartre says of the black poets taught in the missionary schools, learning to speak free words in the language of the oppressors, 'What did you expect when you took away the muzzle closing those black lips? Did you think they would sing your praises?' What the oppressors got they dismissed as 'mere Surrealism'. Jahn retorts that, history or no, it *is Nommo* which rocks the layers of the earth. Cesaire writes: 'I would find again the secret of the great communications, of the great conflagrations. I would speak storm. I would speak river. I would speak tornado.' Stevens concurs: 'His soil is Man's intelligence.' 'The weakness of many men is that they do not know how to become a stone or a tree' since the art of dying to oneself into the blackness and the cloud of unknowing is lost, the art of possession is lost.[145]

It will return: 'One must be able to transform oneself. It brings pleasure.' For the European who has, as we have seen, by all his training and education, a deficient sense of reality, there is a 'fear inherent in the attempt to gain an unmediated, direct sense intuition' equivalent to approaching the snaky countenance of the Gorgon. We are all in the same boat; it is clear that scientific and sociological research is needed in the areas I have indicated throughout this book; but personal research is necessary also, very personal research. Wole Soyinka would prefer to follow Coleridge's example and not set up Manichean opposition between 'thinking' and 'feeling'. However, when he imagines his 'authentic black innocent' in the Masseyan virginal village confronting the pith-helmeted figure of Descartes, he calls out his thought-felt syntactical-diagnosis: 'You are one-who-thinks, white-creature-in-pith-helmet-in-African-jungle-who-thinks and, finally, white-man-who-has-problems-believing-in-his-own-existence.'[146]

FOUR

THE EGYPTIAN DARKNESS

'Neither be anxious to ask whether I actually possess the precious treasure. Ask rather whether I am acquainted with the nature of the Egyptian darkness.'[1]

1 Research

I have tried to provide stimulus and opportunities for research throughout this book by presenting not only the ideas but the sources of the ideas, so that the interested reader can follow his or her own pathways through the notes and 'works cited'. There are some basic exercises, however, that I think most people will find useful. I have no space to give more than outlines, from which, nevertheless, much can come.

Some of the best of these exercises are so simple that most people will not bother to try them. That, then, will be their loss. The best one of these I got from Robin Skelton.[2] I call it 'Sealed Writing'.

It is simply that you write down whatever comes into your head for twenty minutes or so before you go to bed, or at another convenient relaxed time. You persist, whatever you think you have or have not written, or even if you find you can write no more than a single word again and again. Most important of all *you do not read it* – yet. You persist for three months, or a full month at least. At the end of this time, you read it; better still, hand it to a trusted friend to read. He or she will quote something, and you'll say, 'That's good – who wrote it?' Your friend then shows you the page: 'You did!' After this, everything changes.

You can find by this method that there is something in you that speaks better than you know. In such a script there never fails to occur a confusion, then, at the height of this, a relaxation, followed by a synaesthesia: the senses come together in the words and some beautiful image appears; moreover that image and its theme are likely to surface again and again, forming at last a coherent statement which you yourself will be unaware of, until you read it. People who are writers can lift out this new and precious system and allow it to develop by their normal working-methods. In any event, it is an important personal discovery. Language, which can handle all the senses, thought and feeling too, clears like a magic mirror to the supersensible, which includes one's inner senses and further personality. I have supervised hundreds of these scripts, and they have never failed to stimulate development in people who persist with the method. Nobody can believe this who has not tried it; one must simply go at it with a 'willing suspension of disbelief'.

It is a good idea, if one becomes stuck during the twenty minutes, deliberately to move the senses away from the eyes. As Hillman says: 'The place of one's sensitivity may move from eye to ear and then through the senses of touch, taste, and scent, so that we begin to perceive more and more in particulars, less and less in overviews' (see Chapter Three above). After a bit of practice, one can approach the exercise magically: that is, with an intention, which may be put humbly to one's inner self as a request. For example, I could say, 'Please allow me to know more of the Black Goddess,' and continue my sealed writing. After my three months were up, I would look back and see that I had gathered much unconscious information. Many of the patterns of this book were discovered in this way.

One's 'sealed writing' is the companion to all the subsequent exercises, in the sense that it will begin to pick up from everything one does. Another incredibly simple exercise that most people will not bother to try, but which reveals the normally invisible world, is whole breathing. One should get instructions from a good yoga book,[3] but basically whole breathing is filling and emptying, with easy continued breathing, the whole capacity of the lungs: lower abdomen, midriff and upper chest. If you get the way of doing this, and as an exercise start whole breathing while sitting in front of a favourite picture, it is amazing how the colours will change and brighten, new colours and colour relations and planes in the picture emerge, shifting the one over the other. Try it.

One of the most useful *pranayamas* is 'alternate nostril breathing' for which both books I recommend give elaborate instructions. Here, one is in control of an elaborate and sensitive device for perception: nose and lungs. One can distinguish different modes of sensing according to whether one is attending to the in- or out-breath, right or left nostril. It is an excellent experience to do this in a group, with a teacher. One can contemplate changes in body-feeling in the darkness within with eyes closed, or perceive the emergence of previously invisible qualities in the world with eyes open. Every sense is progressively changed by this breathing-work.

There are also walking *pranayamas* in which one can take this new sensitive apparatus outside into nature. The in-breath causes the air to play directly on that portion of the brain which is our smell-organ, about the size of a postage-stamp high in the nose. The consequence is that this powerful dark sense and its associations are stimulated. The sense of smell becomes more acute and its communications are increased. Always the sealed writing is the companion to these practices.

Instructions for sinking within to meet the inner senses by relaxation are also given in yoga books. Penelope Shuttle and I have devised a generally useful combination of these which we give at the back of the 1986 edition of *The Wise Wound*.[4] But these are simply intended as the way to natural relaxation, daydream, and peace of mind, such as we enjoyed when we were children, watching the snow falling or landscapes in a coal fire or the wind undulating in the wheat. The natural relaxation in the presence of animals is particularly important, as will have been understood from Chapter One. Sealed writing will be one's companion, and will pick up things which one ordinarily does not, or merely forgets. For developing relaxation a good idea is to look up a qualified hypnotherapist in the yellow pages and get a 'trance induction for auto-hypnosis' – this will take one further, faster. The reader will find that capability in relaxation is basic and a *sine qua non* to all magical systems, and dream-recall is equally important to most of them, as it is to most systems of psychotherapy.

We have heard a lot about dream interpretation in the twentieth century, but the poets Rilke (who refused to be analysed by Freud) and Valéry knew better when they simply contemplated the sleeping body and found it full of Wisdom.[5] It is useful sometimes to consult a person to whom the dream will speak in their language (thus, for a Jungian, the dream-agent will offer, as in courteous speech, a familiar idiom). However, it is more important to *experience* the dreams consciously. If one now adds a dream-journal to the practice, and applies the three-month rule to that, one finds that dreams that one did not understand now become clear after a lapse of time; reading the journal consecutively reveals themes as well – just like the sealed writing, which is a form of waking dream. People often say, 'I don't dream,' but in my experience they do once they offer the dream-agent a promise of attending.[6] Regular relaxation practice will increase dream-recall, and dreams will often re-dream or dream themselves further if recalled during relaxation.

I believe we have difficulty in understanding dreams because they are synaesthetic events; that is, poetic events. The dream we remember is the 'depressive' interpretation of the synaesthetic 'oceanic' dream of the continuum, which we meet as we descend into sleep. The more we are familiar with synaesthetic or poetic events, the better we are able to enter and participate in the continuum. The likeness between dream and poetic language has long been noted: '. . . are not those basic poetic devices emphasised by recent criticism – paradox, ambiguity, irony, tension – devices whereby the poetic imagination subverts the "reasonableness" of language . . . ?' which is to say its 'depressive position' and we can accept '. . . with Trilling . . . the substantial identity between poetic logic (with its symbolism, condensation of meaning, and displacement of accent) and dream logic'.[7] However, language is capable of reaching from 'depressive' to 'oceanic' and back again in one statement if we will let it; and it is this reach of language we pursue with the sealed writing.

It is important to relate the dream to the fertility cycle if one is a woman or living with a woman; to the moon's phases if one is not; and in a younger family to the cycle-days of all the women in it, which will most likely coincide. The reason for doing this is that dreams carry distinct kinds of information according to the cycle-day, and many can be better understood if related to pre-ovulation, ovulation, pre-menstruation and menstruation. The woman leads with this powerful rhythm, which is reflected in the dreams of those about her, just as these bodily events were at one time commonly treated as influential magical or prophetic utterances, as we have seen in the previous chapter. We have also seen the extent of unconscious communication between people – dream-work helps to bring this into consciousness.[8] Of course, the post-menopausal woman is magical too, and her dreams also radiate power.

Watch the atmosphere if you are relating dreams, and note how it changes. Relaxation, or auto-hypnosis and breathing-practice, will have increased your sensitivity to atmosphere, and you may feel it as a warming or cooling in the skin, as changeable perfumes, or as the switching in the air of charged electrical feelings between people. A content or meaning is likely to dart in from the edge of the mind, or be spoken suddenly by another.

Atmospheres can be felt out, as everybody knows, during the course of all kinds of card game and the like. ESP games can be used,[9] but one must not become superstitious about them; that is, one must not give them too much authority. What we know about the unconscious senses is wonderful enough without going overboard about ESP, or magic for that matter. The same applies to fortune-telling, as by Tarot or I Ching, which should be such a 'feeling out of atmospheres' with the aid of the images of the oracle.

There are many books on the market at present that will take one into new recensions of traditional magic. I cannot for myself say that I like all of these or regard them as useful, but that is most likely due to my own limitations, and I have given my opinion of what I do consider useful in preceding pages. I believe that one should avoid masculinist magic as much as masculinist anything else: Oedipal conflict, competition and hierarchy can arise in this area as in any other field. As S.C. says, 'The litany of the goddess is being newly invented every second . . . ' and it is less that she desires *worship* like an angry parent than 'that she rejoices in being *imagined*'.

If one is looking for a good curriculum, I think Culling's G ∴ B ∴ G ∴ is to be recommended or, in Wicca, the Farrars' in particular.[10] Alternatively one may have the temperament that finds, as in Zen, that one has above everything to kick aside the corpses of all prophets and religions.

My suggestions about magical sex in the above pages are fairly explicit. I consider it vitally important in creating the 'fire-snake', or whatever one wants to call the transformative orgasm, that the female partner should be the leader, as it is from her that the power largely comes at the various sexual highs of her cycle or tides. Very little can be undertaken without investigating this, and Shuttle and I discuss it in more detail in *The Wise Wound*.[11]

The male partner can contribute usefully as switch-gear to the congress by learning how to delay his ejaculation. This will come about by practising yoga *bandhas*, or following Stephen Chang's or Mantak Chia's (op.cit.) instructions. S.C. recommends the exercise called the Deer, which is in effect wagging one's tail. One practises contracting the anus in long sequences, and pulling up the perineum and lower abdomen. This strengthens and sensitises the pubococcygeal muscle with its surrounds and is exactly the same exercise recommended for women after pregnancy to strengthen the pelvic floor. S.C. says that one should also practise interrupting the stream of urine whenever one goes to the loo – being careful to stop if at any time it begins hurting. The Deer is also said to strengthen the prostate in men, which is rumoured to be the lower abode of the fire-snake, Kundalini.

The enhancement of the dark senses of the skin that comes from excellent sex may move naturally to sharing the 'mutual angel', not necessarily in temple work, but in any kind of circle or healing work. Nearly everybody has powers as a natural healer, and sex is a way of developing all these kinds of awarenesses that depend on pheromonal and electrical emissions from the aware body, and contact with the continuum.[12]

There are more recondite matters, which may intrigue some. I cannot find whether there is good medical opinion against drinking one's own or another's urine, and it is a practice many will recoil from. Nevertheless, it is used in Indian and Chinese medicine,[13] and S.C. tells me that as a part of his training he 'drank from his own cistern' daily for some years. He said it seemed to do him no harm, except – and to the unprepared ego this would seem harm – that it increased his weather sensitivity almost intolerably. By the same token, however, it appeared to help make him exquisitely sensitive to the 'auras' of others.

He told me that the best practice was to drink from 'the middle channel' every morning on an empty stomach; that is, to reject substantial quantities of the fluid at the beginning and end of urination. The theory was that all the semiochemicals stimulated by the night's dreaming were present in this elixir, and it brought one closer to the animal senses. Chemicals from weather response also accumulate, so one is, in effect, by feeding back, amplifying weather sensitivity. Obviously such a practice is a risk which not everybody would care to take. Ordinary taboos make this difficult too.

S.C. also tells me that Michelet's experience of the Spirit of the Earth during his mud-baths is an actual one. Unfortunately there are no mineral mud-baths obtainable, so far as I am aware, in the United Kingdom. S.C. said he had improvised during warm summer days in a secret wood and stream, and that it was a most magical event of communion with nature through all the substance of the wood lining his skin and clothes (for some, no doubt electrical, reason, this appears not to work so well 'skyclad'. Alex Comfort in one of his two love-books mentions that showering in a shirt relaxes one for sex extraordinarily, as if circuits in the skin were closed.)

I hope I have convinced the reader *passim* that the creative act and the magical act of communion with the world of reality are identical.

Anton Ehrenzweig has described the process superbly, in terms of artistic creation. He speaks of a 'metaphysical longing for a truly life-giving and life-enhancing pictorial space' and by this he means the 'virtual' or 'imaginal' space in which the action of a picture takes place. But the term equally well applies to the page on which a poet writes; or the magical synaesthetic space created as he or she reads the poem; or the space on which a drama is enacted, in which time and space are controlled by the dramatist and players; or the magic circle or temple; or any of the other magical spaces we have discussed in which symbolic transactions take place which image actual transactions in terms of the subliminal senses.

Ehrenzweig says that this space unconsciously stands 'for the fertile womb' and it may 'prove as potent a stimulus as a more direct libidinous eroticism', as Senghor's friend found, watching High Mass.[14]

When Ehrenzweig says, 'Perhaps a mixture of both the sublime and the crudely sexual may prove potent enough to stir into action our dormant syncretistic sensibilities,'[15] he is speaking roughly of my notion of synaesthesia, in that 'syncretistic' is Piaget's term for the 'still undifferentiated' child's vision of the world: magic stuff vibrates everywhere at a kiss. In such a situation, rapid, almost instantaneous 'unconscious scanning' takes place through all the senses.

For Ehrenzweig there are three phases in the creative act: 'schizoid projection, unconscious integration on an undifferentiated manic level and a final depressive introjection'.[16] In the first stage we are assailed by all the demons, and we must have strength enough to withstand them, and release their power to our purposes, as Schwartz-Salant advocates.

In the second stage ' . . . a new realm of the mind envelops us; we are not engulfed by death, but are released from our separate individual existence. We enter the manic womb of rebirth, an oceanic existence outside time and space.' This '"return to the womb" represents the minimum content of all art; Freud saw in it only the basic religious experience'.[17]

In the final 'depressive' stage (he uses the word in its specialised, Kleinian sense, which does not necessarily mean 'depression' – but it does mean *work*) the artist takes stock, the work assumes an independent existence: 'It is astonishing to see how artists after finishing their work may begin to study it in great detail as though it were the work of somebody else' – which is what happens if you follow the three-month rule with dream-journals or sealed writing. 'A mysterious "presence" reveals itself, which gives the work a living personality of its own . . . '[18]

It is to the 'unconscious scanning' that we go for knowledge and, he implies, rebirth through the work, or magical working. Our sense of reality depends on it, according to Ehrenzweig; without it there would be no sense of felt reality, or what he calls plastic reality: 'The plastic effects in perception rest on a vast unconscious substructure, which does not seem to serve any other biological purpose' – which recalls Alex Comfort's argument for functioning human pheromones.

'Psychotic vision can go dead and irrelevant in this way because of its lack of a "contact barrier" with a rich unconscious substructure.'[19] Without a 'contact barrier', an image or device, a ceremony, a littoral between the worlds, a symbol on which plays the rich black light of the unconscious senses, 'Descartes in the pith helmet' has difficulties in believing in his own or anyone else's reality.

Unconscious vision has superior efficiency in 'scanning the total visual field'; it is a fact that 'the undifferentiated structure of unconscious (subliminal) vision is far from being weakly structured or chaotic . . . but displays the scanning powers that are superior to conscious vision,' so to exercise these greatly enhanced abilities we must 'call on intellect and reason in order to sting into action the powers of the deep'.[20] I believe the whole thrust of Ehrenzweig's argument is that these are powers learnt in the womb, which the creative (or magical) process allows us to recover.

2   The Once and Future Gnosis

'Those pure and virgin apprehensions I had from the womb, and that divine light wherewith I was born, are the best unto this day, wherein I can see the Universe. By the gift of God they attended me into the world, and by His special favour I remember them till now. Verily they seem the greatest gifts His wisdom could bestow, for without them all other gifts had been dead and vain. They are unattainable by books, and therefore I will teach them by experience.' These words from Thomas Traherne are quoted by Ernst

Lehrs, who argues that experience in the womb is the direct source of potent supersensory concepts which can lead to a more humane yet accurate science, based on the 'exact sensorial fantasy' of Goethe: 'the modern re-awakening of man's capacity to remember his pre-natal existence'.[21]

Otto Rank, a favourite 'younger son' of Freud, believed that the source of all anxiety was the birth trauma, and that the processes of healing, sleep and hypnotism represented a return to the womb, and a rebirth somehow but not always bypassing that terror and pain. All hero-tales were of overcoming the pain and fright of birth. If a person could do this, he became the hero of his own tale. 'Birth is both the first of all dangers to life and the prototype of all the later ones that cause us to feel anxiety, and the experience of birth has probably left behind in us the expression of affect which we call anxiety.'[22] Rank says that women are feared and hated because of that original connection with the birth trauma and 'In attempting to make conscious again the repressed primal memory of the birth trauma, we believe that we shall reinstate the high estimation of woman which was repressed simultaneously with the birth trauma . . . ' He says that neurosis arises because in the attempt to overcome this psychological wound a human 'comes to grief at the crossroad of sexual gratification, which most nearly approaches the primal situation . . . ' for it is 'the nearest approach to the pleasure experienced inside the mother as one's original abode'.[23]

We have seen, however, that 'sexual gratification' has many mansions, some more opulently furnished than others. Certainly the 'transformative orgasm' is taking its practitioners, as the creative act does, into a world thriving with that 'vast unconscious substructure . . . ' resembling womb experience which is 'far from being weakly structured or chaotic'.

What of the blood-sacrifice that is seemingly inseparable in some form or another from all magic and religion? As a contemporary poet, Geoffrey Hill, says 'There is no bloodless myth will hold.' Does this sacrifice represent the human birth in blood and pain? It is sometimes suggested that the trauma of birth, like the loss of olfactory sensitivity, was a consequence of humans evolving to stand on two legs. But, as countless deliveries by natural childbirth and the Leboyer method have shown, there need be no foetal distress in birth. Are such children without the birth trauma, and therefore heroes and heroines? Ashley Montagu in *Touching* (op.cit.)

discusses at some length the intense massage that the child receives as it passes down the birth canal, and how essential to good health and development this can be. Stephen Black's arguments and data suggest that altered states of consciousness such as hypnosis involve 'regression to a conditioned reflex established before birth which moulds the foetus to the environment of the womb . . .' In humans this may be 'reinforced by the "swaddling" of infancy'. Rhythmic stimulation 'in the form of stroking or patting, with physical contact, as well as rocking and even a lullaby' sends a child to sleep, and 'rhythmic stimuli' are an essential in hypnotic induction. Thus it may seem that the power of hypnosis draws on womb-conditions, and reflexes set up thereby: 'From this simple system the whole technique of hypnotic induction from Mesmer onwards may be derived.'[24]

Or, to put it another way, this same induction calls upon our non-visual senses,[25] which are our organs of experience in the womb; the eye does not function as an optical instrument before birth (although its apparatus is sensitive to touch and variations of tone). It will be the whole-body responses so vividly evoked by Tromp and Becker and Marino that hold sway. This will apply both to EM and chemical response: the foetus is immersed in the complex elixirs and semiochemicals produced by its own self-making and the womb itself, succussed by the motherly heartbeat. Then the birth comes, and with it the taste and smell of shed blood, the touch of spilt fluids, the first acts of breath and the light and nimble communications of air.

There is now a great deal of information about the child's sentience in the womb. There is the beautiful imagery with its subjective authority of Laing's discussions, who says, 'The forms revealed by microscopic embryology cannot help but deepen the mystery of where some mythic-Gnostic visions come from,' and he quotes Mead on the silver-shining or mother-of-pearl-coloured 'aura'. We have seen that auras are actually *there*; what Laing is telling us is that we also perceive something like them before birth, in the 'amniotic sac and its waters, the umbilical cord and placenta, the uterus and vagina . . .' There is much analytical material that only begins to activate psychological changes, often with great power, when pre-natal sentience is assumed.[26]

Thomas Verney goes much further. He gives us good scientific reasons for believing in the following: that the child leads an active emotional life from the sixth month on; that the foetus can see, hear, taste and even learn; that 'the chief source of those shaping messages is the child's mother'; and that the quality of the father's relationship to the mother is vitally important to the unborn child.[27]

An unborn child grows emotionally agitated if its mother even thinks of having a cigarette (measured by foetal heartbeat). The foetus begins to learn language in utero, and moves its body to the rhythm of its mother's speech. A noted conductor was puzzled that he could play certain passages sight unseen: 'All the scores I knew sight unseen were ones she [his mother, a cellist] had played while she was pregnant with me.' One two-year-old child was found chanting natural childbirth exercises; they were phrases used only in the Canadian version that she could not have known except from the womb. A foetus reacts strongly to altered tastes in the amniotic fluid, and will react to music played, particularly heart-like drum rhythms. Emotional states are communicated to the foetus: ' . . . each wave of maternal hormones jolts him out of the blankness that is his normal state in the womb, and into a kind of receptivity.' I myself wonder if that 'blankness' is right; but one can see from this how important love-making must be to the unborn child. There is certainly an exchange of neurohormones between mother and foetus: they are 'vitally important' because in this way the mother and child 'can carry on an emotional dialogue'. These are 'internal chemical messengers' carried on the bloodstream; we have seen how important, after birth, the 'external chemical messengers', the pheromones, can be.

So it is clear that in the womb there are many opportunities for trauma, and for bliss as well. There is one happening, though, which, if it occurs in awareness, must be a great trauma, and a likely source of that guilt and anxiety and mythic interpretation that so occupies Rank. It may remain, in individuals and in entire cultures, a potent source of activation of that bloody myth of sacrifice and guilt that seems universal, from the sacrifice of Jesus, to the magical fight of the Tanists, the Young King and the Old King; from Cain and Abel to Gilgamesh and Endiku.

It is a fact of nature that we are accompanied in the womb by a Friend, who is made of our own flesh but in whom the mother's blood runs. This Friend supplies us with all food and necessaries, it is the intermediary between us and the mother, it purifies our environment: it is the placenta.

The placenta is like a grail; we sit down to the nine-months' banquet in our mother's womb, and it is the servitor of this banquet. It is our facing-partner beyond the shrouding foetal membranes and our sibling. It responds with its offices in that archaic place, in which we are created from basic life-stuff through all the stages of evolution, and it infuses us with all the substances and elixirs required for these changes. We know it by womb-light in our synaesthesia of the skin in its globe of actively creative waters; and this synaesthesia is gently modulated by all the movements and changes of composition and electrical fields and charges of our womb-liquor, transmitted by the complement of influences that act on our mother in *her* world, as Tromp describes.

We know the picture of that relationship, not merely from photos in biology books, but with the mythic conviction of contemporary fables of regeneration, as at the end of the film *2001: A Space Odyssey* when the star-foetus floats above the great placenta-like surface of the globe. The shaman's ladder or his tree, the rainbow bridge to heaven, Yggdrasil's trunk and the highway of the gods are all likely images of our connection with that heavenly and never-failing abundance. I believe the magical working tools of cord, wand, knife, cup and plate represent a language or prayer of asking for a renewal of womb-experience in that 'virtual space' of the magic circle: the cord and wand are umbilicus; the knife is the blade that cuts us free but equally heals and rejoins; the cup or chalice of wine is the fluid of birth tasted by all; and the plate is the round placenta, which feeds us.

A never-failing abundance – until, at birth, that Brother or Sister dies in cataclysmic blood to give us life. It feeds us like the grail; it dies for us like Jesus on the cross. Perhaps the purpose of all our Masses and Blood-Feasts is to return us to that blood-threshold, the crossing, and reactivate it, so we can pass through it again in awareness and not in dreamless sleep. Then perhaps we can partake of a new draught of Wisdom's living water and eat again of the fruit of her Tree, whose trunk with the snake twining is imaged there, as is her fruitful crown. And in returning for renewal, as for a resurrection, know that the guilt of that necessary murder is washed clean, because it was a willing self-sacrifice to obtain that later renewal as adult humans in full consciousness. We then become united with our other self, as if that womb-companion were a kind of guardian angel who became invisible when we were born.[28]

Thus, in our whole-body experiences, the thriving pictorial or imaginal space of our arts, our magical sex, we return and recapture for our use in *this* world lessons which we learnt in *that* one. We return to a condition of life that draws upon the knowledge in the womb, and activates again all those senses we thought we had lost. From the continuum within our personal mother, we are prepared for continuum in a new outer world that has been waiting for us. The Talmud says that the child in the womb is like the Ancient of Days: it knows all things, the whole Torah. But when it is born, an angel comes and, with a blow of the wings, wipes away that knowledge, which is expunged until the Messiah comes. We have seen that that Messiah may be what we call the Black Goddess.

Perhaps we can now comprehend a little further that great power of the monthly blood which is shed by women in their periodic sacrifice, the odours and magnetic vibrations of it, which are feared and despised and desired by all men. It is only humans who menstruate,[29] and so it is as though in humans the womb were re-made to bleed in order to open that crack between the worlds, *as though menstruation were there to activate the blood-threshold, to render it familiar and kind, to overcome the birth trauma and to give resurrection by womb-knowledge.*

In this way the black body, the invisible mode of the woman, the Egyptian darkness, the winged Isis, fills with new constellations. The Sphinx is truly answered: humans are born for rebirth. This may be the pattern intended from the beginning, when black Wisdom offered the red menstrual fruit of the Tree to the first black Adam. Then our life in the human womb may be an image, a 'Praeparative' and a teaching-model for the life we could live in continuum, as in Eden, with each other and all the species born from the womb of our mother-sister Gaia.

> *Before I knew these Hands were mine,*
> *Or that my Sinews did my Members join;*
> *When neither Nostril, Foot, nor Ear,*
> *As yet could be discern'd or did appear;*
> *I was within*
> *A House I knew not; newly cloath'd with Skin.*

THE EGYPTIAN DARKNESS

Then was my Soul my only All to me,
A living endless Ey,
Scarce bounded with the Sky,
Whose Power, and Act, and Essence was to see;
I was an inward Sphere of Light,
Or an interminable Orb of Sight,
Exceeding that which makes the Days . . .

'The Praeparative', Thomas Traherne[30]

APPENDIX

A POET AMONG THE
BLIND PEOPLE

'I was convinced, by the end of the evening, that even the born-blind see in some way that corresponds very closely to how we see in poetry – i.e., intense visualisation, with shapes and colours – conjured via touch, smell, taste, sound – but especially via conjunctions of words, which – it was generally agreed – carry vision, as they carry weight, etc. It was agreed that too many people who are sighted neglect the other senses to the extent that they can no longer see with them. I was told that, in my poetry, I tend to use touch and sound to create visual images, and that I "see like a blind person" in my work. (I hadn't realised the extent to which I do this until I was in the company of these people. For example, when I say of a quality of light that "you slip it on like sea-silk" – and when I describe a quality "that slips like coloured light between the fingers".)

'Now these blind people told me they could "see" all this, and that the colour "blue" has weight and a smell – that they can smell blue and touch blue and hear and taste blue . . . I noticed a cup of hot coffee placed on the table in front of one blind woman and I was afraid. I thought she might knock it over and scald herself. In fact, she knew exactly where it was – and when she picked it up to drink, she went straight for the handle, as surely as if she saw it there. In other words, she had heard the placing of the coffee, had measured its distance, could feel its heat and which way round the cup was – and all this without even having to think about it. (She was talking while it was happening.)

'So these other senses joined forces to make up for the lack – and they were intensified . . . It seems they can tell depths of colours by heat and weight. The metaphor of "seeing through the tip of the stick", which Penny had put to me, got a whole chorus of agreement. Also, seeing through the dog, of course – via the dog . . .

'Several of the blind-from-birth walked without faltering – straight ahead and edging round furniture without even touching it.

Also, their faces had sight in them, even though their eyes were closed. When they talked to me, they "looked" directly at me with their faces. It was like talking to people who look at you with eyes. The more recently blind were being led and were very hesitant and afraid. A man who'd gone blind in early childhood had cherished and stored every visual memory he had, but admitted that these memories were blinding him a bit to full use of non-sight. It was one particular born-blind man who impressed me most with his sure-footedness, his extraordinary independence. He'd come to the meeting alone, on foot, with a stick and a fluorescent strap around his body – and had walked a few miles, I gathered. He was the one who seemed to have the most completely developed "other sight". He's married and all (to a sighted person – a lecturer, I gather) but he gets around on his own, without a dog – just with his stick. Immensely articulate . . . He's absolutely definite about the fact that he sees – even though he has never had sight. (In the Kingdom of the one-eyed, the born-blind is King . . .)'

> Sylvia Kantaris in correspondence about
> Nottingham University's
> Extra-Mural Course 'Art to Share',
> > Autumn 1986

NOTES

Introduction

1   Redgrove (1973).
2   Shuttle and Redgrove (1986).
3   For arguments concerning Freud's addiction, see Thornton (1983). For objective evidence of the Oedipus complex, see Kline (1972), pp. 95–125; Fisher and Greenberg (1977), pp. 170–230.
4   Edmunds (1985), p. 1.
5   Ibid., pp. 1–6, 38–46.
6   Freud (1900), p. 365.
7   Quoted in Edmunds (1985), pp. 5–6.
8   *King Lear*, IV. i. 19.
9   Bettelheim (1976), p. 197.
10 According to Brown (1986), pp. 240–3, who draws the parallel between Faust and Oedipus and cites Wind (1968), 'Orpheus in Praise of Blind Love', pp. 53–80.
11 Frankl (1974), p. 139, pp. 173–4 and *passim*. Marcuse (1969), Part II, argues similarly, while Deleuze and Guattari (1984) in their book *Anti-Oedipus* mount an 'Introduction to the Non-Fascist Life'.
12 Brown (1959), p. 273 and *passim*.
13 Whitehead (1932), p. 113.
14 Davy (1965), p. 106; Brown (1959), p. 276.
15 Graves (1960), vol. 2, p. 10.
16 Ibid., p. 13.
17 Neumann (1963), p. 238.
18 von Goethe (1976), l. 500.
19 Parry (1981), pp. 70–1.
20 Jung (1956), para. 265.
21 Jung (1964), paras 714–15.
22 Walker (1983), p. 957.
23 Massey (undated), vol. 1, p. 19.
24 Massey (1883), p. 139.
25 Harrison (1962), pp. 165–219.
26 I am indebted to Abrams (1975), pp. 37–54, 'The Correspondent Breeze: A Romantic Metaphor', for his crisp discussion on weather and the eye's despotism; and to Reed (1983). There is a wonderful essay, 'The Eye and the Mind's Eye', in Donoghue (1978) in which he quotes (p. 160) a letter of Rilke's which 'ascribes the work of imagination in nature not to the natural forms of a landscape but to the air between them'. Hartman (1966) is full of ways in which the invisible haunts

Wordsworth, Hopkins, Rilke, and Valéry. Excellent evocative essays on the Aeolian harp by John Hollander and Geoffrey Grigson are to be found in Hartman (1972), pp. 41–84, and Grigson (1947).

27 Freud (1930), p. 43.

One The Fallen Daughter

1   Robinson (1983), p. 34.
2   Achad (1973), p. 87.
3   Beston (1981), p. 25.
4   Tatar (1978), pp. 59–60.
5   Ibid., pp. 68–9.
6   Blackall (1983), p. 145.
7   Tillich (1962), pp. 82–92: 'Nature, also, Mourns for a Lost Good.'
8   Massey (1907), pp. 3–4.
9   Massey (undated; 1883; 1907).
10 Massey (1907), pp. 4–12.
11 McClintock (1971).
12 Quoted in Abrams (1975), p. 4.
13 Massey (1883), pp. 336–7.
14 A point to be returned to, but see, for example, Koltuv (1986), *passim*.
15 Benson (1975).
16 Browne (1928).
17 Parry (1981), pp. 70–1. Roger Cardinal, personal communication.
18 White quoted by Avens (1980), p. 100.
19 James (1960), pp. 26–7.
20 Katcher and Beck (1983), p. 529; ibid., pp. 148–73; Shuttle and Redgrove (1986), pp. 117–18.
21 Katcher and Beck (1983), p. 157.
22 Ibid., pp. 351–9.
23 A superb guide to the waking dream is Watkins (1977).
24 Katcher and Beck (1983), p. 358. My remarks on animals as companions are indebted to this source throughout. Serpell (1983) is a useful short survey.
25 Grinder and Bandler (1981).
26 Parry (1981), 'Kleist on Puppets', p. 18.
27 Dreyfus and Dreyfus (1986).
28 Griffin (1976), pp. 101–3.
29 Tillich (1962), pp. 87–9.
30 Laing (1982), pp. 169–70.
31 Katcher and Beck (1983), p. 532.
32 Ibid., p. 413.
33 Ibid., pp. 461–6.
34 Ibid., pp. 520–1.

35 Wood (1986).
36 Op. cit., p. 521.
37 Harner (1980), pp. 58–61. For a survey of paragnostic powers, see Martino (1972), pp. 13–77.
38 Katcher and Beck (1983), p. 523.
39 Ibid., p. 525.
40 Parry (1981), p. 18.
41 Katcher and Beck (1983), pp. 526–30.
42 Ibid., p. 533.
43 Ibid., pp. 548, 542.
44 Ibid., p. 535.
45 R. M. Rilke, *Duino Elegies*. 'The Eighth Elegy', ll.1–13, author's version.
46 Katcher and Beck (1983), pp. 276–84.
47 The literature on this subject is enormous, and in my brief survey I have chiefly consulted the following, unless otherwise stated: Griffin (1976), Droscher (1971), McFarland (1981), Bright (1984), Winter (1976), Hopson (1979), Dunbar (1984), Brown and Macdonald (1985), Macdonald and Brown (1985), Murchie (1979), Thomas (1980).
48 Ehrenzweig (1967), *passim*.
49 Ouspensky (1937), pp. 98–111, 303.
50 McFarland (1981), pp. 449–50.
51 The discussion and data on animal awareness are much indebted to the excellent and concise Griffin (1976); here especially 'The Versatility of Animal Communication', pp. 15ff. Sophistication in chimp language is reviewed in Dunbar (1985).
52 Bialek and Schweitzer (1985).
53 For animals' responses to earthquakes I have drawn on Tributsch (1982) which is packed with further information.
54 Redgrove (1986).
55 Greig-Smith (1986).
56 Thomas (1980), p. 4.
57 Scott (1985; 1986); leRoith and Roth in Martini and Ganong (1984), pp. 1–25; Simons (1982).
58 Thomas (1980), p. 5.
59 Ibid., pp. 4–7.
60 Sinclair-Gieben and Chalmers (1959).
61 Black (1969).
62 Fabre (1911), pp. 139–67.
63 Townes (1965).
64 'Whistlers' – radio signals at audible frequencies generated by lightning flashes; see Rycroft (1985), p. 46.
65 Konnen (1985), pp. 11, 27, 75 and *passim*.
66 Murchie (1962), p. 463. A wonderful book – Andrews (1966) – shows

authoritatively the continuum between our ideas of music, matter and EM.

67 Hall (1960), p. 42.
68 Rossbach (1985), pp. 12, 21, 25, 29.
69 Grigson (1967), p. 113.
70 Callahan and Mankin (1978).
71 Callahan (1975), pp. 15–17.
72 Jonas and Jonas (1976), p. 24.
73 Callahan (1975), chs 1–4 *passim*. This seminal short book should be read in its entirety.

Two   Extra-Sensuous Perception

1 Walter Hilton in Riehle (1981), p. 112.
2 Beer (1977), p. 86.
3 Greenler (1980), p. 21; Darius (1984), p. 124.
4 Nearly everyone can distinguish black-painted metal from other colours very quickly. Variation between subjects and whether dermo-optical perception is a new sensory channel is discussed by various scientists in *Science*, vol. 152, 20 May 1966, pp. 1,108–10.
5 For instance, the Science Museum, South Kensington, London.
6 Darius (1984), pp. 126–7.
7 Nicholson (1984).
8 Witt (1971), p. 258 (my italics); also pp. 135, 185–97.
9 Bramah (1940), pp. 8ff.
10 Wilson (1838), *passim*.
11 On sonar of the blind, see Kellog (1964); on skin-sight, see White *et al.* (1970) and Montagu (1978), pp. 149–50; on evidence of normal hearing by sonar emission, see Zuccarelli (1983).
12 The painter was Caroline James; the musician Evelyn Glennie.
13 Bramah (1940), pp. 17–21; Murchie (1979), pp. 209, 238, 304, 533; Keller (1902), p. 15 and *passim*.
14 Marcuse (1959), p. 98.
15 Hall (1969), p. 59.
16 Joudry (1984), *passim*.
17 Freud and Breuer (1893–5), p. 92.
18 Marais (1973), pp. 115–31. I am indebted to Ted Hughes for pointing out these experiments.
19 Barber (1969), pp. 64–6; Barber, Spanos and Chaves (1974), p. 125 and Chapter 10 *passim*.
20 Jung (1957), pp. 48–51, 80–6.
21 Personal communication with David-Louis Gouedard. For subliminal perception *per se*, please see notes 121 and 123 below.

22 McFarland (1981), p. 405. Chadwick (1942), p. 79, says of the Poly-
    nesians, 'The *Karakias* or chants, which are regarded by the ignorant
    among the natives themselves as controlling the weather, are often
    merely the memoranda of the more intelligent *tohungas* [shamans], and
    enumerate the winds that blow on a certain coast, or the various types of
    waves which must be encountered on a certain voyage.'
23 Sulman (1980), pp. 8, 12.
24 Please see Works Cited at the end of this book.
25 Wiener (1966).
26 Russell (1976); Cherfas (1985).
27 Bourne (1980).
28 Horrobin (1980), p. 644; Wiener (1966; 1967); Hopson (1979), p. 28.
29 Ibid.
30 Ferry (1985).
31 Thomas (1985), pp. 42–3.
32 Wiener (1966), p. 3,163.
33 Hall (1969), pp. 11, 160–1.
34 Ibid., p. 118.
35 Ibid., pp. 79–80.
36 Ibid., pp. 62, 55.
37 Wiener (1966), p. 3,155.
38 Schneider (1971), p. 163. Like Comfort in Birch (1974), this paper is
    full of insights, although it begs the question on Freudian anality. See
    also Desor and Beauchamp (1974) who emphasise detailed olfactory
    discrimination by training.
39 Wiener (1966), p. 3,159.
40 Hall (1969), p. 56.
41 The noted dress-reformer, Gustav Jaeger, believed this, according to
    Hopson (1979), p. 32, and the idea motivated his influential books in the
    1900s. But it was also an ancient belief; see, for example, Onians (1951),
    p. 172 and *passim*.
42 *Daily Express*, 4 September 1986, p. 12.
43 Sommerville *et al.* (1986), pp. 42–3.
44 Stokes (1978), vol. III, pp. 325–6.
45 Patai (1967), p. 233; Philby (1981) *passim* and p. 73; Kluger (1974),
    pp. 85ff.
46 Proverbs, chapter 8, verses 22ff.
47 Song of Songs, ch. 1, verses 5, 12, 13; ch. 3, verse 3; ch. 4, verses
    12–15.
48 Apocrypha (1894), pp. 172ff.
49 Wiener (1966), pp. 3,166ff.
50 Ellis (1942), part III, pp. 69ff.
51 Winter (1976), p. 80.
52 Iyengar (1981), p. 53. The importance of the *jālandhara bandha* is

heightened by the fact that the salivary glands, which are stimulated, secrete nerve growth hormone into the bloodstream. Many organs of the body which are stimulated by yoga act as endocrine glands with a feed-back regulatory function; see Bergland (1986), p. 114 and *passim* – though his account of brain electricity is very partial.

53 Zuccarelli (1983); Onians (1951), pp. 75-6.
54 Gradman (1980), p. 77.
55 Oliphant (1885); Anon (1906); Evola (1983), p. 29.
56 Onians (1951), chapter III. This book is full of examples; to take only a few: pp. 73-4, the perfumed radiance of Demeter; pp. 74-5, pp. 77-8, the senses as breaths; pp. 158-9, the head fiery with inspiration; p. 172, knowledge or soul in the dying breath; pp. 31-3, sleep as a liquid; and Part I, chapter IV *passim*, perception by radiance and breath.
57 Raine (1986), pp. 23-4.
58 Jung (1976), p. 276; Jung (1977), pp. 320-6.
59 Schneider (1971), p. 168. Plant, animal and human odour responses to the same classes of chemical substances (in this case vanillin and pyrazines) are noticed again in Rothschild (1986).
60 Birch (1974), pp. 386-96. Moncrieff (1967) is a wonderful general survey, as is Wright (1964). It is clear that atmospheric electricity and odour are strongly related.
61 Thomas (1980), p. 18.
62 Shuttle and Redgrove (1986), pp. 144, 313-14.
63 Quoted in Reed (1983), p. 6.
64 Wallace Stevens, 'The Comedian as the Letter C'; Bloom (1977), p. 186.
65 Huntingdon (1945), pp. 344-8.
66 Thomson (1979), pp. 24-5.
67 Von Humboldt quoted by Reiter in Licht (1964), p. 280.
68 Thomson (1979), pp. xi-xii, 3.
69 Brezowsky in Licht (1964), pp. 358-99.
70 Huntingdon (1945), pp. 388-91, 353ff.
71 Reed (1983), p. 4.
72 Hoyle (1983), pp. 134-7.
73 Tromp (1980), pp. 169-71.
74 Quoted in Thomson (1979), pp. 186-7.
75 House (1962), pp. 38-9.
76 Beer (1977), p. 68.
77 Coburn (1957), entry 1,674. See also, entry 1,000 I: 'That Night is brought on by the influence of *dark* Stars that ray out darkness . . . '
78 Beer (1977), p. 256.
79 Sulman (1980), p. 147. Also Montagu (1978), pp. 147-8.
80 Beer (1977), pp. 249-50.

81   Ibid., pp. 255–6, 248.
82   House (1962), pp. 17–18.
83   Discussed in Reed (1983), *passim*; and Hartman (1966), pp. 10ff.
84   'Prelude' (1805–6), Book XIII, ll. 40ff.
85   Coburn (1962), entry 2,546.
86   Grigson (1942), p. 128; Beer (1977), p. 283.
87   Ibid., p. 256.
88   Thomson (1979), pp. 24–5; Reiter in Licht (1964), pp. 308–14.
89   I have drawn chiefly on the following: Presman (1970); Becker and
     Selden (1985); Dubrov (1978); Becker and Marino (1982); Sulman
     (1980); Battocletti (1976); Lund (1947 – with an important bibli-
     ography by H. F. Rosene); König *et al.* (1981); Reiter and Pavlik in
     Licht (1964); Burr (1972).
90   Reiter in Licht (1964), pp. 308ff.
91   Lehrs (1958), pp. 187–8. Reed (1983), p. 5, says 'Goethe's weather
     calls for a book of its own.' There is much evidence for electrical effects in
     earthquakes also; see, for example, Tributsch (1982).
92   Sulman (1980), pp. 5–12, 127–53, 231–3.
93   Ibid.
94   Rossbach (1985), pp. 125–40.
95   Tromp (1949), pp. 287–8, 340ff.
96   Lawrence (1960), p. 358.
97   Bodanis (1986), pp. 40–1.
98   From *The Old Devils* by Kingsley Amis, quoted in the TLS, 12
     September 1986, p. 994.
99   Baker (1981). The failure of the American experiment was reported in
     New Scientist, 25 June 1981, p. 835.
100 *Nature*, vol. 301, p. 78.
101 Dubrov (1978), chapter 5, pp. 235ff, deals with possible mechanisms of
     the biological effect of the geomagnetic field.
102 Tromp (1949), p. 48.
103 Ibid., p. 176.
104 Von Grierke and Nixon in Tempest (1976), p. 139; Townes (1965),
     pp. 839–40.
105 Schafer (1977), p. 99.
106 Becker and Marino (1982), p. ix.
107 Cardinal (1975), pp. 87–91; Becker and Marino (1982), pp. 9–13.
108 Ibid.
109 Brown (1974), pp. 49–118.
110 Becker and Marino (1982), pp. 17–22.
111 Becker and Selden (1985), p. 248.
112 Becker and Marino (1982). An important section on the possible
     mechanisms of the biological effects of EM energy begins on p. 162.
113 Ibid., pp. 169–70.

114 Chou *et al.* (1982). A valuable review with bibliography.
115 Pierce and Whitson (1966).
116 Becker and Selden (1985), pp. 312–13, 318–19. Chapter 15, pp. 271ff.,
     is a fascinating and detailed account of the health hazards involved.
117 Ibid., pp. 315–17, 323.
118 Becker and Marino (1982), pp. 62–3, 69–70.
119 Becker and Selden (1985), pp. 89–102.
120 Cardinal (1981), p. 176.
121 Bertocci (1964), pp. 25, 30, 34. It can be demonstrated that people
     whose thinking shows strong primary processes have an increased recall
     of subliminal stimuli; see Lapkin (1962).
122 Walker (1983), p. 821.
123 Becker and Marino (1982), p. 96. Lapkin (1962) discusses the classical
     evidence for subception, with a short bibliography.
124 'Connubium Terrae', pp. 207–23 in Surette (1979).
125 Cardinal (1981), pp. 176, 170.

Three   Mary Lucifer

1   Goethe quoted in Lehrs (1958), pp. 84–5.
2   Novalis quoted in Hartman (1966), p. 156.
3. Frater S. C., private communication, source unknown.
4   Ecclesiasticus, in the version quoted by Durdin-Robertson (1975),
    pp. 202–3.
5   Hsuan-nu, the Dark Girl who bears 'the sweetest fruits of the Earth' and
    bestows 'lasting transcendence' in *Sex Handbook of the Dark Girl*;
    Parvati, one with Kali, in the dialogue between Shiva and Shakti,
    paraphrased by Douglas and Slinger (1979), pp. 154–62, 131–51. See
    also, 'Nine positions of the Dark Girl', pp. 256–60; Parvati equated with
    the Black Shulamite, Jung (1963), p. 431.
6   Quoted by Moncrieff (1967), p. 14.
7   Pointed out by Iain McGilchrist in the *TLS*, 27 January 1984, p. 77.
8   Walker (1983), pp. 889–90, 929–30, 951–3 and *passim*; Durdin-
    Robertson (1975), pp. 167–8, 199–205, 207–8.
9   Jung (1958), pp. 355–470. For the femininity of the *Ruach Elohim* and a
    discussion of Lilith, see pp. 393ff.
10 Koltuv (1986), pp. xi–xii.
11 Durdin-Robertson (1975), pp. 281–3.
12 Massey (undated), vol. I, p. 2.
13 Sardar (1981); Gall (1979), p. 16.
14 Koltuv (1986), p. xi.
15 Ibid.
16 Koltuv (1986), pp. 121–2; Shuttle and Redgrove (1986), pp. 109, 325;
    Durdin-Robertson (1975), p. 204.

17 Groom (1986); Anon (1986). Massey throughout his work maintains the African genesis of humanity, starting with Massey (undated), pp. 1–47.

18 Author of *God and the New Physics*, quoted by Adam Ford in *The Times*, 19 January 1985, p. 8.

19 Barrow and Silk (1984), p. 28.

20 Anthony (1985), p. 36.

21 Radio 3, 2 November 1986.

22 Brennan (1972), p. 86.

23 Ibid., p. 117.

24 Corbin (1978), chapter V, 'The Black Light', pp. 102, 100.

25 Harding (1976), p. 41.

26 Grant (1980), p. 82.

27 Crowley (1974), p. 112.

28 Cook (1985), p. 19; Hartman (1966), pp. 104–7; also 141–55. The whole makes an absorbing essay on the poet's struggle between optical and visionary contemplation.

29 '*Un Fantome*'. Fred Hoyle's *The Black Cloud* (1957) grazes on the light of the sun and threatens the world. However, it communicates by radio, and turns out to be a being full of knowledge which overwhelms the scientist's brain but which the simple gardener could handle.

30 Richards (1982), pp. 65, 133.

31 Whalley in Beer (1974), p. 14. Ostwald (1964) is an interesting psychologist's discussion of synaesthesia, with a short bibliography.

32 Letter to Georges Izambard, May 1871.

33 Whalley (1953), p. 155.

34 Bertocci (1964), p. 50.

35 Goethe quoted in Lehrs (1958), pp. 84–5.

36 Bardon (1976) gives explicit instructions in terms of electrical and magnetic charges.

37 Mead (1967), pp. 86, 69–71. Avens (1980) is a wide-ranging discussion of the proposition that Imagination is Reality.

38 Chia (1984), pp. 144, 13–15.

39 Chu and Nan (1984), pp. 89–95, 125–7.

40 Walker (1983), pp. 614–15.

41 Ibid., pp. 820–1. Her reference to Campbell (1970), p. 71, on *horasis* I find inconclusive, but you would not expect a biblical work to refer to sexual visions, as the whole thrust of the religion is against this. Whatever its origin may prove to be, I propose to adopt the word as referring to an indubitable fact for which we have no other term. Significantly, though, Skeat (1882) thinks the word 'whore' at first meant 'lover', and connects it with Latin *carus*. 'Whore' is under 'Charitable', para. 2, in Partridge (1966). In Cornish 'whore' is simply a 'girl' – 'Hurs a pretty little whoor': Wright (1904), vol. 6.

42 Chu and Nan (1984), p. 95.

43 Trinick (1967).

44 Von Urban (1952), pp. 74–90. The book has an unfortunate prejudice against female masturbation.

45 Smith (1974).

46 Massey (1900), p. 41.

47 Ibid., p. 40.

48 Armstrong (1969), pp. 8–36 and *passim*.

49 Trinick (1967), p. 97.

50 Ibid.

51 Cento from Riehle (1981), *passim*.

52 Ibid., *passim*. See also 'Shulamite' in Pope (1977), pp. 596–600. The name might also signify that Abishag who warmed the elderly King David in bed by a species of Dianism.

53 Fränger (1976), *passim* and pp. 17, 31, 129.

54 Damon (1924), pp. 99, 101–2.

55 Shuttle and Redgrove (1986), pp. 136ff., 276–9. Certain primates also menstruate, and sexual receptivity at times other than oestrus is, as in humans, an important social factor. An up-to-date summary of psychoimmunology can be found in Martin (1987).

56 Daly (1979), pp. 94–5.

57 G. Wilson Knight discusses the tos and fros of the acceptance of 'disreputable' sexual fantasies, particularly in Knight (1971), pp. 17–109 and 156–96. The upshot is that, correctly handled, they yield up great power, and are a kind of shrinkage of knowledge that has been revealed at a higher level which, because of a cultural censorship, cannot be focused in full consciousness. This would accord with the present argument.

58 Graves (1965), p. 164.

59 Von Franz (1966), pp. 428, 159, 300, 368, 242, 192, 379. Arguments for authorship, pp. 407–31. *Aurora Consurgens* draws heavily both on The Song of Solomon and alchemical literature.

60 Anderson (1980), p. 110.

61 Ibid., pp. 84–5.

62 Ibid., p. 92. The whole question of visionary sexual love is treated with great sympathy and scholarship in this book.

63 Walker (1983), pp. 859–64.

64 Briffault (1927), vol. iii, pp. 477–83.

65 Walker (1983), p. 862.

66 Anderson (1980), pp. 112, 115.

67 Ibid., p. 116.

68 Walker (1983), p. 613.

69 Begg (1985), p. 145 (my italics).

70 '9th Duino Elegy' – author's version.

71 Hartman (1966), pp. 86–9. The whole book in effect studies the

struggle with non-visual perception of Wordsworth, Hopkins, Rilke and Valéry.

72 Begg (1985), p. 14.

73 Jung (1963), pp. 174–5.

74 As, for example, in his first truly Jungian book (Jung 1956) and Jung (1976).

75 Begg (1984), p. 69.

76 Begg (1981).

77 Begg (1982).

78 Begg (1984), p. 80.

79 Begg (1985), p. 12. This book is a thesaurus of further information. Another excellent source is Pope (1977).

80 Begg (1984), pp. 73–4.

81 Baigent, Leigh and Lincoln (1983).

82 Begg (1984), p. 87.

83 Wood (1985), p. 267.

84 Regardie (1969), pp. 248–55. Regardie (1978) compares the magical and psychological views of human alchemy and brings in 'The Magnetic Theory' of mesmerism. Culling (1971) is a practical handbook and Culling (1969) a whole curriculum.

85 Culling's (1969) approach to initiation via dream-work parallels depth psychological practice such as my own derived from Layard.

86 Ladas, Whipple and Perry (1969) confirm from clinical experience the varying taste of the female secretion ('Gluten of the White Eagle' to S.M.). One woman says, pp. 74–5: ' . . . the flavour changes four times during the month. Tangy, sour, tart, and very, very sweet . . . better than any honey.' Honey-tasting liquor seems to be a product of G-spot stimulation. They also discuss multi-orgasm and its varieties in both men and women.

87 Medicines in homoeopathy are potentiated by 'succussion' or shaking with a soft concussion. Homoeopathy also demonstrates the powerful physiological effects of very high dilutions of active substances. The scientific evidence for homoeopathy is very strong; see, for example, Coulter (1981).

88 Ladas, Whipple and Perry (1983), p. 143, discuss types of orgasm in men: the ejaculatory; the pubococcygeal contraction without ejaculation; and the non-convulsive orgasm with oozing of semen. Chia (1984) says the man should never ejaculate; but S.C.'s training taught that ejaculation flooded the bloodstream and the skin with hormones and pheromones, besides being the second ingredient of the elixir. Robins and Jensen (1978) discuss male multiple orgasm.

89 This kind of staircase pattern with 'conjoined climax' is diagrammed in Douglas and Slinger (1979), p. 146. 'Climax' and 'orgasm' were not redefined during our discussion, possibly because an adept's climax is

equivalent to another's orgasm, and the orgasm then goes beyond definition. But, again, 'adept' only means 'a practised human being'. A good working definition is perhaps: 'Climax – the pinnacle of sexual excitement until orgasm. Orgasm – the streaming sensation that continues after climax.' Ladas, Whipple and Perry (1983), p. 146.

90 The literature on bioenergetics is large, but one useful course based on Lowen's methods is Rosenberg (1974). Lowen (1979) is a basic text.

91 Brain laterality appears to alter from left-brain to right during orgasm, which raises all sorts of fascinating testable possibilities of communicating with deeper selves and senses: Cohen, Rosen, Goldstein (1976). Masters and Houston (1973) show the possibilities of 'calling each other down' in a secular and non-orgasmic context. Andersen and Savary (1974) give particularly nice instructions for deepening mutual trance (pp. 138–41).

92 Chang (1978); Chia (1983); Lu (1970).

93 The magical significance of the moth and the honey-bee is vividly given in Grant (1980), pp. 58–60, 200–3.

94 Torr (1984); Rycroft (1985).

95 Quoted from Mumford (1979), pp. 60–3, but it is Mumford (1975) which is particularly recommended.

96 Grant (1972), pp. 27, 29, 31, 45, 126, 128. Chapter 2 in itself is an excellent short summary of the subject. *Kalas* and the practices of bodily alchemy seem to be ancient versions of the complex patterns of neurotransmitters and hormones now being rediscovered; see Bergland (1985), *passim*. The evidence of homoeopathy needs also to be considered; see, for example, Coulter (1981).

97 Ibid.

98 Grant (1973), p. 122.

99 Ibid., p. 17.

100 Avens (1980), p. 103.

101 Grant (1975), pp. 2, 11–12, 20.

102 Ibid., p. 12.

103 Gradman (1980), *passim*.

104 Grant (1975), p. 39.

105 Ibid., p. 65.

106 Coomaraswamy (1971), p. 123.

107 Massey (1883), vol. 2, pp. 272–3.

108 Grant (1975), pp. 70–1.

109 Ibid., p. 73.

110 Grant (1977), pp. 91–2. Chapter 8, Part 1, is especially germane.

111 Grant (1980), p. 9.

112 Grant (1975), p. 173.

113 Strieber (1978), pp. 80, 103, 139, 92, 173.

114 Grant (1975), pp. 147, 181, 194.

115 Butterworth (1970), p. 199.
116 Colonna (1980).
117 Hillman (1979), pp. 25–30, 52, 185–92.
118 Berry (1982), pp. 15–20, 31.
119 Schwartz-Salant (1984).
120 Schwartz-Salant (1982), pp. 63–4, 7.
121 Avens (1980), p. 19.
122 Schwartz-Salant (1984), p. 20.
123 Chadwick (1985), p. 14.
124 *Point du jour*, Gallimard, 1934. I am indebted to Sylvia Kantaris for this reference.
125 Quoted Hartman (1966), pp. 165–6.
126 Kaplan (1977), pp. xi, 27, 47–9, 108–10. Michelet (1965) is available in English.
127 Chadwick (1985), p. 35.
128 Ibid., p. 182.
129 Ibid., pp. 141–2.
130 Ibid., pp. 181, 66.
131 Ibid., p. 143.
132 Orenstein (1978).
133 Colquhoun (1983); also quoted in Chadwick (1985), pp. 182–3.
134 Chadwick (1985), pp. 153–4.
135 Ibid., pp. 187, 200–1.
136 Ibid., pp. 188–9.
137 Ibid., p. 130.
138 Durdin-Robertson (1975), p. 97, says Lilith was originally an Assyrian storm-spirit, that the liliths were credited with 'walking in the air' and the 'greatest kindness to mortals'; and there is a tradition that Lilith was 'one of the Elohim'.
139 Koltuv (1986), pp. 49, 81, 121–2.
140 Massey (undated), vol. I, pp. 14, 17–18, and Chapter 1 *passim*.
141 Senghor (1976), pp. 29–34.
142 Sewell (1960), *passim*.
143 Jahn (1961); pp. 29–155, from which I paraphrase and quote, are particularly powerful and germane.
144 Cardinal (1981), a cento. His book is a revelation, packed with testimony. I recommend particularly pp. 105 ff.
145 Jahn (1961), op. cit.
146 Soyinka (1978), pp. 138–9.

Four The Egyptian Darkness

1 Quoted by Frater S.C., source unknown.
2 Skelton (1971), p. 2. As he says, 'Language itself is a route to perception.'

3   I recommend Van Lysebeth (1979) and Iyengar (1981). The former
    prefaces the practical work with a section on *prana* – the bioelectrical
    properties of air – and remarks (p. 48) how 'the sense of smell opens the
    door to the deepest psychic levels'.
4   Shuttle and Redgrove (1986), pp. 295–7.
5   Hartman (1966), pp. 71–124.
6   For practical advice about dreaming, I recommend Garfield (1974).
7   Brown (1959), pp. 278–9.
8   Shuttle and Redgrove (1986), pp. 270–6. We are exploring these themes
    further in our forthcoming *Creative Menstruation: A Handbook for
    Body, Mind and Spirit*.
9   Hoy (1965).
10 Culling (1969); Farrar (1983); Farrar and Farrar (1984).
11 Shuttle and Redgrove (1986), pp. 279–82.
12 Extra-sensuous perception is a feature of healing by the laying on of
    hands, or by massage. The majority of people can heal. Useful books are
    Gordon (1978) and Downing (1974). To prepare for the magic of touch
    one should work on oneself. Rofidal (1981) is excellent on Do-In, a form
    of Eastern self-massage, and Rofidal (1983) explores its philosophical
    background, using the imagery of *ch'i* force, etc.
13 According to Robertson (1977), auto-urine therapy was the practice of a
    former Indian prime minister. Needham (1983), pp. 307 ff., discusses
    its place in Chinese medicine. Armstrong (1971) recommends it for
    many disorders; and Pauls (1978) discusses its daily use and its place in
    healing practice, quoting relevant passages in translation from the
    Darmar Tantra.
14 Ehrenzweig (1967), p. 141.
15 Ibid.
16 Ibid., p. 119.
17 Ibid., pp. 121–2.
18 Ibid., pp. 103, 84.
19 Ibid., p. 273.
20 Ibid., pp. 33, 146.
21 Lehrs (1958), pp. 144, 206.
22 Roazen (1976), p. 397.
23 Rank (1929), pp. 37, 29, 45.
24 Black (1969), caption to plate IV and p. 161.
25 Grinder and Bandler (1981), op. cit.
26 Laing (1982), pp. 150–1. There is wonderful material in Fodor (1949)
    and Peerbolte (1975) which ought to be read *with* Lehrs (1958).
27 Verney (1982), chapters 1 and 3.
28 The Great Work in Magick (according to Culling) is also said to be the
    'knowledge and conversation of the Holy Guardian Angel' and the
    practitioner's eventual identification with that Guardian. The placenta

treasured as the 'other soul' is much discussed in Frazer (1913); see Index and particularly (i) pp. 182ff. Layard's (1944) discussion of the willing sacrifice arises from a vivid case-history, and is exhaustive concerning the Hare, which I believe the placenta-death images. Massey (1883), vol. 1, pp. 47–8, relates the Hare to the lunar feminine periodicity, with the meaning 'the way is open'.

29   And certain primates.
30   Quoted by Lehrs (1958), p. 149.

WORKS CITED

ABRAMS, M. H. (ed.). 1975. *English Romantic Poets*, London, Oxford University Press, 1975.

ACHAD, Frater. 1973. *The Egyptian Revival*, New York, Samuel Weiser, 1973.

ANDERSON, Marianne S., and SAVARY, Louis M. 1974. *Passages: A Guide for Pilgrims of the Mind*, London, Turnstone, 1974.

ANDERSON, William. 1980. *Dante the Maker*, London, Routledge & Kegan Paul, 1980.

ANDREWS, Donald Hatch. 1966. *The Symphony of Life*, Lee's Summit, Missouri, Unity Books, 1966.

ANON. 1906. 'A curious alleged attempt to prove the existence of a soul', *Annals of Psychical Science*, vol. 3, 1906, pp. 351–2.

ANON. 1986. 'Chromosome maps prove the origins of races', *New Scientist*, 27 February 1986, p. 24.

ANTHONY, Simon. 1985. 'Superstrings: a theory of everything?', *New Scientist*, 29 August 1985, pp. 34–6.

APOCRYPHA. 1894. Geoffrey Cumberlege, London, Oxford University Press, 1951.

ARMSTRONG, John. 1969. *The Paradise Myth*, London, Oxford University Press, 1969.

ARMSTRONG, John W. 1971. *The Water of Life*, Saffron Walden, Health Science Press, 1971.

AVENS, Roberts. 1980. *Imagination is Reality*, Dallas, Spring Publications, 1980.

BAIGENT, Michael, LEIGH, Richard, and LINCOLN, Henry. 1983. *The Holy Blood and the Holy Grail*, London, Corgi Books, 1983.

BAKER, R. Robin. 1981. *Human Navigation and the Sixth Sense*, London, Hodder & Stoughton, 1981.

BARBER, Theodore Xenophon. 1969. *Hypnosis: A Scientific Approach*, New York, Van Nostrand Reinhold, 1969.

BARBER, Theodore X., SPANOS, Nicholas P., and CHAVES, John F. 1974. *Hypnosis, Imagination and Human Potentialities*, New York, Pergamon Press, 1974.

BARDON, Franz. 1976. *Initiation into Hermetics*, Wuppertal, Western Germany, Dieter Rüggeberg, 1976.

BARROW, John D., and SILK, Joseph. 1984. 'The Invisible Universe', *New Scientist*, 30 August 1984, pp. 28–30.

WORKS CITED

BATTOCLETTI, Joseph H. 1976. *Electromagnetism, Man and the Environment*, London, Paul Elek, 1976.

BECKER, Robert O., and MARINO, Andrew A. 1982. *Electromagnetism and Life*, Albany, State University of New York Press, 1982.

BECKER, Robert O., and SELDEN, Gary. 1985. *The Body Electric*, New York, William Morrow, 1985.

BEER, John (ed.). 1974. *Coleridge's Variety*, London, Macmillan, 1974.

BEER, John. 1977. *Coleridge's Poetic Intelligence*, London, Macmillan, 1977.

BEGG, Ean. 1981. 'The archetype of the Black Virgin', *Harvest*, vol. 27, 1981, pp. 119–33.

BEGG, Ean. 1982. 'From Lilith to Lourdes', *Harvest*, vol. 28, 1982, pp. 77–87.

BEGG, Ean. 1984. *Myth and Today's Consciousness*, London, Coventure, 1984.

BEGG, Ean. 1985. *The Cult of the Black Virgin*, London, Arkana, 1985.

BENSON, H. 1975. *The Relaxation Response*, New York, William Morrow, 1975.

BERGLAND, Richard. 1986. *The Fabric of Mind*, Harmondsworth, Viking, 1986.

BERRY, Patricia. 1982. *Echo's Subtle Body*, Dallas, Spring Publications, 1982.

BERTOCCI, Angelo Philip. 1964. *From Symbolism to Baudelaire*, Carbondale, Southern Illinois University Press, 1964.

BESTON, Henry. 1981. *The Outermost House*, Harmondsworth, Penguin, 1981.

BETTELHEIM, Bruno. 1976. *The Uses of Enchantment*, London, Thames & Hudson, 1976.

BIALEK, William, and SCHWEITZER, Allan. 1985. *Physical Review Letters*, vol. 54, 18 February 1985, p. 725.

BIRCH, Martin C. (ed.). 1974. *Pheromones*, New York, Elsevier, 1974.

BLACK, Stephen. 1969. *Mind and Body*, London, William Kimber, 1969.

BLACKALL, Eric A. 1983. *The Novels of the German Romantics*, Ithaca and London, Cornell University Press, 1983.

BLOOM, Harold (ed.). 1970. *Romanticism and Consciousness*, New York, W. W. Norton, 1970.

BLOOM, Harold. 1977. *Wallace Stevens: The Poems of our Climate*, Ithaca and London, Cornell University Press, 1977.

BODANIS, David. 1986. *The Secret House*, London, Sidgwick & Jackson, 1986.

BOURNE, Arthur. 1980. 'A geologist's atlas of wine', *New Scientist*, 18–25 December 1980, pp. 792–4.

BRAMAH, Ernest. 1940. *The Eyes of Max Carrados*, Harmondsworth, Penguin Books, 1940.

WORKS CITED

BRENNAN, J. H. 1972. *Experimental Magic*, New York, Samuel Weiser, 1972.

BRIFFAULT, Robert. 1927. *The Mothers*, London, Johnson Reprint Company, 1969.

BRIGHT, Michael. 1984. *Animal Language*, London, BBC Publications, 1984.

BROWN, Barbara. 1974. *New Mind, New Body*, London, Hodder & Stoughton, 1974.

BROWN, Jane K. 1986. *Goethe's Faust*, Ithaca and London, Cornell University Press, 1986.

BROWN, Norman O. 1959. *Life Against Death: The Psychoanalytical Meaning of History*, London, Sphere Books, 1968.

BROWN, Richard E., and MACDONALD, David W. 1985. *Social Odours in Mammals*, vols I and II, Oxford, Clarendon Press, 1985.

BROWNE, Thomas. 1928. *Magic and the Mysteries*, Calcutta, Statesman Press, 1928.

BURR, Harold Saxton. 1972. *Blueprint for Immortality: The Electric Patterns of Life*, London, Neville Spearman, 1972.

BUTTERWORTH, E. A. S. 1970. *The Tree at the Navel of the Earth*, Berlin, Walter de Gruyter, 1970.

CALLAHAN, Philip. 1975. *Tuning into Nature*, London, Routledge & Kegan Paul, 1977.

CALLAHAN, Philip, and MANKIN, R. W. 1978. 'Correlation between UFO sightings and infestations of spruce budworm moths', *Applied Optics*, 1978, vol. 17, p. 3,355.

CAMPBELL, Joseph. 1970. *Myths, Dreams and Religion*, New York, Dutton, 1970.

CAMPBELL, Joseph. 1984. *The Way of the Animal Powers*, vol. I, London, Times Books, 1984.

CARDINAL, Roger. 1975. *German Romantics in Context*, London, Studio Vista, 1975.

CARDINAL, Roger. 1981. *Figures of Reality*, London, Croom Helm, 1981.

CHADWICK, N. Kershaw. 1942. *Poetry and Prophecy*, Cambridge, Cambridge University Press, 1942.

CHADWICK, Whitney. 1985. *Women Artists and the Surrealist Movement*, London, Thames & Hudson, 1985.

CHANG, Stephen T. 1980. *Chinese Yoga*, Wellingborough, Turnstone Press, 1980.

CHERFAS, Jeremy. 1985. 'How important is the family smell?', *New Scientist*, 24 October 1985, p. 27.

CHIA, Mantak. 1983. *Awaken Healing Energy Through the Tao*, New York, Aurora Press, 1983.

CHIA, Mantak. 1984. *Taoist Secrets of Love*, New York, Aurora Press, 1984.

WORKS CITED

CHOU, Chung-Kwang, GUY, Arthur W., and GALAMBOS, Robert. 1982. 'Auditory perception of radio-frequency electromagnetic fields', *J. Acoust. Soc. Am.*, vol. 71 (6), June 1982, pp. 1321–34.

CHU, Wen Kuan, and NAN, Huai-Chin. 1984. *Tao and Longevity*, Shaftesbury, Element Books, 1984.

COBURN, Kathleen. 1957, 1962. *The Notebooks of Samuel Taylor Coleridge*, London, Routledge & Kegan Paul, vol. 1, 1957; vol. 2, 1962.

COHEN, Harvey D., ROSEN, Ramond C., and GOLDSTEIN, Leonide. 1976. 'Electroencephalographic laterality changes during human sexual orgasm', *Archives of Sexual Behaviour*, vol. 5, no. 3, 1976, pp. 189–99.

COLONNA, M. T. 1980. 'Lilith, or the Black Moon', *Journal of Analytical Psychology*, October 1980, pp. 325–50.

COLQUHOUN, Ithell. 1983. *Osmazone*, Sverige, Dunganon, 1983.

COMFORT, Alex. 1976. *The Joy of Sex*, London, Quartet Books, 1976.

COMFORT, Alex. 1977. *More Joy of Sex*, London, Quartet Books, 1977.

COOK, Albert. 1985. *Thresholds: Studies in the Romantic Experience*, University of Wisconsin Press, 1985.

COOMARASWAMY, Ananda K. 1971. *The Dance of Shiva*, New Delhi, Sagar Publications, 1971.

CORBIN, Henry. 1978. *The Man of Light in Iranian Sufism*, Boulder and London, Shambhala, 1978.

COULTER, Harris L. 1981. *Homoeopathic Science and Modern Medicine*, California, North Atlantic Books, 1981.

CROWLEY, Aleister. 1974. *The Book of Thoth*, York Beach, Maine, Samuel Weiser, 1974.

CULLING, Louis T. 1969. *The Complete Magick Curriculum of the Secret Order G∴B∴G∴*, Saint Paul, Minnesota, Llewellyn Publications, 1969.

CULLING, Louis T. 1971. *A Manual of Sex Magick*, Saint Paul, Minnesota, Llewellyn Publications, 1971.

DALY, Mary. 1979. *Gyn/Ecology*, London, Women's Press, 1979.

DAMON, S. Foster. 1924. *William Blake*, London, Constable, 1924.

DARIUS, Jon. 1984. *Beyond Vision*, Oxford, Oxford University Press, 1984.

DAVY, Charles. 1965. *Words in the Mind*, London, Chatto & Windus, 1965.

DELEUZE, Gilles, and GUATTARI, Félix. 1984. *Anti-Oedipus*, London, Athlone Press, 1984.

DESOR, J. A., and BEAUCHAMP, Gary K. 1974. 'The human capacity to transmit olfactory information', *Perception and Psychophysics*, vol. 16 (3), 1974, pp. 551–6.

DONOGHUE, Denis. 1978. *The Sovereign Ghost*, London, Faber & Faber, 1978.

DOUGLAS, N. K., and SLINGER, Penny. 1979. *Sexual Secrets: The Alchemy of Ecstasy*, London, Hutchinson, 1979.

DOWNING, George. 1974. *Massage and Meditation*, New York, Random House, 1974.

DREYFUS, Hubert L., and DREYFUS, Stuart E. 1986. *Mind Over Machine*, Oxford, Basil Blackwell, 1986.

DROSCHER, Vitus B. 1971. *The Magic of the Senses*, London, Panther Books, 1971.

DUBROV, A. P. 1978. *The Geomagnetic Field and Life: Geomagnetobiology*, New York and London, Plenum Press, 1978.

DUNBAR, Robin. 1984. 'How animals know which way to go', *New Scientist*, 12 January 1984, pp. 26–30.

DUNBAR, Robin. 1985. 'How to listen to the animals', *New Scientist*, 13 June 1985, pp. 36–9.

DURDIN-ROBERTSON, Lawrence. 1975. *The Goddesses of Chaldaea, Syria and Egypt*, Enniscorthy, Eire, Clonegal, 1975.

EDMUNDS, Lowell. 1985. *Oedipus: The Ancient Legend and Its Later Analogues*, Baltimore and London, Johns Hopkins University Press, 1985.

EHRENZWEIG, Anton. 1967. *The Hidden Order of Art*, London, Weidenfeld & Nicolson, 1967.

ELLIS, Havelock. 1942. *Studies in the Psychology of Sex*, vol. 1, New York, Random House, 1942.

EVOLA, Julius. 1983. *The Metaphysics of Sex*, London and The Hague, East-West Publications, 1983.

FABRE, J. H. 1911. *Social Life in the Insect World*, Harmondsworth, Penguin Books, 1937.

FARRAR, Janet, and FARRAR, Stewart. 1984. *The Witches' Way*, London, Robert Hale, 1984.

FARRAR, Stewart. 1983. *What Witches Do*, Washington, Phoenix Publishing, 1983.

FERRY, Georgina. 1985. 'Dementia research sheds new light on old brains', *New Scientist*, 22 August 1985, pp. 33–5.

FISHER, Seymour, and GREENBERG, Roger P. 1977. *The Scientific Credibility of Freud's Theories and Therapy*, Hassocks, Sussex, Harvester Press, 1977.

FODOR, Nandor. 1949. *The Search for the Beloved*, New York, University Books, 1949.

FRÄNGER, Wilhelm. 1976. *The Millennium of Hieronymus Bosch*, New York, Hacker, 1976.

FRANKL, George. 1974. *The Failure of the Sexual Revolution*, London, New English Library, 1974.

FRAZER, James George. 1913. *The Golden Bough*, London, Macmillan, 1980.

FREUD and BREUER. 1893–5. *Studies on Hysteria*, New York, Avon Books, 1966.

FREUD, S. 1900. *The Interpretation of Dreams*, Harmondsworth, Penguin Books, 1976.

FREUD, S. 1930. *Civilisation and Its Discontents*, London, Hogarth Press, 1975.

WORKS CITED

GALL, John. 1979. *Systematics*, London, Fontana-Collins, 1979.

GARFIELD, Patricia L. 1974. *Creative Dreaming*, New York, Simon & Schuster, 1974.

GOETHE, Johann Wolfgang von. 1976. *Faust*, translated by Walter Arndt, edited by Cyrus Hamlin, New York, W. W. Norton, 1976.

GORDON, Richard. 1978. *Your Healing Hands: The Polarity Experience*, Santa Cruz, Unity Press, 1978.

GRADMAN, Barry. 1980. *Metamorphosis in Keats*, Brighton, Sussex, Harvester Press, 1980.

GRANT, Kenneth. 1972. *The Magical Revival*, London, Frederick Müller, 1972.

GRANT, Kenneth. 1973. *Aleister Crowley and the Hidden God*, London, Frederick Müller, 1973.

GRANT, Kenneth. 1975. *Cults of the Shadow*, London, Frederick Müller, 1975.

GRANT, Kenneth. 1977. *Nightside of Eden*, London, Frederick Müller, 1977.

GRANT, Kenneth. 1980. *Outside the Circles of Time*, London, Frederick Müller, 1980.

GRAVES, Robert. 1960. *The Greek Myths*, Harmondsworth, Penguin Books, 1960.

GRAVES, Robert. 1965. *Mammon and the Black Goddess*, London, Cassell, 1965.

GREENLER, Robert. 1980. *Rainbows, Haloes and Glories*, Cambridge, Cambridge University Press, 1980.

GREIG-SMITH, Peter. 1986. 'The trees bite back', *New Scientist*, 1 May 1986, pp. 33–5.

GRIFFIN, Donald R. 1976. *The Question of Animal Awareness*, New York, Rockefeller University Press, 1976.

GRIGSON, Geoffrey. 1942. *The Romantics*, London, George Routledge & Sons, 1942.

GRIGSON, Geoffrey. 1947. *The Harp of Aeolus*, London, Routledge, 1947.

GRIGSON, Geoffrey. 1967. *The English Year*, London, Oxford University Press, 1967.

GRINDER, John, and BANDLER, Richard. 1981. *Trance-formations*, Moab, Utah, Real People Press, 1981.

GROOM, John. 1986. 'Are we all descended from one woman?', *Listener*, 27 February 1986, pp. 10–11.

HALL, Edward T. 1960. *The Hidden Dimension*, New York, Anchor Books, 1969.

HARDING, Esther. 1971. *Woman's Mysteries*, New York, Harper Colophon Books, 1971.

HARNER, Michael. 1980. *The Way of the Shaman*, San Francisco, Harper & Row, 1980.

WORKS CITED

HARRISON, Jane Ellen. 1962. *Prolegomena to the Study of Greek Religion*, London, Merlin Press, 1980.

HARTMAN, Geoffrey H. 1966. *The Unmediated Vision*, New York, Harcourt, Brace & World, 1966.

HARTMAN, Geoffrey H. (ed.). 1972. *New Perspectives on Coleridge and Wordsworth*, New York and London, Columbia University Press, 1972.

HILLMAN, James. 1979. *The Dream and the Underworld*, New York, Harper and Row, 1979.

HOPSON, Janet L. 1979. *Scent Signals*, New York, William Morrow, 1979.

HORROBIN, David. 1980. 'A singular solution for schizophrenia', *New Scientist*, 28 February 1980, pp. 642–4.

HOUSE, Humphrey. 1962. *Coleridge: The Clark Lectures 1951–52*, London, Rupert Hart-Davis, 1962.

HOY, David. 1965. *Psychic and Other ESP Party Games*, USA, Funk & Wagnalls, 1965.

HOYLE, Fred. 1957. *The Black Cloud*, Harmondsworth, Penguin Books, 1960.

HOYLE, Fred. 1983. *The Intelligent Universe*, London, Michael Joseph, 1983.

HUNTINGTON, Ellsworth. 1945. *Mainsprings of Civilisation*, New York, Mentor Books, 1959.

IYENGAR, B. K. S. 1981. *Light on Pranayama*, London, George Allen & Unwin, 1981.

JAHN, Janheinz. 1961. *Muntu*, London, Faber & Faber, 1961.

JAMES, M. R. 1960. *The Apocryphal New Testament*, Oxford, Clarendon Press, 1960.

JONAS, Doris, and JONAS, David. 1976. *Other Senses, Other Worlds*, London, Cassell, 1976.

JOUDRY, Patricia. 1984. *Sound Therapy for the Walk Man*, St Denis, Saskatchewan, Steele & Steele, 1984.

JUNG, C. G. 1956. *Symbols of Transformation*, London, Routledge & Kegan Paul, 1956.

JUNG, C. G. 1957. *Psychiatric Studies*, London, Routledge & Kegan Paul, 1957.

JUNG, C. G. 1958. *Psychology and Religion*, London, Routledge & Kegan Paul, 1958.

JUNG, C. G. 1963. *Memories, Dreams, Reflections*, London, Collins and Routledge & Kegan Paul, 1963.

JUNG, C. G. 1963. *Mysterium Conjunctionis*, London, Routledge & Kegan Paul, 1963.

JUNG, C. G. 1964. *Civilisation in Transition*, London, Routledge & Kegan Paul, 1964.

JUNG, C. G. 1976. *The Visions Seminars*, Zurich, Spring Publications, 1976.

JUNG, C. G. 1977. *The Symbolic Life*, London and Henley, Routledge & Kegan Paul, 1977.

WORKS CITED

KAPLAN, Edward K. 1977. *Michelet's Poetic Vision*, Amherst, University of Massachusetts Press, 1977.

KATCHER, Aaron Honori, and BECK, Alan M. 1983. *New Perspectives on Our Lives with Companion Animals*, Philadelphia, University of Pennsylvania Press, 1983.

KELLER, Helen. 1902. *The Story of My Life*, New York, Macmillan; London, Collier Macmillan, 1964.

KELLOG, Winthrop N. 1964. 'Sonar system of the blind', *AFB Research Bulletin*, no. 4, January 1964, pp. 55–69.

KLINE, Paul. 1972. *Fact and Fantasy in Freudian Theory*, London, Methuen, 1972.

KLUGER, Rivkah Schärf. 1974. *Psyche and Bible*, Zurich, Spring Publications, 1974.

KNIGHT, G. Wilson. 1971. *Neglected Powers*, London, Routledge & Kegan Paul, 1971.

KOLTUV, Barbara Black. 1986. *The Book of Lilith*, Maine, Nicolas-Hays, 1986.

KÖNIG, Herbert L., KRUEGER, Albert P., LANG, Siegnot, and SÖNNING, Walter. 1981. *Biologic Effects of Environmental Electromagnetism*, New York, Springer-Verlag, 1981.

KÖNNEN, G. P. 1985. *Polarised Light in Nature*, Cambridge, Cambridge University Press, 1985.

LADAS, Alice Kahn, WHIPPLE, Beverly, and PERRY, John D. 1983. *The G-Spot and Other Recent Discoveries about Human Sexuality*, London, Corgi Books, 1983.

LAING, R. D. 1982. *The Voice of Experience*, London, Allen Lane, 1982.

LAPKIN, Benjamin. 1962. 'The relation of primary-process thinking to the recovery of subliminal material', *Journal of Nervous and Mental Disorders*, vol. 135 (10), 1962, pp. 11–25.

LAWRENCE, D. H. 1960. *Women in Love*, Harmondsworth, Penguin Books, 1960.

LAYARD, John. 1944. *The Lady of the Hare*, London, Faber & Faber, 1944.

LEHRS, Ernst. 1958. *Man or Matter*, London, Faber & Faber, 1958.

LICHT, Sidney (ed.). 1964. *Medical Climatology*, New Haven, Elizabeth Licht, 1964.

LOVELOCK, J. E. 1979. *Gaia*, Oxford, Oxford University Press, 1979.

LOWEN, Alexander. 1979. *Bioenergetics*, Harmondsworth, Penguin Books, 1979.

LU, K'uan Yü. 1970. *Taoist Yoga*, London, Rider, 1970.

LUND, E. J. 1947. *Bioelectric Fields and Growth*, Austin, University of Texas Press, 1947.

MCCLINTOCK, Martha K. 1971. 'Menstrual synchrony and suppression', *Nature*, vol. 229, 22 January 1971, pp. 244–5.

MACDONALD, David, and BROWN, Richard. 1985. 'The smell of success', *New Scientist*, 23 May 1985, pp. 10–14.

WORKS CITED

MCFARLAND, David (ed.). 1981. *The Oxford Companion to Animal Behaviour*, Oxford, Oxford University Press, 1981.

MARAIS, Eugene N. 1973. *The Soul of the Ape*, Harmondsworth, Penguin Books, 1973.

MARCUSE, F. L. 1959. *Hypnosis: Fact and Fiction*, Harmondsworth, Penguin Books, 1959.

MARCUSE, Herbert. 1969. *Eros and Civilisation*, London, Abacus, 1972.

MARTIN, Paul. 1987. 'Psychology and the immune system', *New Scientist*, 9 April 1987, pp. 46–50.

MARTINI, L., and GANONG, W. F. (eds). 1984. *Frontiers in Neuroendocrinology*, vol. 8, New York, Raven Press, 1984.

MARTINO, Ernest D. 1972. *Magic: Primitive and Modern*, London, Tom Stacey, 1972.

MASSEY, Gerald. Undated. *A Book of the Beginnings*, Secaucus, New Jersey, University Books, 1974.

MASSEY, Gerald. 1883. *The Natural Genesis*, New York, Samuel Weiser, 1974.

MASSEY, Gerald. 1900. *Gerald Massey's Lectures*, New York, Samuel Weiser, 1974.

MASSEY, Gerald. 1907. *Ancient Egypt*, New York, Samuel Weiser, 1973.

MASTERS, Robert, and HOUSTON, Jean. 1973. *Mind Games*, Wellingborough, Turnstone Press, 1973.

MEAD, G. R. S. 1967. *The Doctrine of the Subtle Body in Western Tradition*, London, Stuart & Watkins, 1967.

MICHELET, Jules. 1965. *Satanism and Witchcraft*, London, Tandem, 1965.

MINDELL, Arnold. 1982. *Dreambody*, Santa Monica, Sigo Press, 1982.

MONCRIEFF, R. W. 1967. *The Chemical Senses*, London, Leonard Hill, 1967.

MONTAGU, Ashley. 1978. *Touching*, New York, Harper & Row, 1978.

MUMFORD, John. 1975. *Sexual Occultism*, Saint Paul, Minnesota, Llewellyn Publications, 1975.

MUMFORD, John. 1979. *Psychosomatic Yoga*, New York, Samuel Weiser, 1979.

MURCHIE, Guy. 1962. *Music of the Spheres*, London, Secker & Warburg, 1962.

MURCHIE, Guy. 1979. *The Seven Mysteries of Life*, London, Rider/Hutchinson, 1979.

NEEDHAM, Joseph. 1983. *Science and Civilisation in China, vol. 5, Chemistry and Chemical Technology, Part V, Spagyrical Discovery and Invention: Physiological Alchemy*, Cambridge, Cambridge University Press, 1983.

NEUMANN, Erich. 1963. *The Great Mother*, Princeton University Press, 1963.

NICHOLSON, B. 1984. 'Does kissing aid human bonding by semiochemical addiction?', *British Journal of Dermatology*, vol. 111, 1984, pp. 623–7.

OLIPHANT, Laurence. 1885. *Sympneumata*, Edinburgh and London, William Blackwood, 1885.

WORKS CITED

ONIANS, Richard Broxton. 1951. *The Origins of European Thought*, Cambridge, Cambridge University Press, 1951.

ORENSTEIN, Gloria Feman. 1978. 'Leonora Carrington's Visionary Art for the New Age', *Chrysalis*, no. 3, 1978, pp. 65–77.

OSTWALD, Peter F. 1964. 'Colour hearing', *Archives of General Psychiatry*, vol. II, July, 1964, pp. 40–7.

OUSPENSKY, P. D. 1937. *Tertium Organum*, London, Kegan Paul; Trench Trubner, 1937.

PARRY, Idris. 1981. *Hand to Mouth and Other Essays*, Manchester, Carcanet New Press, 1981.

PARTRIDGE, Eric. 1966. *Origins*, Routledge & Kegan Paul, 1966.

PATAI, Raphael. 1967. *The Hebrew Goddess*, KTAV Publishing House, 1967.

PAULS, Arthur Lincoln. 1978. *Shivambu Kalpa*, Ortho-Bionomy Publishing, 1978.

PEERBOLTE, M. Lietuert. 1975. *Psychic Energy*, Wassenaar, Sevire Publishers, 1975.

PHILBY, H. St John. 1981. *The Queen of Sheba*, London, Quartet Books, 1981.

PIERCE, E. T., and WHITSON, A. L. 1966. 'Atmospheric electricity in a typical American bathroom', *Weather*, vol. 21, no. 12, December 1966, pp. 449–55.

POPE, Marvin H. 1977. *The Anchor Bible: Song of Songs*, New York, Doubleday, 1977.

PRESMAN, A. S. 1970. *Electromagnetic Fields and Life*, New York and London, Plenum Press, 1970.

RAINE, Kathleen. 1986. *Yeats the Initiate*, London, George Allen & Unwin, 1986.

RANK, Otto. 1929. *The Trauma of Birth*, New York, Harper & Row, 1973.

REARDON, Bernard M. G. 1985. *Religion in the Age of Romanticism*, Cambridge, Cambridge University Press, 1985.

REDGROVE, Peter. *In the Country of the Skin*, London, Routledge & Kegan Paul, 1973.

REDGROVE, Peter. 1986. *The Valley of Trelamia*, unpublished radio script broadcast on BBC Radio 4, 6 August 1986.

REED, Arden. 1983. *Romantic Weather*, Hanover and London, University Press of New England, 1983.

REGARDIE, Israel. 1969. *The Tree of Life*, Wellingborough, Aquarian Press, 1969.

REGARDIE, Israel. 1978. *The Philosopher's Stone*, Saint Paul, Minnesota, Llewellyn Publications, 1978.

RICHARDS, Steve. 1982. *Invisibility*, Wellingborough, Aquarian Press, 1982.

RIEHLE, Wolfgang. 1981. *The Middle-English Mystics*, London, Routledge & Kegan Paul, 1981.

WORKS CITED

ROAZEN, Paul. 1976. *Freud and His Followers*, Harmondsworth, Allen Lane, 1976.

ROBERTSON, Jillian. 1977. 'Tonic water', *Spectator*, 8 October 1977, p. 8.

ROBINS, Mina B., and JENSEN, G. 1978. 'Multiple orgasm in males', *Journal of Sex Research*, vol. 14, 1978, pp. 21–6.

ROBINSON, Eric. 1983. *John Clare's Autobiographical Writings*, Oxford, Oxford University Press, 1983.

ROFIDAL, Jean. 1981. *Do-In*, Wellingborough, Thorsons, 1981.

ROFIDAL, Jean. 1983. *Do-In: The Philosophy*, Wellingborough, Thorsons, 1983.

ROSENBERG, Jack Lee. 1974. *Total Orgasm*, London, Wildwood House, 1974.

ROSSBACH, Sarah. 1985. *Feng-shui*, London, Rider, 1985.

ROTHSCHILD, Miriam. 1986. 'The red smell of danger', *New Scientist*, 4 September 1986, pp. 34–6.

RUSSELL, Michael J. 1976. 'Human olfactory communication', *Nature*, vol. 260, 8 April 1976, pp. 520–2.

RYCROFT, Michael. 1985. 'A view of the upper atmosphere from Antarctica', *New Scientist*, 28 November 1985, pp. 44–9.

SARDAR, Ziauddin. 1981. 'Egyptian calamities', *New Scientist*, 29 January 1981, p. 297.

SCHAFER, R. Murray. 1977. *The Tuning of the World*, New York, Knopf, 1977.

SCHNEIDER, Robert A. 1971. 'The sense of smell and human sexuality', *Medical Aspects of Human Sexuality*, May 1971, pp. 157–68.

SCHWARTZ-SALANT, Nathan. 1982. *Narcissism and Character Formation*, Toronto, Canada, Inner City Books, 1982.

SCHWARTZ-SALANT, Nathan. 1984. 'Archetypal factors underlying sexual acting-out in the transference/countertransference process', *Chiron: A Review of Jungian Analysis*, 1984.

SCORER, 1977. *The Clever Moron*, London, Routledge & Kegan Paul, 1977.

SCOTT, Andrew. 1985. 'Messages in evolution', *New Scientist*, 25 July 1985, pp. 30–1.

SCOTT, Andrew. 1986. 'Viruses and cells: a history of give and take?', *New Scientist*, 16 January 1986, pp. 42–5.

SENGHOR, Léopold Sédar. 1976. *Prose and Poetry*, London, Heinemann, 1976.

SERPELL, James. 1983. 'What have we got against pets?', *New Scientist*, 13 October 1983, pp. 80–4.

SEWELL, Elizabeth, 1960. *The Orphic Voice: Poetry and Natural History*, London, Routledge & Kegan Paul, 1960.

SHUTTLE, Penelope, and REDGROVE, Peter. 1986. *The Wise Wound: Menstruation and Everywoman*, London, Paladin, 1986.

SIMONS, Paul. 1982. 'Why plants need aspirin', *New Scientist*, 23 September 1982, p. 847.

SINCLAIR-GIEBEN, A. H., and CHALMERS, D. 1959. 'Evaluation of treatment of warts by hypnosis', *Lancet*, ii, 1959, p. 480.

SKEAT, Walter W. 1882. *An Etymological Dictionary of the English Language*, Oxford, Clarendon Press, 1882.

SKELTON, Robin. 1971. *The Practice of Poetry*, London, Heinemann, 1971.

SMITH, Morton. 1974. *The Secret Gospel*, London, Gollancz, 1974.

SOMMERVILLE, Barbara, GEE, David, and AVERILL, June. 1986. 'On the scent of body odour', *New Scientist*, 10 July 1986, pp. 41–3.

SOYINKA, Wole. 1978. *Myth, Literature and the African World*, Cambridge, Cambridge University Press, 1978.

STOKES, Adrian. 1978. *The Critical Writings*, London, Thames & Hudson, 1978.

STRIEBER, Whitley. 1978. *The Wolfen*, London, Coronet Books, 1979.

SULMAN, Felix Gad. 1980. *The Effect of Air Ionisation, Electric Fields, Atmospherics and Other Electric Phenomena on Man and Animals*, Springfield, Charles C. Thomas, 1980.

SURETTE, Léon. 1979. *A Light from Eleusis*, Oxford, Clarendon Press, 1979.

SÜSKIND, Patrick. 1986. *Perfume*, London, Hamish Hamilton, 1986.

TATAR, Maria M. 1978. *Spellbound: Studies on Mesmerism and Literature*, Princeton, Princeton University Press, 1978.

TEMPEST, W. 1976. *Infrasound and Low Frequency Vibration*, London, Academic Press, 1976.

THOMAS, D. M. 1971. *Logan Stone*, London, Cape Goliard Press, 1971.

THOMAS, Lewis. 1980. *The Lives of a Cell*, Harmondsworth, Allen Lane, 1980.

THOMAS, Lewis. 1985. *Late Night Thoughts*, Oxford, Oxford University Press, 1985.

THOMSON, William A. R. 1979. *A Change of Air: Climate and Health*, New York, Charles Scribner & Sons, 1979.

THORNTON, E. M. 1983. *Freud and Cocaine: The Freudian Fallacy*, London, Blond & Briggs, 1983.

TILLICH, Paul. 1962. *The Shaking of the Foundations*, Harmondsworth, Penguin Books, 1962.

TORR, Marsha. 1984. 'A new image of the atmosphere', *New Scientist*, 23 August 1984, pp. 42–8.

TOWNES, Charles H. 1965. 'Production of Coherent Radiation by Atoms and Molecules', *Science*, vol. 149, 20 August 1965, pp. 831–41.

TRIBUTSCH, Helmut. 1982. *When the Snakes Awake: Animals and Earthquake Prediction*, Massachusetts, MIT Press, 1982.

TRINICK, John. 1967. *The Fire-Tried Stone*, Marazion, Wordens, London, Stuart & Watkins, 1967.

TROMP, S. W. 1949. *Psychical Physics*, New York, Elsevier, 1949.

TROMP, S. W. 1980. *Biometeorology*, London, Heyden, 1980.

VAN LYSEBETH, André. 1979. *Pranayama*, London, Unwin Paperbacks, 1979.

VERNEY, Thomas. 1982. *The Secret Life of the Unborn Child*, London, Sphere Books, 1982.

VON FRANZ, Marie-Louise. 1966. *Aurora Consurgens*, London, Routledge & Kegan Paul, 1966.

VON URBAN, Rudolf. 1952. *Sex Perfection*, London, Rider, 1952.

WALKER, Barbara G. 1983. *The Woman's Encyclopaedia of Myths and Secrets*, San Francisco, Harper & Row, 1983.

WATKINS, Mary M. 1977. *Waking Dreams*, New York, Harper Colophon, 1977.

WHALLEY, George. 1953. *Poetic Process*, London, Routledge & Kegan Paul, 1953.

WHITE, Benjamin W., SAUNDERS, Frank A., SCADDEN, Lawrence, BACH-Y-RITA, Paul, and COLLINS, Carter C. 1970. 'Seeing with the skin', *Perception and Psychophysics*, vol. 7 (1), 1970, pp. 23–7.

WHITEHEAD, A. N. 1932. *Science and the Modern World*, Cambridge, Cambridge University Press, 1932.

WIENER, Harry. 1966, 1967 and 1968. 'External chemical messengers': I. Emission and reception in man, *New York State Journal of Medicine*, vol. 66, no. 24, 15 December 1966, pp. 3,153–70. II. Natural history of schizophrenia, ibid., vol. 67, no. 9, 1 May 1967, pp. 1,144–65; III. Mind and body in schizophrenia, ibid., vol. 67, no. 10, 15 May 1967, pp. 1,287–310; IV. Pineal gland, ibid., 1 April 1968, pp. 912–38.

WILSON, James. 1838. *Biography of the Blind*, Birmingham, printed by J. W. Showell, 48, New Street, and sold only by the author, 1838.

WIND, Edgar. 1968. *Pagan Mysteries in the Renaissance*, New York, Norton, 1968.

WINTER, Ruth. 1976. *The Smell Book*, Philadelphia and New York, J. B. Lippincott, 1976.

WITT, R. E. 1971. *Isis in the Graeco-Roman World*, London, Thames & Hudson, 1971.

WOOD, Clive. 1986. 'Marriage, separation and the immune system', *New Scientist*, 24 April 1986, p. 30.

WOOD, David. 1985. *Genisis*, Tunbridge Wells, Baton Press, 1985.

WRIGHT, Joseph. 1905. *English Dialect Dictionary*, London, Oxford University Press, 1905.

WRIGHT, R. H. 1964. *The Science of Smell*, London, George Allen & Unwin, 1964.

ZUCCARELLI, Hugo. 1983. 'Ears hear by making sounds', *New Scientist*, 10 November 1983, pp. 438–40.

INDEX

Abercrombie, Dr, 50
Aborigines, 44
Abyssinia, 69
Adam, 20
Adamites, 131
Ādi Śesa, 72
Aeolian lyres, xxix
Aesculapius, 4
Africa, 4, 40, 118, 148–9, 168–73
Aivilik Eskimos, 65
alchemy, 140–2, 150, 156
Amis, Kingsley, 97–8, 106
Andreae, Johann Valentin, 139
animal electricity, 102–5
animals, 1–27
apes, 54–5
apocrine glands, 76–7
Aquinas, Thomas, 134, 139
Arabs, 64
Aragon, Luis, 161
Aristotle, 82
aromatherapy, 77
Arthur Koestler Chair of Parapsychology,
    119
aspirin, 86
Aswan Dam, 117
Athene, 49
atmospheres, 93–5, 177–8
auras, 61–2, 63, 108, 183
aurora borealis, 89–90
Austria, 44

Bachofen, Johann Jakob, xxii, 115
Bacon, Francis, 62
Baker, Robin, 98–9
Balzac, Honoré de, 160
Barber, T. X., 55
Barjesus, 49
Barnes, R. Bowling, 46
Barth, Karl, 104
Baudelaire, Charles, 121
Beagle, 26
Becker, Robert O., 101–2, 103, 105, 108,
    109, 183

Beer, John, 84, 104
bees, 18, 19–20, 23–4
Begg, Ean, 136, 138, 139, 142
Benin, 149
Benson, H., 56
Berger, Hans, 104
Bernard, St, 135
Berry, Patricia, 155
Bertiaux, Michael, 152, 153
Bertocci, Angelo Philip, 122–3
Bethe, 60
Bettelheim, Bruno, xxi
Bible, 40, 62, 69–70, 116
Bigelow, 103
Binet, 56
bioelectricity, 102–5, 124–5, 127
biometeorology, xiii, xv, 78–93
Birch, Martin C., 76
birds, 15, 22, 23, 24
birth trauma, 182–3
Black, Stephen, 30, 183
Black Goddess, 115–21, 134–42, *et passim*
black magic, 120
'black theatre', 120
Black Virgin, 136, 137, 138, 139
Blake, Catherine, 131
Blake, William, 17, 44, 48, 52, 65, 72, 85,
    92, 124, 126, 131, 165
blindness, 49–54, 188–9
Bloom, Harold, 78
body-language, 3, 11–12, 59
Boers, 54–5
Bosch, Hieronymus, 130, 131
Botticelli, Sandro, 139
Bowman, J. R., 105
Boyle, Robert, 139
brain, 107–8
Bramah, Ernest, 50
breathing, 72–5, 175–6
Brennan, J. H., 119, 120
Breton, André, 159–65
Breton, Elisa, 162, 165
Brezowsky, H., 81
Brill, A. A., 59–60

218

INDEX

INDEX

INDEX

INDEX

INDEX

INDEX